WILLIAM SHAKESPEARE

A HANDBOOK

S. PAULES CHURCH

Three Cranes

The Gally fuste

Schipes

HAMESIS

The Bear Gardne

The Globe

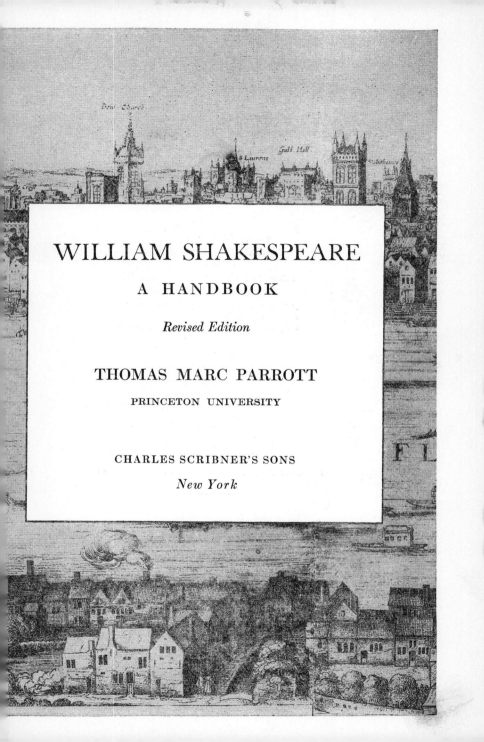

WILLIAM SHAKESPEARE

A HANDBOOK

Revised Edition

THOMAS MARC PARROTT

PRINCETON UNIVERSITY

CHARLES SCRIBNER'S SONS

New York

ACKNOWLEDGEMENTS

ACKNOWLEDGEMENTS are gratefully extended to the following institutions and persons for permission to use pictorial material included in this volume:

The Folger Shakespeare Library, for Visscher's View of London (title-page), the Courtyard of the White Hart Inn (Plate 4), Three Early Drawings of English Stages (Plate 5), and the Title-page of the First Folio of 1623 (Plate 9).

British Railways, for the photographs of Shakespeare's Birthplace (Plate 1) and the Grammar School at Stratford-on-Avon (Plate 2).

The British Travel and Holidays Association for the photograph of the exterior of Holy Trinity Church, and the Travel and Industrial Association of Great Britain and Ireland for the photograph of the Chancel (Plate 3).

The Clarendon Press, Oxford, for the photograph of the Middle Temple Hall (Plate 7).

Sidgwick & Jackson, Ltd., for the title-page of the *Hamlet* Quarto of 1604–5 (Plate 8).

The British Museum, for the page from *The Booke of Sir Thomas More* (Plate 10).

The Brander Matthews Dramatic Museum at Columbia University, for the pictures of Edwin Booth as Hamlet (Plate 12), Ellen Terry as Portia and Sir Henry Irving as Shylock (Plate 13), and E. H. Sothern and Julia Marlowe in *Romeo and Juliet* (Plate 14).

The Garrick Club, London, for the painting of David Garrick and Mrs. Pritchard in *Macbeth* (Plate 11).

Metro-Goldwyn-Mayer Pictures, for the 'still' from the motion-picture of *Julius Cæsar* (Plate 16).

Dr. John Cranford Adams, author of *The Globe Playhouse,* whose reconstruction of the Globe is pictured on the half-title page, on pages 79 and 80, and in Plate 6, in original drawings by Irwin Smith.

CONTENTS

		PAGE
Preface		**v**
CHAPTER		
I.	Environment and Heredity	1
II.	Shakespeare's Youth	10
III.	Shakespeare's London	22
IV.	Shakespeare in London—Under Elizabeth	37
V.	Shakespeare in London—Under James—Last Years at Stratford	53
VI.	Shakespeare's Company	65
VII.	Shakespeare's Theatre	73
VIII.	Shakespeare's Audience	91
IX.	The New Drama	101
X.	Shakespeare's Development	122
XI.	The Poems and Sonnets	184
XII.	The Text of Shakespeare	195
XIII.	Editors and Editions	208
XIV.	Shakespearean Criticism	214
XV.	Shakespeare on the Stage	226
	Appendices	240–258
	Metrical Statisics	240
	Chronological Table	248
	Bibliography	254
	Index	259

LIST OF ILLUSTRATIONS

N.B. PLATES 1–16 WILL BE FOUND IN SEQUENCE FOLLOWING
PAGE 194 OF THE TEXT.

The Exterior of the Globe Playhouse   HALF-TITLE

A Section of Visscher's View of London, 1616   TITLE-PAGE
(The Folger Shakespeare Library)

The Memorial Bust of William Shakespeare *Frontispiece*

The Stage of the Globe Playhouse   PAGE 79

Floor-plan of the Globe Playhouse   PAGE 80

Shakespeare's Birthplace at Stratford-on-Avon   PLATE 1

The Grammar School at Stratford-on-Avon   PLATE 2

Holy Trinity Church at Stratford-on-Avon   PLATE 3

The Chancel of Holy Trinity Church   PLATE 3

The Courtyard of the White Hart Inn   PLATE 4
(The Folger Shakespeare Library)

Three Early Drawings of English Stages   PLATE 5
(The Folger Shakespeare Library)

The Stages of the Globe Playhouse   PLATE 6

The Hall of the Middle Temple, London   PLATE 7

The Title-page of the *Hamlet* Quarto of 1604–5   PLATE 8

The Title-page of the First Folio of 1623   PLATE 9
(The Folger Shakespeare Library)

A Page from the Manuscript of *The Booke*
of Sir Thomas More   PLATE 10
(The British Museum)

xi

David Garrick and Mrs. Pritchard in *Macbeth*   PLATE 11
    (The Garrick Club, London)

Edwin Booth as Hamlet   PLATE 12

Ellen Terry as Portia in *The Merchant of Venice*   PLATE 13

Sir Henry Irving as Shylock in *The Merchant of Venice*   PLATE 13

E. H. Sothern and Julia Marlowe in *Romeo and Juliet*   PLATE 14

Maurice Evans in *King Richard II*   PLATE 15

A Scene from the Motion-Picture of *Julius Cæsar*   PLATE 16

CHAPTER I

ENVIRONMENT AND HEREDITY

ENVIRONMENT and heredity do not determine, but they at least condition and influence genius. It is well, therefore, before beginning the study of Shakespeare's life and work to know something of the town in which he was born, the surroundings that gave form and color to his early life, and the parents from whom he sprang.

The little town of Stratford-on-Avon numbered at the time of Shakespeare's birth about two thousand inhabitants. No greater mistake could be made, however, than to liken it to some American village of this size. It had a local history and tradition stretching back almost to pre-historic times. Its name bears testimony to its historic past. A Roman road (*strata via,* Old English *straet*) crossed the Avon (Welsh *afon,* river) by a *ford,* and the combination of Latin, English, and Welsh gives us Stratford-on-Avon. Near this point there was a Roman military post to guard against raids by the Celtic tribes of the great forest of Arden (Celtic *Ard,* great, *Den,* wooded valley; cf. the *Ardennes* of France and Belgium). In Saxon times the district was under the control of the Bishop of Worcester and a monastery near the site of the present church became the nucleus of a little group of houses. At the time of the Norman conquest, the inhabitants, some 150, were apparently all engaged in agriculture. In the reign of Richard I, how-

1

ever, one of the bishops of Worcester transformed the community into a little town by opening streets, laying out building sites, and granting a charter for a weekly market. The Rother, i.e. cattle market (Old English *Hreother*) has given its name to a main street in the modern town.

The lovely church of the Holy Trinity, where Shakespeare was baptized and in which he lies buried, owes its present form in the main to the benefactions of John of Stratford, a Stratford priest who rose in the reign of Edward III to be Archbishop of Canterbury and Lord Chancellor of England. He enlarged the old church and founded a chantry to sing masses for the souls of himself, his relatives, and his friends. His nephew, Ralph, Bishop of London, built a stone house near the church for the residence of the chantry priests. This building was called the College of Stratford and the church, under the control of the chantry priests, became known as the Collegiate Church of Stratford. A Warden of the College under Edward IV built the beautiful choir, and a later successor completed the building by constructing the double row of large windows above the nave which now form so conspicuous a feature of the church from without and flood its interior with light. During all these changes the church remained what it still continues, the parish church of the community, the centre of the religious life of Stratford.

Another religious organization developed in the Middle Ages which had an even greater influence on the life of the town, the Guild of the Holy Cross. Originally a simple fraternity for mutual aid and the performance of religious rites and duties, it came to be in the fourteenth and fifteenth centuries, the dominant social and administrative body of the community. It was richly endowed and every citizen of good standing in the town was a member. As the brethren were under vow not to enter into litigation with one another without the consent of its officers, it acquired considerable civil jurisdiction. Its fame spread throughout England; rich merchants in distant cities were among its members, and even a Prince of the blood, Shakespeare's "false, fleeting, perjured Clarence" was glad to enroll himself and his wife, daughter of the Kingmaker Warwick, in the fraternity.[1]

Meanwhile the Guild was giving practical and permanent evidence of its wealth and beneficence. The foundations of its noble chapel were laid by Robert of Stratford, the father of Archbishop John. The chapel itself was enlarged and rebuilt in its present form toward the close of the fifteenth century by Hugh Clopton, a citizen of Stratford, who had made his fortune in London and become Lord Mayor of that city. Clopton also built the stately stone bridge which crosses the Avon to-day and left money for the education of poor boys at Oxford and Cambridge. The Guild was specially interested in education and early in the fifteenth century it founded a free grammar school for the children of its members. It was at this school, still in existence, that Shakespeare probably received his education.

The sweeping changes of the Reformation profoundly modified the social life of Stratford. The College was suppressed and the building became a private residence, occupied in Shakespeare's day by his friend John Coombe. The Guild was dissolved and its property passed to the Crown. For a period of six or seven years the little town was left almost wholly without means of self-government. In 1553, however, a charter was

---

[1] The ordinances of the Guild in the reign of Richard II are reprinted in Sidney Lee's *Stratford-on-Avon* and throw much light on the social life of the town.

obtained from Edward VI which remodelled the old
Guild into the new Corporation of Stratford.

The property of the Guild, the chapel and guildhall,
school-house, almshouse, and real estate in the town,
was handed over to the Corporation. The old officers of
the Guild, the bailiff, aldermen, chamberlains, and so
forth, became municipal officials. The town council, composed of these officers and of ten leading citizens, became
the supreme local authority and exercised strict control
over the lives and conduct of the citizens. It fixed the
price and regulated the quality of ale and bread, pre-
scribed the dress of all inhabitants over six years of age,
imposed fines for profanity and non-attendance at
church, set refractory citizens in the stocks, and ducked
scolding wives in the Avon. Stratford became under the
new charter a little self-governing world; but the government lay solely in the hands of a small body, the
"free men of the Corporation," order and degree were
strictly observed, and the idea of personal liberty so
dear to the heart of modern Americans was a thing unknown. Local autonomy and governmental control of
private life count for quite as much in differentiating
Shakespeare's Stratford from an American village as do
the old traditions and monuments in stone that link it
to its past. In Shakespeare's day it was a thriving
country town, humming with industry, the market-place
of a rich farming countryside, and by no means out of
touch with London.

Round about Stratford spreads the lovely country of
central England, far more heavily wooded in Shakespeare's day than now, but less so then than in former
times when, as the saying ran, a squirrel might leap from
bough to bough across all Warwickshire. It was, and is,
a gently rolling country of plough-land and pastures set
off by hedgerows and watered by slow full streams that

rise at times to flood their banks. The rich soil and the mild moist climate give rise to a profuse vegetation; the trees are heavy with leafage and the grassy lanes and green meadows gay with flowers in spring and summer. The streams swarm with fish; the air is vocal with the song of thrush, lark, and nightingale, and in Shakespeare's day there were still deer in the woods and boar in the deeper recesses of the forest of Arden. All this wealth of nature lay at Shakespeare's very door; five minute's walk from his home on Henley Street would take him into the heart of the country, and there is abundant evidence in his plays and poems that Shakespeare knew and loved all the rich and changing aspects of nature that lay about his youth. He is the country-bred poet, as his friend Jonson was the product of the city streets and taverns, and the nature that Shakespeare loved was not the grand, the terrible, nor the stormy nature of the mountains or the sea, but the soft and smiling revelations of beauty of his own English country-side.

One other feature of the country around Stratford is worth noting. It was rich in memories of the Wars of the Roses. Warwick, with its ancient castle, a few hours walk from Stratford, had been the seat of the Yorkist Kingmaker. Coventry, with its old walls, only a little further distant, had been a Lancastrian stronghold. This epoch of English history not much further removed from Shakespeare's day than our own Civil War from us had a peculiar fascination for him. His chronicle plays deal almost exclusively with this period; of earlier English kings and heroes, William the Conqueror, Richard Cœur de Lion, the great Edwards I and III, he has little to say. His great cycle of Histories from Richard II to Richard III deals wholly with the struggle between York and Lancaster, and the lessons that he draws from this struggle, the folly and the wickedness of civil strife, the necessity and blessedness of national unity and civil peace, he was never tired of repeating.

Into Stratford town there came about 1550 the poet's father, John Shakespeare. He belonged to a family, perhaps originally Norman, that had many branches in Warwickshire. Another John Shakespeare, often confused with him, was his fellow citizen, a shoemaker in Stratford. John came of sound yeoman stock; his father, Richard, was a farmer who rented the fifty-acre farm of Asbies from Robert Arden, a rich squire of the neighboring village of Wilmcote. John, however, turned his back upon the farm, and opened a shop in Stratford for the sale of country produce, corn, wool, timber, skins, and so forth, and enrolled himself in the Glovers' guild. His first recorded appearance in Stratford is not exactly to his credit, for in April, 1552, he was fined 12d for failing to remove a dirt heap in front of his house. But in spite of this unpromising beginning John Shakespeare prospered and rose rapidly to be one of the leading citizens of the little town. No doubt his marriage about 1552 to Mary Arden, the daughter of his father's landlord, helped to establish his social position. He bought several houses in the borough, contributed to the relief of sufferers from the plague, and helped to pay the beadle's salary. He took an active part in town affairs and was chosen by his fellow citizens for one office after another. He became first ale-taster (supervisor of the price and quality of ale and bread offered for sale), then town councillor, chamberlain (keeper of borough accounts), alderman, and finally in 1568 bailiff or presiding officer of the Corporation. In this capacity he granted licenses to travelling companies of players, the Queen's and Worcester's Men. The year 1568 marks the first recorded appearance of professional

actors at Stratford and it is quite likely that William
Shakespeare saw his first stage play as a boy of four
standing by John's side in the guildhall where these
companies performed.

John Shakespeare seems, however, to have failed to
retain the honorable position that he had won in the
community. His family and his expenses increased rapidly and he seems to have met with financial losses. We
hear of vexatious lawsuits and heavy fines. He begins
to absent himself from the meetings of the town-council;
in 1578 it is recorded that he was unable to pay the
weekly sum of fourpence for the relief of the poor expected from every councillor. In the same year he mort-
gaged and sold outright property that his wife had
inherited; finally in 1586 he was deposed from his office
as alderman because of his continued absence from council meetings, and in 1592 he was reported as a "recusant"
that is as failing to attend the parish church, and the
excuse was given that he feared to be arrested for debt.

Apart from these recorded facts little is known of the
poet's father. It is probable that he was in our sense
of the word uneducated; indeed it was almost impossible
for a country boy in the early sixteenth century to obtain
even the rudiments of an education. He probably could
read and certainly knew how to keep accounts, but wrote
with difficulty and preferred to use the Glovers' trade-
mark as his signature rather than to sign his name. Tradition reports him as "a merry-cheeked old man" talking
in his shop about his famous son and asserting that "Will
was a good honest fellow but that he (John) durst have
cracked a jest with him at any time." He lived to see
this "good honest fellow" "the best of the family" [1] as

[1] An interesting novel by this name, the work of Caroline
Oman, gives a lively and on the whole accurate picture of
Shakespeare's environment and his life in Stratford and in
London.

an old account calls him, restore their sinking fortunes, purchase New Place, one of the largest houses in Stratford, and secure for him from the Herald's Office a patent of gentility and the well-known coat of arms.

From his father the poet seems to have inherited his interest in practical affairs, his love of landed property, and above all his sanguine temperament and his love of a good jest.

Shakespeare's mother came from a higher class in society than did his father, that of the landed gentry. Her family, the Ardens, was one of the great clans of Warwickshire. As far back as 1438 a Robert Arden had been sheriff of the county and his descendant, Edward Arden, also once high sheriff, was executed in 1583 for alleged complicity in a Roman Catholic plot against the life of Queen Elizabeth. Mary's father, Robert, a distant relative of the main branch, was well-found in this world's goods. He lived at ease in a large well-furnished house hung with "painted cloths." He was the proud owner of many sheep and cattle and the still prouder father of seven daughters. His will shows him a professing Catholic and it is quite possible that Mary adhered in secret to her father's faith. She married John Shakespeare about a year after her father's death, bore him eight children, survived him some seven years and was buried in Stratford churchyard.

Shakespeare's mother, we may well believe, had even less knowledge of letters than his father, but she bequeathed her son two excellent things, a gentle nature and a reverence for the past, the old manners, the old traditions, and the old faith of England. The word "gentle" is almost a stock epithet applied by his contemporaries to William Shakespeare, and in Elizabethan English the word had a more strictly defined meaning than it has with us. It implied race and breeding; a "gentle" man was a gentleman, and there is nothing plainer in Shakespeare's work than his inborn sympathy with refinement, courtesy, and aristocratic charm. He detested the London mob as heartily as any nobleman, and nothing in his life probably gave him greater pleasure than his success in lifting himself out of the despised players' caste and writing himself down "William Shakespeare of Stratford-on-Avon, gentleman." It is worth noting, too, that Shakespeare had nothing of the prejudice partly national, partly religious, against Catholicism which marked so many of his contemporaries. Spenser might symbolize the Roman church in the person of a foul witch; Marlowe introduce the Pope and Cardinals into a scene of gross buffoonery in *Dr. Faustus,* and Dekker entitle an anti-papal play *The Whore of Babylon.* Shakespeare on the other hand has no trace of the Puritan's bitterness or the playwright's readiness to raise a laugh by a jeer at Rome. The figures of priests, friars, cardinals, and bishops that he introduces in his plays are always respectable, sometimes venerable characters, and his references to Catholic doctrines and practices are always reverent. This does not mean that Shakespeare was at heart a Roman Catholic; he lived and died a professing member of the Church of England, and, no doubt, like most Englishmen of his day, felt himself safe in the *via media* that his church marked out for him. Yet the absence in Shakespeare of any trace of religious prejudice in an age of controversy, calumny, and persecution, is not a little remarkable and it is not altogether fanciful to attribute this trait, in part at least, to a filial respect for the faith of his gentle mother.

CHAPTER II

SHAKESPEARE'S YOUTH

Of the early life of Shakespeare at Stratford we have only two recorded facts: the entry of his baptism, and the bond relating to his marriage. Yet we know enough of his environment to be able, in some measure, to reconstruct his early life; and we have ample testimony to his early studies, pursuits, and pastimes in allusions scattered throughout his work. The picture, then, that we may draw of Shakespeare's youth is by no means purely imaginary.

According to the parish register of Stratford, *Gulielmus filius Johannes Shakspere* was baptized on Wednesday, April 26, 1564, the festival of England's patron saint, St. George. The exact day of his birth is unknown; the tradition that he was born on April 23, the day of his death in 1616, is late and unreliable. In those days, however, children were baptized as soon as possible and it is unlikely that William was born before the 21st or 22nd of April. He saw the light in one of the two contiguous houses in Henley Street, probably not in the one now shown as the Birthplace, which did not become John's property till 1575, but in the other, now called the Museum, which John had bought just before his marriage.

William was the oldest surviving child; two girls born before him had died in infancy; but a numerous brood succeeded him, three brothers, Gilbert, Richard,

10

and Edmund, and two sisters Joan and Ann. In Shakespeare's home the strict discipline of the Middle Ages still prevailed. The boy rose early, waited on his parents at table, kept silent in their presence, capped to his elders on the street, and, no doubt, was whipped for any petty fault. Yet his parents must have been proud of their vigorous, handsome eldest son and arranged at the first moment for him to enjoy the education which had been denied to them.

The old Guild school had been transformed by Edward VI in 1553 into the King's New School of Stratford-on-Avon. The salary of the master was fixed at £20 a year, a much higher figure than was usual in Elizabethan schools, and a succession of able scholars conducted the teaching. The school offered free education to all the sons of Stratford citizens, and when we consider John Shakespeare's position in the town it seems incredible that he should have neglected to avail himself of this opportunity for his son. A lively appreciation of the advantages of a classical education was one of the distinguishing characteristics of Elizabethan England, as is shown by the founding of almost as many free schools during the Queen's reign as had been in existence up to her time, and John Shakespeare, town-councillor and bailiff of Stratford, was not the man to deprive his son of such an advantage.

Before William entered the grammar school, however, he must have mastered the alphabet in the horn-book, learned to spell out simple English, and to write in the old-fashioned script which he continued to use all his life.[1]

[1] The only certain specimens of Shakespeare's handwriting that remain are six signatures of his to various documents—three of them to his last will. It is possible that three pages of the MS. play of *Sir Thomas More* (cf. p. 181) now in the British Museum, are in Shakespeare's hand. The apparent illegibility

The curriculum of an Elizabethan grammar school was almost entirely composed of Latin and Latin was the vehicle of instruction, for the end of education was conceived to be the ability to read, speak, and write this common language of scholars. The Latin Grammar of Colet and Lyly had been authorized by royal proclamation as the only textbook to be used in English schools. The rules were written in Latin and the unhappy schoolboy was forced to learn them by heart before he understood the language in which they were written. Along with the study of grammar came exercises in Latin conversation, based on phrase books like the *Sententiae Pueriles*, which the boys also had to learn by heart. The bits of Latin dialogue between the schoolmaster, Holofernes, and the parson in *Love's Labour's Lost* are modelled on such exercises and show how well Shakespeare remembered his early training. Along with these studies came the reading of Latin: *Æsop's Fables* and the *Eclogues* of Baptista Mantuanus, the popular Renaissance poet,—"for style and matter very familiar and grateful to children," says an old schoolmaster; one wonders what the boys thought of Baptista. Holofernes both quotes and praises him. Then came Cicero, the idol of the Renaissance, in his *Epistles, De Officiis, De Amicitia,* and other works. The Latin poets and playwrights, Virgil, Ovid, Terence, Plautus, and the much praised tragedies of Seneca, were also read, usually in selections. Ovid was evidently Shakespeare's favorite; he prefixes a quotation from the *Amores* to his first poem, *Venus and Adonis,* makes innumerable references

of his handwriting has led some uninstructed persons to think of him as an illiterate person, but scholars know that his handwriting is the usual old English script taught in all provincial schools in his time. The new Italian script, now current, was only used in the most cultured circles at that time.

to the stories of the *Metamorphoses,* and borrows from that poem the name of his fairy queen, Titania.[1]

The question has sometimes been raised whether Shakespeare knew Greek. The masters of the Stratford school in Shakespeare's day were Oxford scholars no doubt qualified to teach Greek, and Jonson's well-known statement that Shakespeare had "small Latin and less Greek" seems to imply that the poet had at least an acquaintance with that language; otherwise Jonson might have written "no Greek." But the question, after all, is idle since there is no reason whatever to believe that Shakespeare read Greek or had any acquaintance with Greek literature—except Plutarch—either in the original or in translations. With Latin the case is different. What seemed "small Latin" to such a scholar as Jonson would be a very respectable quantity today. A boy must have been dull indeed who could spend six or seven years devoted almost exclusively to the study of Latin for about ten hours [2] a day and yet emerge from the process without a very fair command of the language.

Apart from the Latin classics the only book studied was the Bible in the Geneva version with which Shakespeare's plays show a perfect familiarity. There is some reason, however, to believe that Shakespeare had studied the formal Rhetoric which was taught only in the most advanced forms of such schools.

What may we believe, then, to have been the final result of Shakespeare's schooling? A possible smattering of Greek may be discarded, but he must have had such

[1] An old copy of the *Metamorphoses,* now in the Bodleian, bears on the title-page the abbreviated signature Wm Shre and opposite the signature the entry in a seventeenth-century hand: "This little Booke of Ovid was given to me by W. Hall who sayd it was once Will. Shaksperes, T. N. 1682." The supposed signature is probably a forgery.

[2] School began in Shakespeare's day at 6 or 7 a. m. and lasted with brief intermissions till 5.30 or 6 p. m.

a knowledge of Latin as enabled him to read the best authors with ease and fluency. More important still was a real mastery of English composition acquired by the constant practice of translating Latin into English and English back into Latin. Along with this went a thorough grasp on the Latin element in the English language; no author could use this with the precision and power that Shakespeare displays unless he had enjoyed a sound classical education.

Even in such a school as Shakespeare's a boy's life was not all work. There were the legal holidays, the holidays granted at the request of a graduate or a patron of the school (Master Slender gets the boys leave to play, *Merry Wives* IV, i), and the happy hours stolen by the truants. The boyish games with which these hours were filled were well-known to Shakespeare and there is frequent mention of them in his works. We have no reason to imagine him a shy, retiring, bookish lad. On the contrary in his youth as in his manhood he must have loved the society of his fellows, and revelled in such games as hide-and-seek and blind-man's buff (the *Hide, fox* and the *hood-man blind* of *Hamlet*), prisoner's base (*Cymbeline,* V, iii, 20), football (*Comedy of Errors,* II, i, 82), and the nine-men's morris (*Midsummer Night's Dream,* II, ii, 98). Like Falstaff in his youth he probably plucked geese, played truant, and whipped the top (*Merry Wives,* V, i, 26), and if he were beaten for his pranks, weighed the pain against the pleasure, shrugged his shoulders, and continued in his ways with the fat Knight's own equanimity. He swam and fished in the Avon and made an early acquaintance with the field sports which seem to have had a decisive influence on his career some time later. In short, as Shakespeare was a man's man in London, we may well believe him to have been a real boy in Stratford.

It was usual then for boys to spend some seven years in the grammar school, and if Shakespeare entered it at the age of seven, he would have been ready to leave in 1578. His first biographer, Rowe, says that Shakespeare's father withdrew him from school at an early age because of his financial difficulties. It is not, however, until 1577 that John's financial difficulties appear in the records and it is hard to see how these would have been lessened by withdrawing his son from school. There were no school bills for John to pay and William could hardly have been a help to him in business before his fourteenth year. It is possible that John's increasing troubles prevented him from sending his son to one of the universities, but whether William lost much thereby is an open question.

Upon leaving school then, about 1578, Shakespeare was probably bound over as apprentice to his father, possibly later, according to an old tradition, to a Stratford butcher. This was the usual, in fact the necessary practice for a boy who was expected to take his father's place in such a town as Stratford. Without passing through an apprenticeship to a recognized craft no one could open a shop, practice a trade, or become a free citizen of the town. No doubt John Shakespeare expected William to take over his business, restore his sinking fortune, and succeed him in his various offices.

It is not likely, however, that William shared his father's expectations. The traditions of his youth at Stratford may be late and uncertain, but they point to a life quite unlike that of the industrious apprentice. The story of his drinking bout with the "sippers" of Bidford and his subsequent night's lodging under a crabtree would hardly have been told about a man whose youth was remembered as one of sobriety and self-restraint. More particularly Shakespeare's familiarity with field sports, hawking and hunting, and with the care and training of horse, hawk, and hound, point, like that efficiency in billiards on which Emerson once remarked, to many ill-spent hours in youth. It is hard to exaggerate the significance of this familiarity. Madden, whose *Diary of Master William Silence* is the recognized authority on this matter, comments on Shakespeare's knowledge of the most intimate secrets of woodcraft and falconry and of the nature and disposition of the horse. He notes, moreover, that this knowledge is peculiar to Shakespeare; no such familiarity with field sports and horses appears in the work of any other Elizabethan playwright. Now it is certain that the young Shakespeare, son of a busy Stratford shopkeeper, never owned a hawk, much less a kennel of hounds, and never bestrode a horse, except perhaps a heavy plough horse on some country farm. Nor could he have acquired this familiarity during his busy years in London. It comes from the period of his youth that lies between his schooldays and his departure to London, and points to hours on hours spent in following on foot the chase of stag and hare as practiced by gentlemen about Stratford and to more hours spent in hanging about the stables, mews, and kennels of such a country house as Charlecote in intimate converse with grooms, falconers, and huntsmen, and in loving observation of their charges. Such hours, after all, were not mis-spent; they have left their traces in delightful passages in his work, but they were not likely to lead to success in business or gladden the heart of an anxious father.

Another pastime which must have delighted young Shakespeare was the drama. Coventry was within walking distance of Stratford and at Coventry some scenes of a famous cycle of miracle plays were annually performed on Corpus Christi day in early summer as late as 1584. Shakespeare may well have seen such a performance more than once and as a boy of eleven he may have gone with his father to see the splendid pageants and masques with which Leicester in 1575 entertained the Queen at Kenilworth some fifteen miles from Stratford. There were, moreover, opportunities for seeing plays at home of which Shakespeare would surely have taken advantage. A travelling company performed at Stratford in 1568 while John Shakespeare was bailiff. They must have given a good report of the little town, for in the seventies and early eighties a number of companies appeared there.[1] It seems more than a guess that the young Shakespeare never missed a chance to attend these performances and that as a boy at Stratford he made his first acquaintance with the crude early work of the Elizabethan drama to which he was destined to contribute its greatest plays.

Shakespeare was hardly more than a boy—not yet nineteen—when he took the most important step in a man's life and married. Such a cloud of controversy has gathered about this marriage and so many inferences have been drawn from it that it seems best simply to state the known facts and leave the inferences to be drawn by the reader.

Shakespeare's bride was Anne, daughter of Richard Hathaway, a farmer at Shottery near Stratford, who died in the summer of 1582. Anne was eight years older than William and apparently quite uneducated. Some months after Richard's death, on November 28, 1582, two friends of his filed a bond with the Bishop of Worcester, in whose diocese the town of Stratford lay, freeing him from all liability if any lawful impediment

[1] In 1573 Leicester's Men; in 1576 the companies of Warwick and Worcester; in 1577 Leicester's and Worcester's; in 1579 Lord Strange's; in 1580 Derby's; in 1581 Worcester's and Lord Berkeley's.

prevented a marriage between Anne and William Shakespeare. The purpose of this action was to obtain the Bishop's license permitting the couple to marry without the customary delay of a triple asking of the banns in church. Such a delay would have carried them into the Advent season and by the old church law marriage was forbidden from Advent Sunday till about the middle of January. And there was urgent reason for a speedy marriage. The Bishop accordingly granted a license [1] and the young couple were married, not in Stratford, as would have been most natural, but in some unknown church. To Stratford they came, however, and there Anne's child was born and baptized Susanna in Trinity Church on May 26, 1583.

It is an interesting fact that John Shakespeare seems to have taken no part in this marriage. His consent, however, must have been obtained as William was still a minor, and it must have been to his house that William brought his bride, for neither he nor Anne had the means to take a house of their own. John can hardly have approved his son's marriage with a poor girl eight years his elder, and it is unlikely that he had consented to or been aware of a formal betrothal before the filing of the bond, an engagement which some apologists for Shakespeare conjecture to have taken place.

Less than two years after Susanna's birth Anne presented her husband with twins who were baptized Hamnet and Judith in Trinity Church on February 2,

[1] A license preserved in the Bishop's register dated Nov. 27, 1582, authorizes the marriage of William Shaxpere to Anne Whately of Temple Grafton. Most scholars believe this to be the license granted to our William and Anne, and explain the discrepancy as due to a clerk's careless copying. On the other hand it may be a license to a quite different pair. The name, William Shakespeare, was not uncommon in the district and Anne Whately of Temple Grafton seems a long remove from Anne Hathaway of Stratford.

1585. After this there is no record of Shakespeare in Stratford for years to come, and there is reason to believe that shortly after the birth of the twins he left his home, his wife, and his children to seek his fortune in the world.

There has been much idle talk about the married life of Shakespeare. The simple facts are that he left his wife at Stratford—their son, Hamnet died and was buried there in 1596 and there is no evidence that Anne ever joined her husband in London—that no children were born to them after 1585, that about 1611 he installed his wife and daughters in New Place, the fine house in Stratford that he had bought in 1597, that he joined them there and died in that house in 1616, leaving Anne his "second best bed" in his will.[2]

These facts do not suggest a congenial and happy marriage, but rather a hasty wedding, a brief life together, a long separation, and late in life an amicable reunion. Further than this we have no right to inquire.

Shakespeare's departure from Stratford is by old tradition connected with a poaching affair. His first biographer states that he had robbed a park belonging to Sir Thomas Lucy and was prosecuted by that gentleman so severely that he was forced to fly to London. There is independent and old corroboration of this story and it is so in accord with what we know of Shakespeare's love of sport and the reckless spirit which led to his hasty marriage that we may well accept it as in

[2] This bequest and the fact that it was an afterthought interpolated into the first draft of the will have been taken to show Shakespeare's disregard of his wife. This is quite improbable. Mrs. Shakespeare, now over sixty, was apparently regarded as incapable of managing property; she was left in charge of Susanna, who with her husband, Dr. Hall, lived in New Place after Shakespeare's death. The bed, probably the one she had used for years, was bequeathed to her as her own personal property, perhaps at her special request.

the main correct. The only question is why such a trivial offence as poaching, punishable at that time by fine and a brief imprisonment, should have driven the culprit into exile. The question, however, is answered when we realize the social position of the two parties in the case. Sir Thomas was the greatest magnate in the neighborhood of Stratford; he was not only a Knight, but a member of Parliament and at one time high sheriff of Warwickshire and Worcestershire. He was interested in preserving game and a rigorous enforcer of the law. When he visited Stratford the Corporation formally entertained him with food and drink at an inn. Shakespeare, on the other hand, though married and the father of three children, may still have been an apprentice, and was certainly a doubtful character; there is no evidence that he had become a free citizen of the town. His father was rapidly losing the high position he had once held, and Shakespeare himself possessed no independent means of support. It is plain that the vindictive wrath of such a personage as Lucy, fanned into flame, the story goes, by a scurrilous ballad which Shakespeare wrote against him, might well render the poet's life at Stratford intolerable.

Another tradition, even older and resting on better authority, comes from a certain William Beeston, whose father, Christopher, had played as a boy in Shakespeare's company. He told the antiquary Aubrey that "Shakespeare understood Latin pretty well for he had been in his younger years a schoolmaster in the country." This is by no means impossible for Shakespeare's training in the Guild School would qualify him at least for a subordinate position in a country school. Nor is the report incompatible with the poaching tradition. There is a gap of seven or eight years between the last record of Shakespeare in Stratford and his appearance in London, and it is quite possible that a period of school-teaching intervened between the two. If so, Shakespeare spent this time in all probability in the neighboring country of Gloucester. The names of Shakespeare and Hathaway occur repeatedly in that district, so that William may have found friends and relatives there who would help him to a position in a school, and in one of his plays (*2 K. H. IV*) he shows an intimate acquaintance with family names, localities, and local customs of the Cotswold district. A year or two of school-teaching, however, was probably enough for Shakespeare and he began to turn his eyes longingly toward London. It is not at all likely that he thought of taking up a trade there, as his fellow Stratfordian, Richard Field, later the publisher of *Venus and Adonis* and of *Lucrece,* had done. He would have heard reports of the building of theatres, the formation of new companies of actors,[1] perhaps even of the brilliant success of Lyly's courtly comedies and the popular triumph of Kyd's *Spanish Tragedy*. It was no doubt with a view to sharing in the bright future dawning for the English drama as an actor, perhaps as a playwright, that Shakespeare, some time about 1587 or 1588, threw down the schoolmaster's rod, closed his books, and took the road to London.

[1] The Queen's new Company was organized in 1583 and its members were allowed wages and liveries as grooms of the chamber—a privilege accorded many years later to Shakespeare himself.

CHAPTER III

SHAKESPEARE'S LONDON

SHAKESPEARE probably came to London about 1587 or 1588—there is no certainty as to the date—and remained there except for short visits to Stratford for some twenty-five years, that is, all his working life. The life of London, the pursuits and pleasures of the citizens, influenced and colored all his life and work. It was for Londoners that he wrote his poems and produced his plays. The country youth had perforce to adapt himself to an urban environment, but there is nothing to show that he shrank from this adaptation. On the contrary it would seem that he plunged gladly into the tide of London life and swam strongly with the current. He won his success, in part at least, by the truth and beauty with which he reflected in his work the spirit and the color of his new surroundings.

London in Shakespeare's day presented the spectacle of a medieval city bursting its bonds, physical and spiritual, under the stimulus of the Renaissance. It was the one city in England which had come fully under the influence of this movement and it was rapidly concentrating in itself all the life in England that was touched by this new spirit. It was not only the capital of the kingdom, but the centre of its social, commercial, and intellectual life. The Queen held her court at Whitehall in Westminster just outside the city proper, or at Greenwich on the Thames below, or at Richmond or Windsor above London. The road along the Thames from the city to Westminster, the Strand of to-day, was lined with the town-houses of great nobles. The Royal Exchange, built by Sir Thomas Gresham in 1566, was the sole building in England devoted to the meetings of merchants for the transaction of business. The quays along the Thames were crowded with shipping from all parts of the world, for English commerce with East and West was increasing with leaps and bounds, and the customs duties paid at London constituted a substantial part of the royal revenue. Except for the university presses at Oxford and Cambridge all the printers and publishers in England were gathered in London, and it was only in London that theatres for the public performance of the drama were to be found. To this great centre of the kingdom there flowed a steady stream of students from the universities, young gentlemen from the homes of the landed aristocracy, and apprentices from provincial towns like Stratford. London was indeed the heart of England, and in Shakespeare's day this heart was beating high with a full consciousness of its supreme importance.

No greater contrast can well be imagined than that between the huge metropolitan London of today and the city of Shakespeare's time. The Thames, a tidal river, swarming with fish, as yet unpolluted by the refuse of factories on its banks, ran all along the old town. It was crossed by a single bridge, London Bridge, reckoned one of the wonders of the world with its score of arches through which the tide rushed with tremendous force. The bridge was built up with shops and houses like the Ponte Vecchio at Florence, and defended at its southern end by a tower and gate over which grinned the rotting heads of traitors fixed on spikes. Flocks of swans sailed gracefully upon the river and hundreds of little boats—some two thousand in Shakespeare's day—plied busily up and down stream with cries of "Westward Ho" and "Eastward Ho," serving the same function of transportation as is today performed by the underground railway, the bus, and the taxi-cab. It is worth noting that coaches were unknown in London streets before 1564, the year of Shakespeare's birth, and wheeled vehicles were still rare in the narrow streets when Shakespeare came to town. The river was the main artery of traffic and served also as a highway for stately pageants and solemn funerals.

The city proper was still surrounded by its mediæval walls describing an arc of over two miles from the Tower in the east, to a brook called the Fleet in the west. The Tower, according to common opinion first built by Julius Cæsar and enlarged from age to age, at once fortress, armory, prison, mint, and menagery for the royal lions, still frowned upon the city. The walls were pierced by gates, closed at the curfew hour, whose names still survive in the London districts of Ludgate, Aldgate, Newgate, the western gate by which Shakespeare entered London, and Bishopsgate. The growing pressure of population, however,—London rose from ca. 100,000 at the beginning of Elizabeth's reign to double that number under her successor—had long since pushed the inhabitants outside the circle of the walls. There were almost as many people living in the suburbs, Southwark, Moorfields, and Charing Cross, as in the city. The suburbs, like one or two small districts within the walls, were not under the jurisdiction of the city authorities. They were known as the "liberties" and were not of the best repute; one angry contemporary calls them "dens for adulterers, thieves, murderers, and every mischief-worker." It was in these "liberties" that the first theatres were built.

Within the walls lay the city proper traversed by a few main crowded thoroughfares intersected at irregular intervals by narrow lanes, unpaved, dark, and dirty. Open sewers ran along them to the river and sanitary conditions were so bad that the city was seldom free from the plague and during Shakespeare's residence was devastated by terrible epidemics in 1593 and 1603. To modern notions the policing of the city was quite unsatisfactory; there was no police force at all by day, and at night the dim streets were protected only by a volunteer guard, of whose efficiency we may form some idea from Shakespeare's humorous picture of the night watch in *Much Ado*. Yet London in his day seems to have been singularly free from crimes of violence.

The closely crowded houses were built of brick and timber and many private dwellings as well as shops and taverns were distinguished by large hanging signs. Yet there were gardens behind many houses and just without the walls there were open fields where the citizens enjoyed their sports. Gentlemen hawked and hunted where today the buildings of the British Museum cover the ground. It is probable that the Londoners of Shakespeare's time spent many more hours in the open than the citizens of to-day. The shops themselves lay open to the air, their goods exposed for sale on benches protected from the rain by penthouses springing from the main building and projecting over the narrow street.

London was a city of churches; the one hundred and twenty steeples of its parish churches rose toward heaven like a forest of stone. Yet it was by no means a religious city. To this the extraordinary condition of its great cathedral, St. Paul's, bears amazing witness. Shortly before Shakespeare's birth a flash of lightning struck the lofty spire and the fire that followed left only the stone walls standing. The church was promptly

rebuilt, all but the spire, but in the years that followed
it became quite as much a meeting and lounging place
for Londoners as a house of prayer. Divine service was
performed daily in the choir, but the transept became
a city thoroughfare and the great central aisle, known
as Paul's Walk, was a combination of business exchange
and city club. Merchants made appointments to meet
at this or that pillar and lawyers transacted business
there with clients. One pillar was reserved for jobless
serving men to post up their qualifications—Falstaff engaged Bardolf in St. Paul's—young gallants strolled up
and down to show off their fine clothes, and tailors hung
about with tablets to take note of the latest fashions and
with tape to measure customers. Penniless adventurers
lounged about the tomb known as Duke Humphrey's
waiting for an invitation to dinner or a chance to fasten
upon some country gull; courtesans and their attendant
squires hunted the place in pursuit of prey. And all the
while the solemn liturgy of the church was being chanted
in the choir. The service, however, was liable to sudden
interruption, for by a local rule, if a gentleman entered
the choir with his spurs on during worship, he was subject to a fine which was collected on the spot by the
choir boys who left their posts to swarm about him like
a flock of white butterflies. Paul's Churchyard—the
walled enclosure of the cathedral—and the lanes adjoin-
ing were the centre of the book trade—over half of
Shakespeare's plays published in his lifetime issued from
Paul's Yard, and he must have spent hours at the book-
stalls reading some new poem or turning over a book of
old tales in search for a plot for a play.

This conversion of the great cathedral to secular uses
was characteristic of the spirit of London in Shakespeare's day. The busy, eager, many-colored life of the
town, was pre-eminently a worldly life. The old religion

had lost its hold upon the people and Puritanism, though growing ever stronger among the middle classes, had not yet become predominant. If London had a real religion it was that of patriotism. The great city was devotedly loyal to the Queen. There was a fierce outburst of popular wrath when a Catholic posted on the door of the Bishop of London's palace a papal bull, excommunicating and deposing Elizabeth, and it was only appeased by the public execution of the offender in St. Paul's Churchyard. It is worth noting in this connection that Catholics were prosecuted in Elizabeth's reign on civil, not on religious grounds, and that the victims were executed as traitors, not as Catholics; a loyal Catholic was as a rule left unmolested. London merchants joined with the Queen in financing the plundering and colonizing expeditions which challenged the power of Spain in the New World. At the approach of the Armada Elizabeth called on London for fifteen ships and five thousand men; the loyal city promptly offered double the number of both and raised an additional force of ten thousand men to meet a possible invasion. The wealth of the city, due in the main to its commerce, was rapidly increasing and the citizens were well aware that their peace and prosperity rested upon the firm rule and wise policy of the Queen.

London was not only a busy and patriotic city; it was passionately addicted to pleasure. In spite of the attempted restrictions of a Puritan magistracy the spirit of the citizens at large was still that of Merry England. They poured out of the walls on Sundays and holidays to seek their pleasure in the open fields and suburbs, to play at bowls or football, to shoot at the butts, to watch the baiting of bulls and bears, or to see a play in some inn courtyard or theatre.

In the life of pleasure-loving London the taverns

played a principal part. Originally mere inns for the reception of travellers, these houses had in Shakespeare's day developed a variety of functions. They served not only as lodging places but as restaurants where a guest might either eat at the host's table, the so-called "ordinary," or order what food he wished served to him in a private room. It was customary for a gentleman visiting a tavern to engage such a room for himself and his friends, male or female, where he might eat and drink, transact business, gamble, or make love, undisturbed except by the entrance of the "drawer"— the waiter—or by the appearance of a band of musicians—"a noise" in Elizabethan English—who wandered from tavern to tavern to offer their services to gentlemen inclined for a little music. Such rooms were distinguished, not by numbers as now-a-days, but by proper names, the Rose, the Angel, the Dolphin, etc., with corresponding signs over the doors and the amount consumed therein was charged up to the room at the central bar— "score a pint of bastard"—a sweet Spanish wine—"in the Half Moon" is the drawer's cry in *I King Henry IV*. In such rooms, where visitors were assured of a certain amount of privacy, groups of friends assembled for social intercourse and so made a beginning of the modern club. We hear, for instance, of the famous group comprising Shakespeare, Jonson, Beaumont, Fletcher, and other wits, poets, and playwrights, who used to meet at the Mermaid tavern, and somewhat later Jonson presided in state over a club which met in the Apollo room of the Devil tavern at Temple Bar. Here the old scholar-poet wrote the club rules in Latin and engraved them in marble over the fireplace and here he formally adopted young wits and poets into "the tribe of Ben."

In the large common room before the bar all sorts of conditions of men assembled to drink a cup of sack meet a friend, chaff the drawer, and kiss the hostess. Here was the soldier, full of strange oaths, back from the Low Countries, the sailor from the Indies, the traveller from the Continent, the scholar from Oxford or Cambridge, the flat-capped city prentice, and the county squire open-eyed in wonder at strange sights and sounds. The Elizabethan drama, not only of Shakespeare, but particularly of such city playwrights as Jonson, Dekker, and Middleton is redolent of the London tavern.

There was, moreover, a particular bond between the tavern and the new drama. From early times the inn courtyard had been a common place for dramatic performances. Entered from the street by a single arch through which the carriers led their horses, and surrounded by galleries opening on the adjacent rooms of the inn, the courtyard was easily adapted to a crude sort of theatre. A scaffold projecting into the·yard was erected for the stage opposite the entrance and a curtain hung from the gallery over the scaffold gave a backdrop to the actors who entered the stage from their dressing-room in the inn behind the curtain. They could also use, if they wished, a part of the gallery just above the scaffold to represent an upper chamber or the wall of a town. One of the actors stood at the arch to exact the penny entrance fee which admitted the spectator to standing room in the flagged courtyard. Such spectators were the "groundlings" of Shakespeare's plays. Visitors of higher rank, with heavier purses, hired a room in the tavern, sat on stools in the gallery and witnessed the performance at their ease. There were no theatres in or near London till some years after Shakespeare's birth and the natural home of the new drama was the inn courtyard. Performances within the city limits were indeed forbidden by a local ordinance in

1567, but the prohibition, like other prohibitions, was not strictly enforced; plays long continued to be given at such London taverns as the Crosskeys, where Shakespeare himself may have acted, at the Red Bull, and at the Boar's Head. The inn which he made immortal as the hangout of Sir John Falstaff was in Eastcheap.

Performances at such places were attended by a motley throng of spectators. The dregs of the city, harlots and pickpockets, plied their trade and jostled sober citizens with their wives, while rowdy prentices rubbed elbows with country squires. London citizens delighted in shows of every sort; malicious gossip declared that city wives would sell their honor for a sight of masques at court. The city fathers presented gorgeous pageants in the streets or on the river on every fit occasion. All this thirst for pleasure in the form of spectacle found a quick gratification in the lively action, the songs and dances, the clownage, the broad-sword combats, and the dumb-shows of the new drama. The rapid building of theatres and the amazing development of the drama in Shakespeare's day show how heartily the city supported this new art. It must not be forgotten that Elizabethan drama was a popular entertainment; it was neither endowed by the state like the Attic drama nor supported by the court as later in France. It appealed directly to and depended mainly upon audiences composed of London citizens.

There were, however, two institutions which exerted a very considerable influence upon the new drama, neither of which were in any sense popular. The first of these was the Inns of Court. These famous London law-schools, through which alone admission to the Bar was possible, were and still are, something more than law-schools. Dating back to the thirteenth and fourteenth centuries the four great Inns, the Inner and the Middle

Temple, Lincoln's Inn, and Gray's, resembled the colleges of Oxford and Cambridge. They required the residence of students within their walls or in subordinate Inns, such as Clement's, Staple's, and Furnivall's, which were attached to them. Their members dined together, summoned to table by the blast of a horn, and attended worship together in their own chapels. The Inns were self-governing bodies, outside the jurisdiction of the city, and ruled by their senior members, the Benchers. Even the King's writ did not run in the precincts of an Inn of Court and a story is told of an unlucky royal messenger who was shaved, ducked, and beaten by the students for venturing within their grounds to serve a warrant on one of them. Membership was strictly limited to the upper classes, for all students were required to be sons of "persons of quality." Many famous Elizabethans were members of these Inns; Sidney and Bacon belonged to Gray's, Sackville and Beaumont to the Inner Temple, John Donne to Lincoln's Inn. It was customary for a student to retain his membership in his Inn long after he had completed his studies. Bacon, for example, through his long and busy life, retained an active interest in the affairs of Gray's, devised their Court masques, contributed generously to these costly shows, and laid out the lovely gardens of the Inn where his statue now stands. Thus the Inns of Court were social as well as educational institutions. Members had as a matter of course the entry of the royal court. They were taught dancing and courtly manners as well as law and it was not only the privilege, but in a sense the duty, of the Inns to entertain the sovereign with revels, masques, and dramatic performances.

Now the interest of these Inns in the drama of Shakespeare's day was lively and intelligent. Members of the Inns acted in works of their own composition and sometimes called in professional actors on state occasions; *The Comedy of Errors,* for instance, was acted at Gray's in 1594 and *Twelfth Night* at the Middle Temple in 1602. A large proportion of the members came from the universities; all of them had probably received the common classical training of the grammar-schools. It is, therefore, not surprising that they were for the most part admirers of classical drama. Indeed the attempt to domesticate Senecan drama in England was closely connected with the dramatic activities of the Inns of Court. Sackville and Norton led the way with their *Gorboduc,* performed at the Inner Temple in 1562 and later before the Queen at Whitehall. At the same Inn in 1566 Gascoigne and Kinwelmersh produced *Jocasta,* their translation of an Italian version of the *Phoenissae* of Euripides. *Gismond of Salerne,* revised and published as *Tancred and Gismonda,* was written by five members of the Inner Temple and played at Court in 1568. Finally *The Misfortunes of Arthur,* the most purely Senecan of Elizabethan tragedies, was the work of a member of Gray's.

The influence of the Inns of Court upon the new drama must have been profound and lasting. Members of the Inns were constant and enthusiastic supporters of the theatre. They furnished a group of auditors at once appreciative and critical who cared less than the "groundlings" for mere action, jigs, and clowning, but demanded lofty rhetoric, classical allusions, regular structure, and polished verse. They not only attended the theatres but conversed with the playwrights and actors at the tavern and elsewhere. Jonson boasts of his friendship with "divers members of the Inns of Court" and though we have no record of such an intimacy on Shakespeare's part, it is most likely that as a popular playwright and an actor in the best company of his day he must have been well acquainted with the dramatic enthusiasts of the Inns. One can imagine how these gentlemen would urge their views upon the playwrights and it is fairly certain that the classical influence which helped to transform the crude popular drama of the first decades of Elizabeth's reign came in large measure through the Inns of Court.

The second great influence upon the new drama was that of the Court. It is hard for us today to appreciate the extent of this influence upon life in Shakespeare's London. The Queen was, of course, the sole fount of honor; her favor could raise any man to the highest pinnacle of fortune; her wrath could break the proudest noble; and both her favor and wrath were exhibited in most capricious fashion. The Court constantly intervened in private affairs and in the daily business of the city. The Queen apparently thought herself possessed of the power of veto on the marriages of her courtiers; she granted and withdrew trade monopolies by which fortunes were made and lost. Even in the provisioning of the city the Court played a part, for its caterers had the first choice on every shipload of fish or cartload of country supplies that was brought into town.

The Court circle, too, was larger than it is today. It was open, as a matter of course, to all members of the landed gentry who swarmed to London to share in the new life of the realm. It was open at certain times under certain restrictions to the citizens themselves. From time to time the Queen made stately progresses through the city and was feasted by rich merchants or city magistrates. A host of Londoners were in one way or another dependent on the Court, holding minor offices about it, supplying its needs or satisfying its pleasures. Court intrigues, the rise and fall of favorites and factions, were as interesting to the Londoner of Shake-

speare's day as local and national politics are to us.
The Court certainly influenced the daily life of Shakespeare's London far more intimately and powerfully
than it does the London of today.

Now the Court of Elizabeth was not only pleasure-
loving, but it found a main source of its pleasure in spectacles, masquing, and the drama. The Queen herself, a
true Renaissance sovereign, at once cultured and lux-
urious, was an ardent lover of such entertainments. She
had a special official, the Master of Revels, whose business it was to prepare and supervise all masques and
plays at Court and who finally came to exercise the function of licenser and censor of all plays. Through her
Privy Council Elizabeth more than once intervened to
protect the players from the attacks of the city magistrates. In 1583, for example, when they were waging an
aggressive war upon actors and theatres, the Queen
selected twelve of the best actors from various organi-
zations to form her own company, the Queen's Servants,
and gave them a special license to play in London and in
the country. The Children of the Chapel, that is the
choir-boys of the Court Chapel, were under her special
protection. They began at an early date to present plays
at Court and later began giving public performances in
a hall in the former monastery of Blackfriars. The
Queen helped to pay their expenses, lent her musicians
to accompany their performances, outfitted them from
her magnificent wardrobe, and seems once at least to
have attended a performance at Blackfriars along with
her maids of honor.

As a rule, however, when Elizabeth wished to see a
play she commanded a performance at Court. We have
numerous records of such performances by various companies, but from 1594 on Shakespeare's company was
the Queen's favorite. Shakespeare and his fellows ap-

peared at Court every year from 1594 till the Queen's
death in 1603, often several times a year. Their popularity was due not only to their ability as actors, but
also to the fact that they alone could present Shakespeare's plays. We know that *Love's Labour's Lost, The
Comedy of Errors, The Merchant of Venice, King
Henry IV, King Henry V,* and *Much Ado about Nothing*
were acted before Elizabeth, and there is an old tradition that *The Merry Wives of Windsor* was written at
her command. The favor that she showed this company
was increased rather than diminished under her successor. James took Shakespeare and his fellows under his
direct patronage, gave them the title of the King's Servants, and attached them officially to the royal household
as grooms of the Chamber. It is even credibly reported
that James once wrote Shakespeare a letter with his own
royal hand.

As a result of this intimate connection between the
Court and the drama, Shakespeare as actor and playwright came into close touch with the aristocracy of
England. Some of the great nobles of the day, Stanley,
Essex, Southampton, the Pembroke brothers, William
and Philip, were among his patrons, acquaintances, and
even friends. The public audiences to which he played
were almost exclusively masculine, but at Court he saw
and met the loveliest, wittiest, and most cultured ladies
of the realm. It was from them that he drew such
gracious and charming figures as the Princess and her
ladies in *Love's Labour's Lost,* Portia, Rosalind, Beatrice, and Imogen; and the influence of the Court is no
less noticeable in the dialogue of his plays, in the high-
flown style, the conceits, affectations, and sparkling
repartee with which his comedies abound. Lacking this
connection with the Court, Shakespeare would doubtless
have been a great dramatist, but his plays would not

have been what they are without the deep and lasting influence to which this connection exposed him.

Enough has been said to show the difference between Shakespeare's London and the environment of his early life in Stratford. He must have felt when he settled down to work in the city as if he had been transported into a brave new world. The rich, busy, pleasure-loving city, the lively, intelligent, and critical gentlemen of the Inns of Court, the royal Court with its circle of splendid nobles and fair women, formed a world of which he could hardly even have dreamed at Stratford. Yet he was quick to recognize that the life of this new world was altogether human. Unlike his Miranda he did not mistake its inhabitants for immortal spirits. He saw, no one more clearly, their affectations, follies, and vices. Yet Shakespeare was a child of the Renaissance and the Renaissance atmosphere which surrounded him for a quarter of a century in London was the very environment needed to bring his genius to its full and splendid flower.

CHAPTER IV

SHAKESPEARE IN LONDON—UNDER ELIZABETH

THERE is no certain record of Shakespeare's life or activities between February, 1585, when the twins, Hamnet and Judith, were baptized in the church at Stratford, and the year 1592 when he was at work as actor and playwright in London, as we know from Robert Greene's attack on him referred to below.

This period from 1585 to 1592 is sometimes spoken of as "the lost years"; some part of it may have been spent as a school-teacher, but to have obtained such a position in London as is shown by Greene's onslaught, he must have been active there for a considerable period. It is a fair guess, but only a guess, that he came to town to seek his fortune about 1587 or in the Armada year of 1588. No doubt he plunged at once into the world of play-acting and play-making. An old tradition that his career in London began by holding horses outside one of the new theatres is hardly credible. It is more likely that he attached himself at once to one of the companies of actors. The parish clerk at Stratford told a visitor in 1693 that Shakespeare was at first received into the play-house as a "serviture," which means that he was engaged by one of the companies to do odd jobs and play minor parts, in other words that he was one of the "hirelings" (see below p. 67). It has long been believed that this company was that of Lord Strange with which

we find him associated from 1594 for the rest of his life.
Recent scholarship inclines to the view that he joined a
company organized under the patronage of Lord Pembroke about the year 1590. There are arguments, not
very convincing for either view, and it does not after all
make much difference. Of one thing we may be sure, that
Shakespeare was both busy and successful in his new
career by 1592 when we next hear of him.

In the late summer of 1592 Robert Greene, the brilliant and dissolute poet, playwright, and pamphleteer,
lay on his death-bed. In extreme poverty and deserted
by his former friends he roused himself to write an
autobiographical tract, *Green's Groatsworth of Wit
bought with a Million of Repentance* which he hoped to
sell for enough to pay his debts. After narrating the
rather scandalous life of a certain Roberto, i.e. Greene
himself, he closes with a sharp warning to his former
friends and fellow playwrights, Marlowe, Peele, and
Nashe, to beware of the players who will desert them
as they have deserted him. "Yes, trust them not:" he
continues, "for there is an upstart crowe beautified with
our feathers that with his *Tyger's hart wrapt in a
Player's hyde* supposes he is as well able to bombast out
a blanke verse as the best of you; and beeing an absolute
Johannes fac totum, is in his owne conceit the onely
Shakes-scene in a countrey." The phrase, a *Tyger's
hart, etc.,* is parodied from a line in *III K. H. VI* (I,
iv, 137), a play by the young Shakespeare who is directly pointed at in the pun on his name, "Shakes-scene."
It is plain that Greene was provoked by the success of
Shakespeare both as an actor, "a crowe beautified by
our feathers," i.e. famous by speaking the poetical lines
of Greene and his fellows, and as a rising dramatist
able, at least in his own conceit, to write blank verse
with the best of them.

The *Groatsworth* was edited for publication by Henry Chettle, an old friend of Greene's, and appeared in print shortly after his death, September 3, 1592. It caused a distinct sensation; Marlowe, who had been accused of atheism, a very dangerous accusation at that day, when even a Unitarian like Kett of Cambridge might be burnt as a heretic, was naturally furious, and Shakespeare, or his friends, seem to have been deeply offended. At any rate pressure was brought to bear on Chettle who in a preface to his *Kind-Hart's Dreame,* entered in the Stationers' Register, December 8, 1592, made a formal apology. Chettle's reference to Shakespeare is so interesting that it deserves to be quoted in full.

After noting that Greene's address to "diverse playmakers is offensively by one or two of them taken" he goes on to say that "With neither of them that take offence was I acquainted, and with one of them [Marlowe, of course] I care not if I never be. The other, whome at that time I did not so much spare, as since I wish I had . . . that I did not, I am as sorry as if the originall fault had beene my fault, because my selfe have seene his demeanor no lesse civill than he exelent in the qualitie he professes [i.e. acting]: Besides divers of worship have reported his uprightnes of dealing, which argues his honesty, and his facetious grace in writing, that approves his Art."

There are several interesting things to be noted in this statement. Chettle seems to have met Shakespeare for the first time—no doubt in connection with the controversy over Greene's pamphlet—and to have been as much impressed with his "civil demeanor," well-bred manners, as by his ability, generally recognized, as an actor. Apparently, moreover, "divers of worship," i.e. noblemen or gentlemen of standing, had testified to Shakespeare's "uprightness in dealing"—he was too

honest to steal another man's work as Greene had in-
sinuated, and to the charm and grace of his writing—
he did not need to steal. Evidently Chettle recognized
at once that Shakespeare was something better than the
"upstart crowe, the Johannes fac totum" of Greene's
attack.

It seems likely that a combination of circumstances
turned Shakespeare in the autumn of 1592 from his work
as actor-playwright to a more ambitious undertaking,
the effort to establish himself as a true poet. A scandalous riot of apprentices in June, 1592, brought about
the closing of all theatres for a period of three months.
Before this time had elapsed the plague broke out in
London with such severity that the theatres were forced
to remain closed, except for a few brief intervals, until
the summer of 1594. The chief companies, Pembroke's
and Lord Strange's, went on tour in the provinces, but
Shakespeare did not accompany either of them. On the
contrary he remained in London and devoted himself to
the composition of a long poem in the fashionable erotic
manner of the time, his *Venus and Adonis*.

Every poet in that day needed a patron; the Elizabethan public might support, after a fashion, a popular
playwright; it was quite incapable of buying enough
books of verse to keep a poet alive. And so, naturally,
Shakespeare looked about for a benefactor. It may be
that "divers of worship" suggested to him the name of
the Earl of Southampton, young, rich, and extravagant,
but in the words of a contemporary "a dear lover and
cherisher as well of the lovers of poets as of poets
themselves." To him Shakespeare dedicated *Venus and
Adonis,* which he called "the first heir of my invention,"
in a respectful epistle remarkable for the absence of
the customary fulsome flattery of Elizabethan dedications.

The little volume, printed by Richard Field, appeared some time in the early summer of 1593 and was sold for the usual price of 6d. It is interesting to note that some years ago a copy was sold in London for £15,000. The work had a phenomenal success; eight editions were published in Shakespeare's lifetime and his rank as one of the leading poets of the day was at once established. From 1593 on there are repeated references to "honey-tongued" Shakespeare and to his popularity especially with young lovers of poetry. More than this the poem seems to have brought Shakespeare into familiar and friendly association with Southampton and the brilliant circle of which the young earl was an ornament. There is a tradition going back to Davenant that Southampton once gave Shakespeare £1,000 "to enable him to go through with a purchase." The figure is probably much exaggerated, but a handsome gift is more than likely.

In January, 1594, during a brief lull in the plague the theatres were re-opened and a minor company, Sussex's Men, presented *Titus Andronicus* at the Rose. Henslowe, the owner of this theatre, marked this play in his account book "ne"—probably meaning that it was played in a new and revised form, and there is some reason to believe that he engaged the popular poet Shakespeare to make this revision.

Shakespeare's revision of *Titus* was probably the product of a few hours withdrawn from a more serious undertaking. This was the composition of a long narrative poem on the story of Lucretia. It may be that the frequent references to the erotic quality of *Venus and Adonis* provoked Shakespeare to attempt a poem on a graver subject. He completed it in the spring of 1594 and published it in the summer of that year. Like *Venus and Adonis* it was dedicated to Southampton, but this time in an epistle that shows the nature of the relation

that had grown up between the poet and his patron.
"The love I dedicate to your Lordship" wrote Shakespeare "is without end—what I have done is yours;
what I have to do is yours; being part in all I have,
devoted yours."

Lucrece was at once successful. It never quite attained the popularity of *Venus and Adonis,* but five
editions were called for in Shakespeare's lifetime and
there was a consensus of opinion that the poet had
done well to leave "love's foolish lazy languishment"
and turn to a theme that could "please the wiser
sort."

It was in these years 1593-94, apparently, that Shakespeare following again the fashion of the time began the
composition of his sonnets. These were intended for
private circulation among his friends; it is possible that
some of them were addressed directly to Southampton.
But the whole vexed question of the sonnets needs fuller
treatment than can be given here. (See below, pp. 189-
194.)

With the cessation of the plague in the summer of
1594 the theatres re-opened. Two main companies of
actors re-organized—one headed by Alleyn playing under
the patronage of the Lord Admiral; the other formerly
Lord Strange's, under that of the Lord Chamberlain.
It was to this company that Shakespeare now attached
himself, if, indeed, he had not been connected with it
before, and with this company he remained as actor and
playwright for the rest of his life in London. A warrant
for payment of two performances at Court in the Christmas season of 1594 joins Shakespeare's name with those
of Kemp, the clown of the company, and Burbage the
famous tragedian, and reveals his position as one of the
full-fledged members of the company. In 1595-96 we
find him living in the Parish of St. Helen's near the
theatre where his company was acting. He must have

been a very busy man, rehearsing in the morning, acting in the afternoon, and busily engaged in touching up old and writing new plays for his fellows. Most of the older playwrights, Lyly, Greene, Marlowe, Peele and Kyd had died or stopped writing by 1594—a group of younger writers had yet to win their spurs upon the stage—and Shakespeare rose rapidly into eminence as the most popular and successful dramatist of the day. The years from 1594 to 1600 must have been among the busiest and happiest of Shakespeare's life.

A couple of interesting documents discovered lately among old court records in London show that in the autumn of 1596 Shakespeare had shifted his lodging from St. Helen's Parish to the Surrey side of the Thames. The one of these that concerns us is a petition by a certain William Wayte, stepson of William Gardiner, Justice of the Peace in Surrey, praying that William Shakespeare, Francis Langley, builder of the Swan Theatre, and others, might be bound over to keep the peace since they had put him in the fear of death. This petition is part of a long wrangle between Gardiner and Langley in which only a few weeks before Langley had filed a similar petition against Gardiner and Wayte. What Shakespeare's part in the quarrel was we shall never know, but it is interesting to learn that at one time of his life he is at least alleged to have put the fear of death into a fellow citizen.

These were the years in which he began to amass a quite considerable fortune. The first evidence of this is seen in 1596 when his father at Stratford applied to the Herald's Office for the grant of a coat of arms which would permit him and his son after him to write themselves down as "gentlemen." It is probable that William suggested the application; other members of his company, Phillips, Pope and Burbage were securing such patents of gentility and Shakespeare was not the man to fall behind in the race. After due consideration and the receipt of the customary fee the Heralds granted John Shakespeare the well-known coat of arms with a falcon shaking a spear—the pun on the name is evident —and the motto *Non sanz droict*.

A more substantial sign of his increasing prosperity appears in his purchase in 1597 of New Place, one of the finest houses in Stratford, originally built by Sir Hugh Clopton, and often spoken of as "the Great House." It had fallen into considerable decay and Shakespeare acquired it for the small sum of £60, but he repaired and restored it till it became one of the glories of the town, surrounded by orchards and gardens and boasting the extreme luxury of ten fireplaces. Fifty years later during the Civil Wars when Queen Henrietta Maria came to Stratford at the head of a Royalist Army, she took up her residence at New Place, then occupied by Shakespeare's daughter Susanna and his grandchild Elizabeth. This was the first of several purchases of landed property that Shakespeare made. As late as 1613 we find him purchasing a dwelling-house in the fashionable quarter of Blackfriars; but New Place was his country home. He seems to have established his wife and daughters there at once—the boy Hamnet had died in 1596—and it was to New Place that he finally retired. One can imagine the sensation in Stratford when it was known that young Shakespeare who had left the town under a cloud and joined himself to the "roguish players" in London was now the master of New Place. The re-action of the townsfolk was characteristic; they at once attempted to get Shakespeare to invest more money at Stratford and one of the Stratford Quineys on business and in debt at London tried to borrow £30 of him.

In 1598 Francis Meres, a scholar and clergyman, living at that time in London wrote a book with the high sounding title of *Palladis Tamia, Wits Treasury*. It was in the main a review of English literature from the time of Chaucer and a comparison of English authors with their classical prototypes. He paid particular attention to Shakespeare and after declaring that "the sweet witty soul of Ovid" lived again in Shakespeare's verse, he went on to speak of his work as dramatist. The passage deserves quotation in full: "As Plautus and Seneca are accounted the best for Comedy and Tragedy among the Latines: so Shakespeare among the English is the most excellent in both kinds for the stage; for Comedy, witnes his *Gentlemen of Verona,* his *Errors,* his *Love labors lost,* his *Love labours wonne,* his *Midsummers night dreame* & his *Merchant of Venice:* for Tragedy, his *Richard the 2. Richard the 3. Henry the 4. King John, Titus Andronicus* and his *Romeo and Juliet."*

There are some interesting facts about this famous list. In the first place out of the twelve plays named only six —*Titus, Richard II, Richard III, Henry IV, Romeo and Juliet* and *Love's Labour's Lost*—had appeared in print when Meres published his book (entered S. R. Sept. 15, 1598). Of these only three, the second editions of *Richard II* and *Richard III,* and *Love's Labour's Lost* bore Shakespeare's name on the title-page. It is plain that Meres must have seen the other six upon the stage, or at least have talked with men who had seen them and that he had been assured that these six as well as the three printed but unsigned plays were the work of "honey-tongued Shakespeare." In other words Meres must have been closely in touch with the world of the theatre in London in 1597–98.

In the second place there is a curious addition and an interesting omission in this list. No play bearing the name of *Love's Labours Won* has come down to us. It is most unlikely that a play with this title has been lost and it is probable that it was the first name of *All's Well That Ends Well,* later revised, re-named, and printed for the first time in the Folio of 1623. It has also been identified, less probably, with *The Taming of the Shrew.* The omission is that of the trilogy on the reign of Henry VI. (See below, p. 126.) We may assume that if these plays were on the stage when Meres wrote, which is rather doubtful, he did not feel justified in claiming them for Shakespeare. On the other hand, we note that he did so claim *Titus Andronicus* and his testimony may at least assure us that this repulsive tragedy passed for Shakespeare's in Meres' day.

We may assume that Meres meant to give and gave, as far as his knowledge allowed, a complete list of Shakespeare's plays up to the date of his writing, i.e. to the summer of 1598. The list seems complete; there is no extant play by Shakespeare with the possible exceptions of *The Shrew* and the *Henry VI* trilogy which can be dated before this time.

Finally the list throws an interesting light on the character of Shakespeare's work for the theatre up to 1598. Apart from his revision of *Titus* and the early poetic lyric tragedy of *Romeo and Juliet,* it consisted entirely of comedy—Meres lists six plays—and of chronicle plays which Meres groups under tragedy. The chronological order of these plays is discussed below. (pp. 126-143.)

Another interesting proof of Shakespeare's popularity appeared in the following year, 1599, when an enterprising publisher, W. Jaggard, secured a manuscript which included among other poems two of Shakespeare's sonnets, yet unprinted, two others from *Love's Labour's Lost,* and a song from that play. The manuscript was probably a gentleman's commonplace book in which the

owner had copied poems printed and unprinted that
he had come across. Jaggard had the impudence to label
it *The Passionate Pilgrim* and to publish it as by W.
Shakespeare. The fraud seems to have been successful,
for a second edition appeared some time later—no copy
has come to us and the exact date is unknown—and a
third in 1612. To this last Jaggard prefixed the statement "newly augmented and corrected by W. Shakespeare" and added a pair of poetical epistles between
Helen and Paris which he lifted from *Troia Britanica*
a poem by Shakespeare's contemporary playwright,
Thomas Heywood. Heywood naturally protested vigor-
ously against the theft and in an epistle added to his
Apology for Actors, 1612, remarked that Shakespeare
was "much offended with M. Jaggard that (altogether
unknown to him) presumed to make so bold with his
name." This is, I believe, the only bit of evidence
we have that Shakespeare ever took offence at the im-
proper use of his name or the piratical publication of
his work.

In 1599 a very important change occurred in Shakespeare's fortunes and his relation to his fellow actors
which deserves attention. His company, the Chamberlain's Men, had been acting for some years at the Theatre
in the suburbs north of London. This building had been
erected by James Burbage, father of Shakespeare's
friend Richard, in 1576 on ground for which he had taken
a twenty-one year lease. Shortly before its expiration he
had attempted to open a new playhouse in the fashionable district of Blackfriars in the very heart of London.
The residents of the district entered an emphatic protest and the Privy Council forbade Burbage to proceed
with his undertaking. He died in 1597 leaving his
troubles to his sons Cuthbert and Richard. Cuthbert, to
whom the Theatre had been left by his father's will, tried

in vain for a year or more to secure an extension of the
lease from Giles Alleyn, the landlord, but in the last
days of 1598 he realized that Alleyn not only was determined to refuse, but meant to seize and tear down the
building. Thereupon Cuthbert secured the services of a
master-builder, tore down the Theatre himself, and
transported the material across the Thames to the sport-
ing district of the Bankside where the builder promptly
erected a new playhouse for him, the famous Globe
Theatre. This must have been a very expensive business
and Cuthbert, who seems to have inherited his father's
business ability, devised a scheme for financing it which
was new in his day and of great importance to the leading players of the company. He formed a stock company
consisting of ten shares of which he and Richard took five
and invited the actors to subscribe for the remaining
half. Five of the company, Shakespeare, Heminges,
Phillips, Pope, and Kemp, responded taking one share
each. This little group—the "housekeepers" they were
called—along with the Burbage brothers thus became
the owners of the Globe which they then leased out to
the company on profitable terms. This excellent arrangement secured the loyalty of the chief actors to the company—only one of the housekeepers, Kemp, ever left
them,—increased their profits, and made it possible to
admit in later years deserving actors to this favored
inside ring. Henceforth Shakespeare as one of this
group enjoyed a triple source of revenue; as a dramatist
he was paid for the plays he furnished the company, as
an actor he received his proportionate share of the net
profits on all plays acted at the Globe, and in addition
as a housekeeper, he received a tenth, later somewhat
more, of the rent the company paid the owners of the
theatre.

The Globe opened probably in the summer of 1599.

Jonson's *Every Man out of his Humor* was one of the early productions and it was quickly followed by a group of Shakespeare's comedies, *Much Ado, As You Like It,* and *Twelfth Night.* These are the so-called Joyous Comedies and, as we have seen, there was every reason at this time for Shakespeare to be in the best of spirits. But clouds were beginning to gather.

In the spring of 1599 Essex, a popular hero since his raid on Cadiz, started for Ireland to put down the dangerous Tyrone rebellion. In his company went Shakespeare's friend and patron Southampton. The expedition set out with high hopes which are reflected in a well-known passage in the Chorus to the last act of *Henry V* where Shakespeare pictures Essex returning from Ireland "bringing rebellion broached on his sword" and the Londoners pouring out to welcome him. But the expedition proved a complete failure; instead of crushing Tyrone Essex made a truce on favorable terms with him and rushed back to England to regain the favor of the Queen which his ill-success had forfeited. In this too he was unsuccessful; he was brought to trial, stripped of his offices, and driven at last to open rebellion. Early in February, 1601, he and Southampton and a group of discontented nobles and gentlemen determined to march into London at the head of an armed force, rouse the city, and seize the person of the Queen. They may even have planned to depose her, for a day or two before the rising some of the conspirators came to the Globe and asked the actors to give a performance of "the play of the deposing and killing of *King Richard II*" with the idea, probably, that representation of such a precedent would win the sympathy of the audience for their proposed rebellion. The prudent actors demurred but were induced by promise of a special bonus to accede to the request, and accordingly revived the old play on Saturday, February 6, before a house packed by the friends of Essex.

On Sunday the 7th Essex with a body of 200 armed men marched into London and attempted to raise the city. The loyal Londoners, however, were in no mood to join even such a popular hero as Essex. The mad attempt collapsed at once; Essex was arrested, tried and convicted of high treason and, on February 25, beheaded on Tower Hill. Southampton, too, was condemned to death, but the sentence was commuted at the last moment to life imprisonment and he was accordingly confined in the Tower for the remaining years of Elizabeth's reign.

The rebellion and death of Essex ended the glorious period of Elizabeth's reign. "The Queen," it was said, "had no comfort thereafter and the people were wrathful at the death of their favorite. . . . The death of Essex like a melancholy cloud did shade the prospect of her people's affection." And over Shakespeare this cloud must have cast an especial shadow. The sudden and tragic fall of so brilliant a figure as Essex, the danger and long imprisonment of his beloved Southampton, contributed not a little, we may well believe, to the gloomy outlook upon life which shows itself in his work for years to come. It is not without significance that when a chorus of poets burst out in mournful strains at Elizabeth's death, March 24, 1603, Shakespeare was noticeably silent. His company, in fact, had been involved in the rebellion and one of its oldest and most respected members, Augustine Phillips, was called on to testify at the trial of Essex and Southampton to their innocency in performing *Richard II* at the request of the conspirators. Phillips seems to have cleared his companions of all blame, for no punishment of any kind was inflicted on the company, and Elizabeth actually invited them to play before her on the eve of the execution of Essex.

One would like to know what play was acted and in what mood Shakespeare performed before her Majesty.

Another cloud that appeared on the horizon meant less, no doubt, to Shakespeare personally than the ruin of Essex and Southampton, but even more to his company. This was the new and lively competition in the theatrical world thrust upon them by the sudden rise to favor of the Children of the Chapel. Their enterprising manager, Evans, secured permission to give so-called private performances in the hall of Blackfriars where James Burbage had been forbidden to put on plays and which Evans now rented from Richard Burbage. The closed hall was a far more pleasant place in which to sit and watch a play than the open air theatre of the Globe. The Children were well trained and accomplished actors; the music, vocal and instrumental, was excellent, and the high prices charged for admission kept the audience select. A little group of poets and playwrights began selling their works to the Children and before long the whole fashionable world of London was crowding to Blackfriars. That Shakespeare's company suffered from and resented this competition is plain from the well-known passage in Hamlet referring to the "little eyases" [the unfledged birds] that are now the fashion and carry away "Hercules and his load"—the swinging sign of Shakespeare's theatre was, of course, Hercules with the Globe on his shoulders.

This competition was intensified, moreover, by what is known as the "War of the Theatres." Jonson for some reason turned his back on Shakespeare's company who had produced his two *Every Man* plays and began writing for the Children. In the plays they staged for him Jonson indulged not only in general satire, but gave free rein to personal animosities which culminated in his *Poetaster,* 1601, with some very ill-natured slurs on his old friends at the Globe, the "common players." In revenge Shakespeare's company secured the right to present at the Globe *Satiromastix* a play written by two of Jonson's enemies for the private theatre where the Boys of Pauls were playing. In the play Jonson himself under the name of Horace was brought on the stage, scolded, laughed at, tossed in a blanket, and crowned with nettles instead of the poet's laurel. It is not likely that Shakespeare contributed anything to this abusive performance, but the laughter which it provoked seems to have put an end to the War; and since Shakespeare's company had staged the play, Shakespeare himself was credited with having given that "pestilent fellow" Horace-Jonson "a purge that made him bewray his credit." That Shakespeare's company had regained their own credit is shown by the fact that they were called on to play before the Queen three times in the Christmas season of 1602. A little over a year later in February, 1603, they played to her at Richmond for the last time. Elizabeth died in March of that year and with the coming of her successor Shakespeare and his company enter upon a new period which deserves special consideration.

CHAPTER V

SHAKESPEARE IN LONDON—UNDER JAMES —LAST YEARS AT STRATFORD

THE death of Elizabeth and the accession of James mark the beginning of a new period in Shakespeare's life.

Much has been said of the personal clumsiness, the pedantry, and the political stupidity of James, but one thing must not be forgotten. He like all the Stuarts was a lover and patron of the arts, and the art that he most loved was that of the theatre. Even in Scotland where the grim elders of the Kirk threatened to excommunicate players and playgoers, he had contrived to enjoy performances by a company of visiting English comedians in 1601, headed by a certain Lawrence Fletcher. James, in fact, seems to have given Fletcher the right to call a company which he led on tour in England in 1602 "His Majesty's Players," and this title may have suggested to James an interesting step that he took immediately upon his arrival in London in May, 1603. He took Shakespeare's company, the Chamberlain's Men, under his own patronage with the name of the King's Men, added his favorite Fletcher to their number, and gave them a patent to play, not only at the Globe, but anywhere else in his "realms and dominions." Each member of the company was granted a small annual salary and in addition received an issue of scarlet cloth to be worn on state occasions as cloak and cap with the royal arms embroidered in gold on the sleeve to mark them as indeed His Majesty's Servants. Furthermore James promoted Shakespeare and his fellows to the honorary rank of Grooms of the Chamber. We may well believe that Shakespeare, already signing himself Gentleman of Stratford-on-Avon, was gratified by these marks of royal favor; probably he was made even happier by the release from imprisonment of his friend and patron, Southampton, which followed shortly after the King's arrival in London.

The gloom that seems to have settled over Shakespeare's mind in the last days of Elizabeth's reign was not lifted by these signs of royal favor. He had already entered into what is known as his tragic period. Even the comedies of this time, *All's Well, Troilus,* and *Measure for Measure,* show a bitter humor far other than the happy mirth of his earlier plays and the shadow deepens as he goes on to write, *Othello, Lear,* and *Macbeth.* The change of tone and temper in his work has been explained by the changing dramatic fashion of the time, shifting from romantic comedy and the chronicle play to realistic satiric comedy and tragedy; but this is hardly a sufficient cause. His change of theme may have been due in part to his unceasing desire to explore new realms of art; a deeper cause, no doubt, was his growing realization of the powers of evil that lay beneath the brilliant surface of Renaissance culture and that were to show themselves in abhorrent forms during the reign of the first Stuart king.

It may have been with the idea of rehearsing at the Globe a play likely to please their learned master when presented at Court that Shakespeare's company some time in 1603 staged Jonson's grave classical tragedy *Sejanus.* The play has a special interest for us because of the fact that Shakespeare himself acted in it, the last play in which we can be certain that he ever played a part. More and more he was devoting himself from this time on to his true work, play-writing, and letting his old business as actor fall to his fellows. Whether the ill success of *Sejanus,* which was hissed off the stage by an angry audience had anything to do with Shakespeare's withdrawal from public performances we cannot say, but it is at least not impossible.

Before the end of May, 1603, the plague had grown so hot in London that all theatres were closed. A vivid account of this visitation of the plague in Dekker's *The Wonderful Year* shows how all that could leave the stricken city fled into the country. The King was forced to postpone his formal entrance into London and Shakespeare's company went on tour in the provinces. On December 2nd they were summoned to play before the King at Wilton, the country seat of the Earl of Pembroke, who according to the dedication of the First Folio "prosecuted" the author of the plays "with so much favor." Later the King shifted his residence to Hampton Court and there between December 26th and February 18th the Company presented six plays, for which they were paid £53. In addition the King gave Burbage £30 "for the mayntenaunce and releife of himselfe and the rest of his company being prohibited to p'sente any playes publiquelie in or neere London . . . till it shall please God to settle the cittie in a more p'fecte health."

By March, 1604, conditions had so far improved that James was able to make his formal entrance into London. There was a grand procession through the city from the Tower to Whitehall and Shakespeare and his fellows received a special grant of red cloth for liveries, though we do not know that they took part in the procession.

On April 9th the London theatres were allowed to

open and Shakespeare's company settled down to their
regular spring and summer season at the Globe. *Measure for Measure* and *Othello* seem to have been Shakespeare's offerings at the Globe this year and both of
them were presented at Court in November and December of 1604.

In August the Company was called on to assist in
the entertainment of the Ambassadors of Spain and
Austria who had come to London to negotiate a treaty
of peace. They were invited in their capacity of
Grooms of the Chamber, not as actors. They certainly
did not perform before the Ambassadors and their
retinue, few of whom probably understood a word of
English. They only served as their official attendants
during the Ambassadors' stay of a fortnight or so at
Somerset House. The Company was paid the sum of
£21 12s for this service and the Spanish Ambassador was
very bountiful in his gifts "unto all that attended him."
It is possible that Shakespeare received from him at
this time the silver-gilt bowl which he left in his will to
his daughter Judith, or the sword which he bequeathed
to his friend, Thomas Coombe. The rise in favor of the
King's Men at Court is shown by the fact that in the
holiday season of 1604-5 they were called on for eleven
performances at Whitehall as against two by other companies and of these eleven eight were plays by Shakespeare. An interesting letter which has come down to
us shows that Queen Anne, the pleasure-loving wife of
James, was not satisfied with the regular programme at
Court, but insisted on having a new play presented to
her privately between New Years and Twelfth Day.
There was much running to and fro to fulfill her Majesty's request and at last Burbage, who stated that there
was no new play which she had not seen, suggested that
she attend a revival of *Love's Labour's Lost* "which for

wit and mirth" he said "would please her exceedingly."
Accordingly this early work of Shakespeare's, furbished
up perhaps for the occasion, was played before the
Queen in a nobleman's house in London.

Shakespeare's personal fortune was so largely increased by the popularity of his plays and their frequent
performance at Court that in July, 1605, he was able
to put through the largest transaction of his life, the
purchase of certain fixed rents at Stratford, for the sum
of £440, a purchase that turned out very favorably for
his heirs.

From about 1602 to 1607 Shakespeare was living in
the house of a French refugee, Mountjoy, in the heart
of the city. It has recently been discovered that Shakespeare interested himself in the marriage of Mountjoy's only child Mary to Mountjoy's apprentice. The
marriage led in the end to a law-suit brought by Mary's
husband against her father and in 1612 Shakespeare was
dragged, against his will no doubt, into the case. Certain questions as to a promised dowry and legacy were
put to him to which he returned somewhat inconclusive
answers. The case is interesting to us only because
the formal interrogatory laid before William Shakespeare of Stratford-upon-Avon, Gentleman, preserves
for us one of the half-dozen of his autograph signatures
which still remain.

It may have been the family troubles of the Mount-
joys that drove Shakespeare away from their house in
1606-7. He seems to have been living on the Bankside
in the latter year when his younger brother Edmund, "a
player," was buried in St. Saviour's in Southwark the
special church of the actors "with a forenoon toll of the
great bell—20 shillings"—a fee no doubt paid by
William.

A happier event had called Shakespeare back to Stratford in the preceding June. In that month his oldest child, Susanna, was married to John Hall, a doctor of good family and skill in his profession—*medicus peritissimus,* the burial register calls him. The Halls settled in a little house, Hall's Croft, not far from Shakespeare's New Place and the doctor became the close friend and medical adviser of Shakespeare in his later years. We know of at least one occasion when he accompanied him to London. The one child of this marriage, Elizabeth, was born in February, 1608, to become the darling of Shakespeare's last days.

The winter of 1607-8 was the most severe that England had known for years. The Thames was frozen over for weeks and the bitter weather must have had a most discouraging effect upon the audiences of the open-air Globe. This may have had a bearing upon a decision taken in the spring of 1608 which led to important results in the history of the King's Men and had a direct influence upon the later life and work of Shakespeare himself. When James came to the throne, the Children of the Chapel, long a thorn in the side of Shakespeare's company, were taken under royal protection, and given the title of the Children of Her Majesty's Revels. Their manager, however, was indiscreet and ungrateful. In 1605 he produced a lively comedy, *Eastward Ho,* with some pointed satire on the King's countrymen; in this play indeed a boy actor went so far as to mock the King's broad Scotch accent. The royal patronage was withdrawn and the theatre was closed. Evans, however, managed to get it re-opened and the boys continued to act under the title of the Children of Blackfriars. Once more however the managers in their efforts to create a sensation over-reached themselves. In 1608 two plays in quick succession gave bitter offence. In one, the name of which is unknown, the King himself

was brought on the stage, drinking and swearing; in the
other, Chapman's *Conspiracy of Byron,* the French
Queen was shown quarrelling with and boxing the ears
of her husband's mistress. The French Ambassador entered an energetic protest and King James swore that
the children "should never play more but should first
beg their bread." Evans saw that the game was up and
entered into negotiations with Burbage for the surrender
of his lease.

This was a heaven-sent opportunity for the King's
Men. Secure now in the royal favor they could take
over an enclosed theatre in the heart of the town where
they could produce plays in winter protected from the
weather while charging a higher price of admission than
was possible at the Globe. Burbage at once formed a
syndicate to take over the management. He invited
Shakespeare, Condell, Heminges, and Slye of the company to participate, and associated with them his brother
Cuthbert and Evans himself. The undertaking proved
immensely successful; it was alleged in a law-suit in
1612 that the King's Men got "more in one winter by a
thousand pounds than they were used to get on the
Bankside." A good share of these profits of course
went into Shakespeare's hands.

It reached him in all probability at a most opportune
time. The strain on Shakespeare as actor, playwright,
and man of business in the last ten years must have been
prodigious. There is indeed some reason to believe that
about 1608 he suffered some sort of physical breakdown.
With the acquisition of the Blackfriars, the enlargement
of his company—two able actors from the old Revels
Company were added to the King's Men at this time—
the engagement of two promising young playwrights—
Beaumont and Fletcher—who had already been delight-
ing the Blackfriars audience with their romantic and

courtly plays, a period of rest and relaxation began for Shakespeare. He seems to have spent more time at home in Stratford and to have felt less of an obligation to furnish his company with a couple of plays a year as had been his earlier practice. And the plays that he wrote from 1609 on were of a quite different type from the histories and tragedies that had poured from his active brain for a period of years. They have been called "romances"; tragi-comedies would be a better word. It has even been suggested that he was influenced by the work of the young pair of playwrights with whom he was now associated. This is, perhaps, too sweeping an assertion; Beaumont and Fletcher did not invent tragi-comedy. They, Beaumont in particular, learned more from Shakespeare than he from them. But the Blackfriars theatre had specialized in romantic drama; Chapman had written for the children acting there the first play, *The Gentleman Usher,* ca. 1602, that seems a genuine forerunner of the later fully developed tragicomedy. No doubt when the King's Men began to play to the Blackfriars audience in 1608 or 1609 they felt obliged to offer, in part at least, something of the fare to which their hearers were accustomed; and the Company naturally looked to their fellow, the most popular playwright of the day, to furnish something of this fare. It must have been a great relief to Shakespeare after the storm and stress of *Othello, Lear,* and *Macbeth* to turn to the composition of the plays that mark his last period. He patched up an old popular success in *Pericles,* dramatized a novel by Greene in *The Winter's Tale,* and apparently was willing to furnish a partly written play, *The Two Noble Kinsmen,* for Fletcher to put in shape for production. *The Tempest,* 1611, seems to show that Shakespeare was looking forward to retirement from active life, and after *Henry VIII,* in which he collaborated with Fletcher, he wrote no more. This play was put on at the Globe with great splendor in June, 1613. At the first performance a bit of burning wadding discharged from a small cannon behind the stage set fire to the thatched roof of the galleries; the fire spread downward, and although the audience and actors escaped unhurt—except for one unlucky man whose burning breeches had to be extinguished with a bottle of ale—the famous theatre was burnt to the ground.

Shakespeare may have been in London at the time of this catastrophe. He certainly was there in March, 1613, when he bought a piece of property in Blackfriars; two of his six remaining autograph signatures are on documents connected with this transaction. In the same month he devised an *impresa*, a symbolic device with motto, for the Earl of Rutland to display at a Court tournament. It is interesting to note that Shakespeare's old friend, Burbage, received the same amount, 44 shillings, for painting the device, that Shakespeare did for designing it. A creditable tradition also relates that he coached Lowin of the King's Men in the rôle of Henry in the ill-fated play, a task which would probably keep him in town at least until the first performance.

A heavy assessment was levied on the "housekeepers" of the Globe and the theatre was rebuilt, "the fairest that ever was in England," and ready for the players by June, 1614. Shakespeare probably saw it when he was in London, attended by his son-in-law and physician, Dr. Hall, in November of that year, but by that time the Company would have been playing in their winter house, the Blackfriars. This is Shakespeare's last recorded appearance in London and from this time we must imagine him living quietly in Stratford, the most distinguished and perhaps the wealthiest citizen of the little town.

It is difficult to estimate Shakespeare's income in these last years and still more difficult to appreciate its actual value in purchasing power. The statement of the Stratford vicar, John Ward, ca. 1662, that "he spent at the rate of £1,000, a year" is a wild exaggeration based no doubt on Stratford gossip. Probably Shakespeare received from all sources less than a quarter of that sum, say £200, which might, perhaps, be worth some $4,000 today. On this income we may be sure that Shakespeare lived well and comfortably in Stratford. He practiced hospitality; the Corporation sent him "a quart of sack and a quart of claret wine" when a preacher was stopping at his house. He worked in his garden and planted the famous mulberry tree that flourished till the middle of the next century when it was cut down by a peevish clergyman. He cultivated friendly relations with various Stratfordians, the Coombes, the Sadlers, Julius Shaw, and others. He must have been disturbed by the slander that was circulated about his daughter Susanna, and still more by the imprudent marriage of Judith. In 1616 she married an old friend of the family, Thomas Quiney, in February, the "closed season" without a special license. Cited and failing to appear before the Church Court to explain their irregular action she and her husband were formally excommunicated. There is some reason to believe that Shakespeare took cognizance of this affair in the alterations made in the will he had already drawn.

According to a tradition preserved by the Vicar of Stratford, "Shakespeare, Drayton and Ben Jonson had a merry meeting and it seems drank too hard for Shakespeare died of a fever there contracted." This meeting must have taken place early in March, 1616, when Jonson was visiting Drayton, then staying with friends near Stratford. We need not believe that Shakespeare was the victim of a wild drinking bout; in his enfeebled health the excitement of such a meeting, late hours, and over-indulgence may well have brought about the attack to which he succumbed. Certainly on the 25th of March, 1616, he sent for his lawyer, Francis Collins, to make certain changes in his will. He arranged for a marriage portion for Judith, cancelled his gift of plate to her in favor of his little grandchild, Elizabeth, left memorial rings to Burbage, Heminges, and Condell, and, in an often discussed interpolation, his "second best bed" to his wife. The probable explanation of this bequest has already been given (p. 19, *n.*).

Shakespeare signed the rewritten sheets of the will in a hand so faltering that he was evidently very ill or quite exhausted; the signatures contrast most unfavorably with the final "by me William Shakespeare" written some weeks before. He lingered on for about a month, died on the 23rd of April, and was buried in the Stratford church. Over his grave is a flagstone with the well-known inscription:

> Good frend for Jesus sake forbeare,
> To digg the dust encloased heare:
> Bleste be ye man y^t spares thes stones,
> And curst be he y^t moves my bones.

A credible tradition reports that Shakespeare himself composed these lines and ordered them to be carved on his gravestone. The reason for such an action is plain enough. Burial inside the church was a favor highly esteemed at Stratford and elsewhere. As claimants for this favor multiplied and available space diminished, it was customary to dig up the bones of those who had no friends or descendants left to protect them and pitch them into the charnel-house outside the church. This is exactly what happened to the bones of Susanna in 1707 when her grave near her father's was wanted for a fresh occupant. Shakespeare, if we may judge from the grave-diggers' scene in *Hamlet,* had a not unnatural horror of such a fate, and, as a seventeenth-century visitor to Stratford tells us, laid a curse on any who should disturb his repose and composed it in language simple enough to be understood by "clarks and sextons, for the most part a very ignorant sort of people." Whether the tradition is true or not, the inscription has had the desired effect; Shakespeare's grave has never been opened since his death.

Some years after his burial a firm of Dutch tombmakers in London, the brothers Johnson (originally Janssen) were commissioned to prepare the monument which is still to be seen in the Stratford church. It contains a half-length bust of the poet "in his habit as he lived" in a scarlet doublet—perhaps representing the royal livery of a King's Man—a black gown, and a white collar. The rather heavy face may have been modelled after a death mask; it has been stigmatized as the portrait of a "self-satisfied pork butcher"; but it is the only portrait of Shakespeare—except for the engraving prefixed to the First Folio which seems to be derived from it—that has any claim to authenticity, and we must accept it for what it is worth, remembering always that the Johnsons who made it were architectural designers and not portrait sculptors. It was originally painted, then whitewashed, and repainted in 1861 in the original colors.

The terms of Shakespeare's will seem to show that he had hoped to found a family. Since his only son had died in childhood all his estate was to go to Susanna and her children. But Susanna's only child, Elizabeth, herself died childless in 1670 and the three sons of Judith had died long before. The descendants of Shakespeare were soon extinct; his heritage was left to the world in his immortal works.

CHAPTER VI

SHAKESPEARE'S COMPANY

APART from the work of the playwright there are three factors to be taken into account in any successful dramatic performance: the actors, the theatre, and the audience. That Shakespeare's plays were successful from the first we have not only contemporary testimony but the fact of their long survival in the English-speaking theatre and their conquest of foreign stages. To what extent did these three factors influence the work of the playwright William Shakespeare? Let us consider first the actors who originally presented his plays.

In the first collected edition of Shakespeare's plays, the Folio of 1623, Heminges and Condell, who furnished the copy for the printers, included on the page just preceding the "catalogue" of the plays a list of "the names of the principal actors in all these plays." There are twenty-six names beginning with that of Shakespeare himself and ending with that of John Rice, who had been Heminges' apprentice in 1607 and had become a regular member of the Company only a few years before the publication of the Folio. These twenty-six were Shakespeare's "fellows" with whom he acted and for whom he wrote.

An Elizabethan company of actors was such a different thing from the group gathered now-a-days for the presentation of a play by the producer that some account of its development and organization seems neces-

sary. The increasing taste for dramatic performances in
the late fifteenth and sixteenth centuries led to the
formation of little groups of players, five or six in number, with a boy or two for female parts, who wandered
about the country, giving shows of various sorts, especially the so-called "moralities" and interludes, in town-
halls, inn-yards, or noblemen's houses. These groups
were looked on with increasing disfavor by the authorities and were finally included in the famous statute of
1572 as "masterless men" and therefore "rogues and
vagabonds." To escape the penalties denounced against
such undesirables the actors sought to shelter themselves
under the protection of a nobleman by becoming, nominally at least, members of his household. As early as
1559 we find Robert Dudley—later the Earl of Leicester, Elizabeth's first favorite—writing to a fellow nobleman in behalf of "my servants—players of interludes"
and requesting his friend's license for them to play in
his county of Yorkshire. In 1574 Dudley secured from
the Queen a royal "patent" which permitted his "servants" to act in London or elsewhere in spite of local
rules to the contrary, on the condition that their plays
had been approved by the Master of the Revels.
Dudley's example was followed by many other noblemen. The Earls of Worcester, Pembroke, and Warwick,
and the great Admiral, Lord Charles Howard, each had
his own company. Some of these were more or less permanent bodies; others broke up and re-formed, but until
the end of the Queen's reign there were always two or
three companies of adult actors under the patronage of
a noble lord acting in London, while other less distinguished companies toured the provinces. In 1583 the
Queen herself ordered the formation of a company of
twelve to be known as the Queen's Company, perhaps by
way of demonstrating the royal patronage of the pro-

fession as opposed to the ceaseless efforts of the city authorities to prohibit it altogether. This company included among others James Burbage, the father of Shakespeare's friend, and the famous clown, Dick Tarleton. When James came to the throne in 1603, the privilege of retaining a company of actors was withdrawn from the nobility and henceforth till the closing of the theatres in 1642 all companies were under the direct patronage of the King himself and other members of the royal family.

The organization of such a company was somewhat along the lines of a medieval guild. It consisted in the first place of a small and limited number of full members, corresponding to the "masters" in a guild. It is probable that each of them had a more or less definite "line" in the profession; one played clown's parts, another the old man's, a third the young hero, and so on. Some allowance must be made, of course, for the actor's versatility; Burbage, for example, played the young lover Romeo, the villainous Richard III, and the old magician Prospero; but in the main it is probable that each member held fairly closely to his "line."

It is evident, of course, that the small group of members could not possibly, even by doubling, fill all the parts demanded by the average Elizabethan drama. To fill these parts the company hired for a limited time minor actors, corresponding in a way to the "journeymen" of the guild. These were paid the regular wage of a skilled workman, but had no share in the company's profits, and seem rarely to have been admitted into full membership.

The third class in the company was composed of the apprentices. These for the most part were young boys engaged at about the age of ten. Each of them was apprenticed to an individual member who trained him in

all the routine of the profession and when he was able
to play in public hired him out to the company. All the
parts for women in Elizabethan plays were taken by
these boys since the actress was unknown to the public
stage until after the Restoration. It was possible, though
rather unusual, to take on a grown man as an apprentice, and it has been suggested that Shakespeare himself was an apprentice for the usual period of seven
years in the company of which he was later a full member. It was, in fact, from these well-trained young actors,
boys or youths, that the company was accustomed to add
to its membership as vacancies occurred.

The first requisite for such a company, of course, was
a place to play in. In the early years of Elizabeth's
reign, the actors played for the most part in the inn
courtyards of London. Five of such inns were more or
less adapted as regular playing-places, but after the
building of the first playhouse, the Theatre, 1576, it
became of course the desire of every company to find a
footing in this or one of the rapidly succeeding theatres.
This they did by renting the building for a term from
the owner, James Burbage at the Theatre, or Henslowe
at the Rose. Rent was paid by allotting to the owner
half the admission money charged for seats in the galleries, which naturally cost more than standing room on
the ground floor. The balance of the admission money,
after expenses had been paid, was divided equally among
the full members.

The expenses, however, were by no means limited to
the rent; there was the wage to be paid the hired men
and the fee to the actor whose apprentice was actually
playing. More costly still would be the outlay for
properties of all sorts, especially for the gorgeous costumes in which the actors strutted their hour upon the
stage. The initial outlay for all such charges was as a

rule met by the owner of the theatre who recouped himself by levying on that half of the gallery money which went to the company. When the leading members of Shakespeare's company formed a syndicate (cf. p. 48) to build the Globe and later to lease the Blackfriars, this syndicate took the place of such an owner as Henslowe; its members, the so-called "housekeepers," met all expenses and in return received a larger share of the receipts than their less fortunate fellows.

The Elizabethan company, we see, was a self-governing and self-perpetuating body. It owed, indeed, a certain allegiance to its patron and was liable to be disciplined by royal authority acting through the Master of the Revels for trenching upon forbidden topics—religious or political themes, or offensive personal satire. Apart from this it was free, and it was particularly free in its relation to the poets who furnished it with plays. A dramatist to-day writes his play according to his own best will and judgment; he finds a producer who undertakes to stage it and assembles a company to act the parts. In rehearsal, it is true, lines may be struck out, passages added, and various changes made, but on the whole the play stands or falls according to the author's design. In Elizabethan times, on the other hand, a play was written for a particular company and we know from records still preserved that the company sometimes furnished the book which was to be dramatised or the old play that was to be re-written. The author sketched his plot for the actors, received their approval, read the first couple of acts to them at a tavern after their acting for the day was done, and received an advance payment. He then finished the play, incorporating, no doubt, whatever suggestions the actors offered, wrote out a clean copy which would be sent up to the Master of the Revels for licensing, and received his final

payment. At every stage in his work the playwright
was conditioned by the company for whom he was writing; he must have a good part for each principal actor,
if there were not sufficient parts in the tale he was
dramatizing, he must work up a sub-plot which would
furnish them. This, by the way, is one of the reasons
for the frequent appearance of the sub-plot—sometimes
a comic one in a tragic play—in Elizabethan drama. He
must so far as possible adapt the characters of this
play to the "lines" of the actors who were to perform it.
For example while the comedian Kemp was a member of
Shakespeare's company the poet created for him such
low comedy rôles as those of Peter, Bottom, and Dogberry. When Kemp's place was taken by the brilliant
and witty Armin, Shakespeare furnished his new fellow
with such high comedy parts as those of Touchstone and
Feste. Perhaps the most striking instance of Shakespeare's consideration of an actor occurs in *King Lear.*
In *Othello,* the play immediately preceding this tragedy,
there is indeed a part for the Clown (Armin) but it is
so short and so slight—indeed is cut out in all modern
acting versions—that we may well imagine Armin
strongly objecting to so poor a rôle. As if to recompense
him Shakespeare introduced into his next play, *King
Lear,* the part of the Fool—for which there is no corresponding part in the old source—a rôle which would at
once tax and exhibit all of Armin's quality as an actor.

The boy apprentices in the company were not only
carefully trained by their masters but had special parts
written for them by the dramatist. Granville-Barker
has noted how carefully Shakespeare avoids what we call
"sex-appeal" in his boys; they are gay, witty, mocking,
at times sentimental, never, except in the case of Cressida, sensuous. When they could sing, Shakespeare
exploited their voices as in the rôles of Ophelia, Desde-

mona and Ariel. In addition to women's parts Shakespeare wrote for the boys the rôles of roguish pages, such as those of Moth in *Love's Labour's Lost* and Falstaff's page who carries over into *Henry V*. When Shakespeare wrote *A Midsummer Night's Dream,* there were evidently two boys in the company who differed greatly in size; one of them played Helena the tall "maypole," the other Hermia the little "dwarf."

Since Shakespeare never wrote for the Children who played at Blackfriars and Paul's we need not dwell at length upon the constitution of these companies. It is sufficient to say that they were in no sense independent self-governing bodies like a company of adult actors. Their managers had a royal license to impress children for singing and acting which they strained so far as actually at times to kidnap children on the streets of London. The manager supported and trained the boys, produced their plays, which were characterized by an unusual amount of music, vocal and instrumental, and pocketed all the proceeds. The training in these companies was no doubt excellent; when the Children of the Chapel were dissolved in 1608-9, Shakespeare's company took over two of the best young actors; one of them, Nat Field, was to become a rival of Burbage himself as an actor of tragic parts.

The history of the company to which there is good reason, though not positive certainty, to believe that Shakespeare belonged throughout his career may be briefly traced. It began in the first years of the Queen's reign as Lord Leicester's Men. It is possible that Shakespeare became attached to this company shortly after their visit to Stratford in 1587. At Leicester's death in 1588 the principal actors joined a company under the patronage of Ferdinando Stanley, Lord Strange. They acted for a time in 1592 at Henslowe's theatre, the Rose, where they were joined by Edward Alleyn, the leading tragedian of the Admiral's Men. With him they, or most of them, toured the provinces in the plague years of 1592-94. While on tour their patron, Lord Strange, became, in September 1593 by the death of his father, the Earl of Derby, and the Company accordingly took over this new title, and became the Earl of Derby's Men. The new earl, however, lived only till April of 1594, shortly after which the Company secured the patronage of Henry Carey, Queen Elizabeth's cousin, at that time Lord Chamberlain. On his death in 1596 they became the "servants" of his son, George Carey, Lord Hunsdon, and when he succeeded his father as Lord Chamberlain in 1597 they once more regained the title of the Lord Chamberlain's Men. This title they bore until the accession of James who, as we have seen, took them under his direct patronage and they remained the King's Majesty's Servants from 1603 till the closing of the theatres in 1642.

The various names borne by this company appear from time to time in records of their performances and on the title page of published plays. It is well to remember, however, that under these various titles the Company remained essentially the same, adding of course new members and losing old ones by death or resignation, at least from the re-organization as Lord Strange's Men in 1588 to the dissolution of the Company in 1642. All things considered it was the most stable, the most prosperous, and the most talented of all Elizabethan companies, and its success was due in no small measure to the fact that it early secured and long retained the services of William Shakespeare as its regular playwright.

CHAPTER VII

SHAKESPEARE'S THEATRE

IT is a commonplace of criticism that the technique of acting drama is of necessity strongly influenced by the physical conditions of the theatre for which the dramatist writes. The plays of the Greek tragedians, for instance, were written to be represented in vast open air theatres; those of Molière for the small closed "tennis-court" theatre of seventeenth-century France; Ibsen's for the modern "picture-frame" stage. Recent developments in lighting and staging are having a profound effect upon the technique of contemporary drama. Strangely enough, however, it is only in comparatively recent years that this self-evident truth has been taken into account in a consideration of Shakespeare's plays. His first editors divided them into acts and scenes and equipped them with stage-directions and indications of locality in accordance with the practice of the eighteenth-century theatre, a theatre, by the way, different in many important respects from that for which Shakespeare wrote. Modern producers find it difficult to present his plays on the "representational" stage, i.e., one which represents by scenery and setting the locale of the action. To do so they often make cuts and alterations to fit the plays to this stage. There is even a tendency at times to find fault with Shakespeare's technique because it does not suit later methods of production. This is as foolish as it would be to blame the Greek dramatists for writing plays with choral songs and dances. We sometimes hear that if Shakespeare had enjoyed the advantages of the modern theatre he would have used them. From this it is supposed to follow that a modern producer has the right to adapt Shakespeare's plays to the "picture frame" stage. On the other hand, his plays have recently been well performed when the producer has availed himself of the resources of the present-day theatre in lighting and setting; Margaret Webster's direction of *The Tempest,* for example, resulted in a first-rate production of this sort. After all, however, Shakespeare wrote for the Elizabethan theatre, and, to understand his work as a playwright, we must know something of his stage.

The patient researches of a group of scholars, based largely upon a contemporary sketch of the Swan, an Elizabethan theatre, the contract for the building of the Fortune upon stage-directions and other indications in the texts of Elizabethan plays, have dispelled certain misconceptions handed down from the past and enabled us to form a fairly accurate idea of the Elizabethan stage. It is no longer possible to think of it as a bare platform without decoration or properties of any kind. It did not seem poor or bare to contemporaries. There is abundant testimony to the fact that Englishmen and foreigners alike regarded the London theatres of Shakespeare's day as magnificent structures and the stage as admirably equipped. De Witt, the Dutchman who sketched the Swan, mentions their beauty, and Coryat, the famous traveller, remarks that the theatres of Venice were "beggarly and bare in comparison with our stately playhouses in England." So far from the stage being bare it was strewn, like the halls of gentlemen's houses with rushes, or on special occasions covered with matting. Elaborate properties were often brought upon the

stage, the chariot, for example, in which Tamburlaine
was drawn by captive Kings, the arbor in which Don
Horatio was hanged by the neck (see the frontispiece
to the 1615 edition of the *Spanish Tragedy*), a fountain with real water, a well-head down which a body
could be dropped, trees, possibly pushed up on the stage
through a trap, substantial enough for an actor to climb
upon them, rocks, mossy banks, shops, beds, thrones,
tents and wayside crosses. The back-stage was hung
with arras, sometimes painted in perspective—Henslowe
had a "painted cloth" of the City of Rome—sometimes
with scenes from the Bible or from classical mythology.
In the *Knight of the Burning Pestle* there is an allusion to such a picture which the Citizen's Wife thinks
may be "The Confutation of St. Paul," but which her
wiser husband calls "Rafe and Lucrece." Extravagant
sums were spent upon the actors' costumes. Henslowe,
who usually paid about £8 for a play, once laid out
£20 upon a single cloak. Garments of silk and satin
decked with gold and silver lace, trimmed, cut, and
slashed with all the fantasy of Elizabethan tailoring,
were the ordinary apparel of the Elizabethan actor.
The Puritan opponents of the stage were loud in their
denunciation for such extravagance of dress, but it must
have added more than a little color to Shakespeare's
stage.

Sometimes the actors presented great spectacular
shows and gorgeous processions upon the stage. Sir
Henry Wotton wrote to a friend in 1613 "The King's
players had a new play called *All's True* [*Henry VIII*]
—which was set forth with many extraordinary circumstances of pomp and majesty even to the matting of the
stage; the Knights of the Order with their Georges
and Garters; the Guards with their embroidered coats
and the like; sufficient in truth to make greatness very

familiar, if not ridiculous." When we add to such spectacles the introduction into Elizabethan plays of elaborate masques, calling at times for the employment of complicated machinery, such as appear, for instance, in *Cymbeline* and *The Tempest*, it is plain that the old notion of the Elizabethan stage as a bare scaffold must be altogether rejected.

Such matters as properties, costumes, and spectacles are, however, non-essential. Of greater importance to the art of the dramatist is the physical structure of the stage itself. On this point there is now a practical agreement among scholars; differences remain only on a few minor details.

The Elizabethan theatre may be regarded as evolving from the inn courtyards which were, long before the first playhouse was built, favorite places for dramatic performances by the old companies of actors.

A description of these courtyards and of their adaptation for dramatic performances has already been given (p. 29).

When James Burbage built the Theatre in 1576 he naturally designed it along the lines of the inn-yards in which he had been accustomed to play. The building had two entrances—one in front for the audience; one in the rear for the actors, musicians, and the personnel of the theatre. Inside the building a rectangular platform projected far out into what was called "the yard" —we know that the stage of the Fortune, ran halfway across the "yard," some twenty-seven and a half feet. Here the common herd of spectators, the "groundlings" stood—there were no seats on the ground floor in the old public theatres—in front and on both sides of the stage. Around and above the yard ran three galleries approached by interior stairs and divided into "rooms" or boxes where the better class of spectators who paid an additional price for the accommodation, sat more or less comfortably on stools. There was no front curtain and the performance was viewed not from the front alone but from three sides by the spectators in the yard and in the galleries. On this projecting platform the greater part of the action took place. As a rule the playwright made no attempt to localize such action; the platform was, so to speak, neutral ground. It might be any place, outdoors or in, and if the poet wished to designate a locality he wove an allusion to it into the dialogue. "This is the forest of Arden" says Rosalind when the scene has shifted from the Court to the greenwood.

Over a large part of this platform there extended a wooden roof, called "the heavens" or "the shadow," which served partly to protect the actors from bad weather, but primarily to contain the machinery needed to let down on the stage certain properties—"the creaking throne" at which Jonson laughed—or actors impersonating fairies or gods. In the sketch of the Swan we see this "shadow" supported by strong pillars resting on the platform. These, one would suppose must have interfered with the action, but they could no doubt be used by an actor to conceal himself from others on the stage. We hear once of a pick-purse caught plying his trade in the yard who was hoisted up on the stage and tied to a post for the rest of the performance.

Across the back of the platform ran a wall partly concealed by arras, woven or painted cloth set on frames standing out three feet or so from the wall. This cloth was sometimes painted in perspective, but rarely, if ever, presented a realistic background and certainly was not shifted to denote a change of scene. It served a decorative rather than an illusion-producing purpose. In the narrow space between the arras and the backwall an actor might hide himself, as Polonius does in *Hamlet*, and it was here that Falstaff was found "fast asleep and snorting like a horse" by the Prince and Peto.

Directly behind the backwall, in the centre under the balcony, was a recess, variously known as the "rear-stage" or the "alcove." It was cut off from the front by a "traverse," i.e. a curtain hanging before it. This was drawn back to disclose an action taking place in the rear-stage and pulled over it again at the close of such a scene. This "alcove" was an essential feature of the Elizabethan stage. Since it was concealed from the front by a curtain it could be set beforehand with properties to suggest a definite locality, a scholar's study (*Dr. Faustus*), a lady's bed-chamber (*Cymbeline*), a magician's cell (*Tempest*), or a tomb (*Romeo and Juliet*). An action beginning in this alcove, like the last scene of *Othello*, might be transferred to the front stage—the alcove being too small for the numbers of actors involved—which then became for the time the same locality as that indicated by the setting of the alcove. At the close of such a scene the curtain was drawn and the front stage became again "neutral ground," ready for whatever action the playwright needed. It may be noted here, that the sketch of the Swan shows no trace of this alcove, only a flat back wall of the front stage pierced by two doors. But the existence of such a recess on the Elizabethan stage is quite certain; either the Swan differed from the other theatres of the day in this respect or, which is perhaps more likely, De Witt failed to represent it.

To right and left of the alcove were doors, set flat in the back wall, as in the Swan sketch, or possibly set on the bias, so that actors emerging from them would meet each other in the centre of the stage. These doors connected the stage with the "tiring-room," the modern "green room," from which another entrance was possible through the alcove to the front stage.

The Huts

The Music Gallery

The Chamber is behind these curtains, and the Tarras is in front

Window Stage

Stage Door

The Rear-Stage or Alcove is behind these curtains

The Platform; with the "Hell" beneath

THE MULTIPLE STAGE OF THE GLOBE PLAYHOUSE

As reconstructed by John Cranford Adams

Above this rear-stage was the upper-stage, a gallery, slightly projecting over the platform and provided with a curtain by which it could at need be cut off from the view of the audience and like the alcove could be set with properties. This space seems at first to have been occupied by specially favored spectators and was known

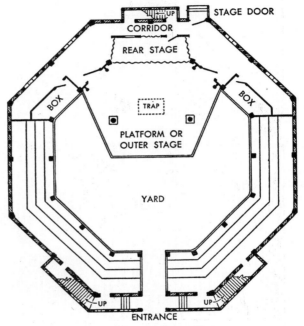

FLOOR-PLAN OF THE GLOBE PLAYHOUSE

As reconstructed by John Cranford Adams

as "the lord's room"; occasionally the musicians needed for a performance were placed here. Its peculiar value in the presentation of plays, however, was soon realized and it became a positive asset to the playwright. It was used especially to designate a locality above the plane of

the main action on the lower stage: the wall of a city
from which the defenders could converse with an oppo-
nent below, the window, or the balcony of a private
house, a high rock, or Cleopatra's monument up to which
she and her women draw the dying Antony. This upper-
stage was entered as a rule by back stairs from the
tiring-room, but it was also possible to reach it from the
front by temporary stairs, by a practicable tree set on
the main-stage, or by a rope-ladder. It is by such a
ladder that Romeo is seen to descend from Juliet's balcony after their wedding-night. In some of the later
theatres there seem also to have been boxes over the
back doors which could be used at need for the windows
of an upper room.

Such was in general the structure of the Elizabethan
stage in one of the large public theatres; the Swan
seated, De Witt reckons, about three thousand people.
There was no essential difference in the so-called "private" theatres. These consisted simply in the adaptation of a hall in a private house for theatrical purposes.
The private theatre like the public had its uncurtained
front stage, its curtained alcove and balcony. The whole
space stage, pit, and gallery was under cover, whereas
in the public theatre the "yard" was open to the sky and
only the galleries and the shadow were roofed with
thatch or tile. An upper room or attic served the purpose of the shadow in providing space for the necessary
machinery. Performances took place by artificial light
and there is reason to believe that the alcove was larger
and better lighted. The same plays were produced at
public and private theatres, as when Shakespeare's company played both at the Globe and the private Blackfriars; and there is no evidence that any reconstruction
of these plays was necessary. The main part of the audience sat on benches on the floor or in the one gallery

which sufficed the private theatre. The custom of sitting on a stool upon the stage itself which seems to have originated in public theatres became especially fashionable, and objectionable, in the private houses where a more select audience was ready to pay as much as a shilling extra for such a seat.

The stage, then, for which Shakespeare wrote consisted of three parts, the front stage, uncurtained and visible from three sides, the rear-stage which could be cut off from public view by a curtain and set with properties, and the balcony which could also be cut off and disclosed by a curtain hanging before it and withdrawn at need. There was no scenery at all in our sense of the word. The use of set properties to suggest a definite locality was in the main confined to the rear-stage, although at times a bed was thrust out or a throne dropped from the shadow upon the front stage and necessary properties like the caldron in *Macbeth* were raised to the stage and dropped again through traps in the floor. It is quite unlikely that the medieval practice of permanent properties to denote separate and distinct localities upon the same stage was long retained, though there are traces of it, in the public theatres early in Shakespeare's day. Sometimes signboards were hung over the back doors to indicate the place of action, but this naïve device seems soon to have been discontinued.

Over these three stages the action of a play of Shakespeare's flowed smoothly and swiftly without pause for scene-shifting or change of properties. There were, to be sure, brief intermissions, for music, though there was not much of this at the Globe. There is no act division in any of the old texts of Shakespeare which we may imagine to have been printed from his manuscript, so that it is at least doubtful whether he thought of a play as a thing to be composed in the regulation five acts. The word "act," indeed, occurs at times in the old texts to denote the intermission, as when we learn in a stage direction that the lovers in *A Midsummer Night's Dream* "sleep all the act" that is lie sleeping on the stage throughout the intermission. A bit of action beginning in the alcove might shift to the front stage and vice-versa. Both stages might be occupied at once as when in *Hamlet* the *Mouse-Trap* is presented by the strolling players in the alcove while Claudius and his court occupy the front stage. Balcony and front stage could be used together as when Juliet at her window converses with Romeo below in the orchard.

The absence of a front curtain made it impossible for the dramatist to work up to some effective situation on which the curtain falls. Since the greater part of the action took place on the front stage it was incumbent on him to get his characters off at the close of the play. Thus in tragedy dead bodies are[1] dragged or carried off, in *Hamlet* to a funeral march; in comedy the characters often dance off together as at the close of *Much Ado*. In comedy and tragery alike there is a relaxation of tension before the close, not a swift ending on the highest note with the curtain dropping on the "tableau" beloved by modern playwrights.

Change of place during the play was effected by the simple process of getting all the actors off the stage; the rhymed tags so common in Shakespeare are often a device to mark the end of a scene. When the stage was

---

[1] Exceptions to this rule occur when death has taken place in the alcove. Thus in *Othello* the bodies of the Moor, Emilia, and Desdemona are on or in the bed in the alcove and at the close of the play are concealed by simply drawing the curtain. In *Romeo and Juliet* the bodies of the lovers within the tomb in the alcove were similarly concealed while the survivors file out in procession.

deserted, it became for a moment no man's land, so to
speak, only to become another place with the entrance
of a fresh group of actors. In the first act of *Cymbeline*,
for example, the scene shifts from Britain to Rome and
back again. We know where the scene is laid by the
presence of certain actors, not by a scenic background.
Decorations and properties were employed to suggest a
certain locality rather than to give as on the modern
stage a realistic illusion. Shakespeare was not bound by
the necessity of fixing every scene in his plays in a definite locality realistically represented on the stage. His
stage, in fact, has been well characterized as symbolic
rather than as producing the illusion of reality.

The influence of the physical structure of the Elizabethan stage upon the dramatic technique of Shakespeare
has never been quite fully appreciated. Certain aspects
of this influence, however, seem fairly clear. In the first
place this stage allowed the playwright an almost bound-
less freedom as to the place of any action; like the writer
of scenarios for the cinema he could shift his scene at
will. He could, if he pleased, localize a scene by the
use of setting and properties, but he was under no com-
pulsion to do so. We must always remember that the
indications of place in modern editions of Shakespeare—
"a room in the palace," "another room in the same," etc.,
are the addition of modern editors; there are no such
scene-headings in the original texts. The scene-divisions
themselves are, for the most part, supplied by modern
editors. Shakespeare apparently thought of a play as
a continuous whole, interrupted, to be sure by brief act-
pauses for relaxation, but otherwise running an unbroken course; certainly he never dreamed of such
breaches of continuity as occur when the attempt is made
upon the modern stage to provide each of his short scenes
with its appropriate setting. The possibility of swift

continuous action was one of the main gifts of the Elizabethan stage to Shakespeare and his contemporaries.

It was this speed of presentation which made possible
the length of Shakespeare's plays as compared with the
modern drama. The time allowed for the performance
of an Elizabethan play was, as we know from contemporary evidence, about the same as is required today,
some two and a half hours. To produce *Hamlet* uncut
in its complete form, would require today a much
longer time. It is probable, indeed, that Shakespeare's
plays were originally produced in a somewhat shorter
form than that in which they appeared in print; but
even in this shorter form they would be too long for a
production interrupted by constant pauses for scene-
shifting as on the modern picture-frame stage. It seems
clear that the speed of performance on the Elizabethan
stage gave the dramatist an opportunity of which Shakespeare fully availed himself to get more of the story,
the background, and the environment, into his play than
is possible to the writer for the stage today.

It is by no means certain, however, that this liberty
and speed of action were unalloyed benefits. The liberty
tended at times to degenerate into a license which im-
paired concentration and dramatic power. The forty-
two scenes of *Antony and Cleopatra* scattered all over
the known Roman world could indeed be represented on
Shakespeare's stage as they cannot be on ours, and
Shakespeare obtained in this manner a scope and breadth
of effect which is lacking in all other dramatic versions
of this story. But it is equally clear that the third and
fourth acts of *Antony and Cleopatra* which contain together some twenty-eight scenes are on the whole the
least dramatic of the play. In the last act of *Macbeth,*
again, Shakespeare obtained a unique effect by the rapid
alternation of short scenes within and without the castle

of Dunsinane, an effect impossible of realisation on the modern stage. Yet it is undeniable that the last act of *Macbeth* lacks the concentrated dramatic force of the closing scenes of *Lear, Othello,* and *Hamlet.* Of these single scenes of unbroken action that of *Lear* is but a few lines shorter than the whole fifth act of *Macbeth,* while the closing scenes of *Othello* and *Hamlet* are even longer. The great central scene of *Othello,* perhaps the finest single specimen of Shakespeare's dramatic power, is about one-third longer than the last act of *Macbeth.* It would appear, then, that while Shakespeare exploited the opportunities of his stage to the fullest extent, he was led away at times from the highest perfection of his art by the very opportunities presented by his stage.

Other characteristic features of Elizabethan drama are probably due in part to the influence of the Elizabethan stage. It has been remarked by critics from the time of Sidney to the present day that there is something too much of narrative method in Elizabethan drama. This was due in part to mediæval tradition, in part to the delight of an unsophisticated audience in the mere story presented; but another cause may be found in the stage itself. Its freedom from fixed locality, the speed of action which it allowed, positively tempted the unwary playwright to compose in something like a narrative form. Many Elizabethan plays are stories in action, a mere sequence of events with little or none of the causal connection which marks true drama. This is especially true of the popular chronicle plays in which the events of a king's reign were presented in chronological order with little care for dramatic sequence. Shakespeare himself is by no means free from this fault; *Henry V,* for example, hardly conforms to strict dramatic requirements, and even *Macbeth,* which approaches the chronicle play more nearly than do the other great tragedies, shows in the first and last acts something of this loose method of narrative technique. A good story, of course, is always popular, a story represented in action doubly so, as is shown by the vogue of the "photoplay," and the Elizabethan stage like the modern cinema afforded special facilities for this style of easy popular dramatic composition. To this cause, too, we may ascribe in part the Elizabethan fashion for double and multiple plots. Shakespeare, indeed, knew how to get genuine dramatic effects of contrast and parallel from the use of minor plots, but in many of his contemporaries the under-plot is a mere device to get in more story and entertain the audience by variety of incident.

Another aspect of the influence of this stage upon Elizabethan drama also calls for notice. In the absence of anything like scenery and the comparative insignificance of properties and setting, the attention of the audience was directed primarily to the action. The elaborate and beautiful stage-settings of today too often divert attention to non-essentials. In Shakespeare's day the play was the thing, not the trappings of the play. Moreover the projection of the stage into the very midst of the yard drew and fastened all eyes upon the actor. He was not separated from his audience as he is today by the orchestra and the proscenium arch. In fact at times the most critical and influential part of his audience sat upon the stage itself. The actor was seen not at a distance, moving like a figure in an animated picture, but in the round, so to speak, in close and intimate relation with his hearers. Words, gestures, facial expression, must all have gone home with a directness and force that is hardly even conceivable today.

This intimate contact of actor and audience gave to the playwright, himself at times like Shakespeare an actor on this stage, an impulse, an inspiration, a lively

sense of the reality of his action. Whatever else the
Elizabethan drama lacks it abounds in life-like characters and this is largely due to the fact that the actors
were not puppets seen at a distance, but live men moving among their fellows and in close touch with them.
How real the action on this stage seemed to unsophisticated hearers may best be realized from the delightful
running commentary of the Citizen and his wife in *The
Knight of the Burning Pestle.*

There was, to be sure, another side to this intimacy
between actor and audience. It gave rise at times to
certain tricks that were later abandoned. The soliloquy,
whether used as a method of exposition or as a self-
revelation of character, was credible upon that stage, but
has been generally discarded in realistic drama. The
aside, rather absurd in plays attempting the illusion of
reality, was a natural and easy device when the speaker
was perhaps nearer to a part of his audience than to his
fellow actors. Still worse was the direct appeal to the
audience in the form of improvised "gags" against which
Hamlet warned the players, a striking proof by the way
of Shakespeare's dislike of this breach of dramatic illusion. Yet some such "gags" seem to have crept into the
text of his plays as it has been handed down to us. A
somewhat similar breach of illusion appears in the customary epilogue when a player, still in costume, stepped
forward to beg a *plaudite,* punctuating his appeal at times
by more or less witty comments on his auditors, as Rosalind does at the close of *As You Like It.* Akin to this
last, was the address by a Presenter or Chorus at the
beginning or between the acts of a play. Yet we should
remember that an Elizabethan audience lacked such an
aid to the understanding of a performance as is furnished
by our programmes which give the actor's names, sometimes with a bit of characterization, and specify the

localities in which the scenes are laid. We need not be too severe on the first author of *Pericles,* who prefaced each act with a speech by Gower as Chorus informing the audience of the present situation and naming the characters about to enter, a naïve device left unchanged by Shakespeare in his revision of the old play.

One last point deserves consideration. The absence of scenery and the prominence of the actor on the Elizabethan stage forced the playwright to rely for his effect primarily upon the spoken word. Now it is a patent fact that Shakespeare's plays, like other Elizabethan dramas, contain much beside pure dramatic dialogue; they are packed with rhetorical, descriptive, and lyrical passages. Something of this redundancy was due to the temper of the times. The Elizabethans, like other Renaissance people, had a very passion for words; they delighted in word-play, puns, conceits, and far-fetched images; in set orations, grandiose tirades, and lyrical interludes. Now the very nature of the Elizabethan stage forced the playwright, to appeal to this passion. His stage was comparatively bare; the setting and properties were suggestive only. To create that illusion of reality which is the life of the drama he was forced to address himself to the imagination of his audience— consider Shakespeare's appeal in the choruses of *Henry V*—and he appealed to their imagination through the spoken word. Hence instead of the present stage-picture of Macbeth's castle we have the spoken description of it by Duncan and Banquo, a description packed, by the way, with dramatic irony. It is for a like reason that we get so often in Shakespeare's plays the lovely songs which give tone and atmosphere to a scene. To stir the imagination of his audience the dramatist had first of all to rouse his own and thus he became, by necessity as it were, poet as well as playwright. The

Elizabethan drama as a whole is poetic drama because the Elizabethan stage demanded from the playwright the exercise of his poetic imagination. It was by recognizing and complying with this demand that Shakespeare became early in his career a popular playwright, and it is because he rose steadily to even loftier heights of poetic imaginative utterance that he towers over the heads of his contemporaries and remains, in Jonson's noble words "not of an age, but for all time."

CHAPTER VIII

SHAKESPEARE'S AUDIENCE

A THIRD influence on the drama is, of course, the audience for whom the dramatist writes. No other art demands as peremptorily as the drama a prompt and sympathetic response, and in every age the character of the drama has been conditioned by the audience to whom it appealed. The religious drama of Athens, the miracle plays of medieval times, were addressed to hearers of an age of faith; the drama of the golden age of France to a society dominated by the social and political conventions of the period. The Elizabethan drama at once springs from and reflects the Elizabethan age as expressed in the Elizabethan audience.

What was the character of the audience that thronged to Shakespeare's plays at the Theatre and the Globe? A rather unfavorable picture has too often been drawn, reflecting the hostile traits embodied in Puritan denunciations or the objections of the staid city fathers. We are led to think of this audience as composed of the lowest classes of London society, riotous apprentices, courtesans and pickpockets plying their disreputable trades, with perhaps a sprinkling of dissolute court gallants. This is quite wrong. The truth is that Shakespeare's audience was a representation in miniature of Shakespeare's nation, the English people of Elizabeth's day. Apprentices and criminals came to his plays, but so did sober citizens and their wives, so did the flower of Elizabethan gentry and nobility. The students of the universities and members of the Inns of Court were devoted lovers of the drama. We hear from a contemporary witness that in 1599 Shakespeare's patron, Southampton, and his friend Lord Rutland "come not to court" but "pass away the time merely in going to plays every day." We know that scholars and courtiers took notebooks to the theatre with them to jot down jests, epigrams, and poetic phrases that they might use when wooing a mistress. Marston, a satirist of Shakespeare's day, laughs at a gallant who courts Lesbia "from out some new pathetic tragedy"; from his lips

> doth flow
> Naught but pure Juliet and Romeo.

To stigmatize Shakespeare's audience as a recent poet-critic has done, as "those wretched beings who can never be forgiven their share in preventing the greatest poet and dramatist of the world from being the best artist" is to misunderstand both the audience and the dramatist. Shakespeare was himself an Elizabethan; he sympathized with the tastes of his audience and gave them what they wanted; but he was artist enough to give it to them in a form better than they expected.

The Elizabethans we must remember were what we could call today "temperamental" people, quick to anger, to laughter, and to tears. They were accustomed to swift and sudden changes of emotion and behavior. Philip Sidney, "the president of noblenesse and chevalree," threatened on mere suspicion to thrust his dagger into his father's faithful secretary. Elizabeth struck her favorite Essex across the face in the council chamber and Essex with a savage curse laid his hand upon his sword. Yet not long after the Queen sent Essex to Ireland as commander-in-chief with almost regal powers and Essex

on his return from his unfortunate campaign burst into
the Queen's chamber all stained with travel to find her
half dressed with her hair about her ears. The notion
of "decorum" so dear to later ages was unknown to the
Elizabethan people as to Elizabethan drama.

What the people wanted in a play was first of all
action—serious or comic, but even the serious must be
interspersed with comedy. The popular play of *Cambyses,* written about the time of Shakespeare's birth,
was printed with a title page describing it as a "lamentable Tragedie mixed full of pleasant mirth." The clown
was always the favorite actor; Tarleton was a darling
of the public before Alleyn or Burbage rose to fame.
It was customary, indeed, to end every performance
with a "jig," a comic dance which developed into a
rough farce spoken or sung. Shakespeare's early plays
have good parts for the comic actor Kemp, another
popular idol, and even in his latest there are such rôles
as those of the merry rogue Autolycus or the uncouth
monster Caliban. In serious action the audience wanted
plenty of fighting, armies on the stage, or duels to the
death. Every Elizabethan gentleman wore a sword;
their retainers walked the street with swords and
bucklers. There were frequent street fights, such as
Shakespeare showed in *Romeo and Juliet;* frequent
single combats, such as that in which Jonson killed his
fellow-actor Gabriel Spencer. "Masters of fence" gave
exhibitions of their art to crowded houses in the public
theatres. We may be sure that Shakespeare's audience
watched the rapier duel of Tybalt and Mercutio with
keen interest and howled disapproval when the villain
slew Mercutio with a foul thrust. Such broadsword fights
as those of Hal and Hotspur or Macbeth and Macduff
were not the tame affairs that one sees on the stage
today, but genuine exhibitions of the art followed with

the same keen interest that a crowd today watches a
prize-fight. In many ways the Elizabethans were thicker
skinned than men of today. Royalty itself delighted in
the bloody sports of bull and bear-baiting. Executions
were public spectacles and crowds, women as well as
men, gathered to see the savage punishment inflicted on
traitors. Such mimic mutilations as we get in the Senecan plays, in the *Spanish Tragedy* and *Titus Andronicus,* could not shock an audience that had witnessed more
horrid things at Tyburn. Shakespeare did not stoop as
often as some of his contemporaries to gratify the taste
of his audience for such sensations, but he had no objec-
tion to weaving scenes of physical agony into a play
where they were in accord with the theme. He brings
in King John dying of poison in the play by that name
and in his most powerful tragedy he shows the blinding
of Gloucester on the stage—"a blot" on his work, says
a Victorian critic, rather a master-stroke showing to
what depths of cruelty wicked cowardice can sink.

On the other hand Shakespeare's audience was capable
of something better than clownage and bloodshed. For
one thing it was intensely patriotic. Satirists might
mock at English follies, more especially the English
imitation of foreign manners, but the average Elizabethan believed most sincerely that an Englishman was
the noblest work of God—*Englishmen for my Money* is
the title of a popular play of Shakespeare's time—and
that England was the best and noblest of all countries.
With this went a keen interest in England's past, an
interest which the playwrights gratified with a long roll
of chronicle plays stretching from the mythical times of
Cymbeline and Lear to the defeat of the Spanish Armada in 1588. Shakespeare contributed something more
than his share to this type of play and has done more
than most historians to tell the story and fix the char-

acters of certain English kings. The great Marlborough
said that he had learned all the English history he knew
from Shakespeare. And again Shakespeare did something more than stoop to gratify a taste of his audience;
he raised and purified it. There is no such exalted expression of love of country in English, perhaps in any,
literature, as that which he puts into the mouth of the
dying John of Gaunt. The other and less pleasing side
of this patriotism is a rather cheap contempt of foreigners, not so marked in Shakespeare as in many of his
contemporaries, but evident enough in his caricature of
the French nobles in *Henry V*.

Like most audiences in most ages the Elizabethans
sometimes came to the theatre to escape from the sordid
realities of daily life; they loved tales of chivalry, of
magic, of enchanted islands, of witches and fairies. But
even in these they liked a touch of the familiar daily
life, and so when Shakespeare sent his lovers wander-
ing in the fairy-haunted wood near Athens, he brought
in Bottom and his crew, typical English homespuns, to
give a note of realism to his fantastic play. For the
same reason he introduced the tavern scenes and Shallow
in his orchard into the chronicle plays of *I* and *II*
Henry IV. On the whole, it seems, Shakespeare cared
less than most of his contemporaries for the drama of
everyday life. He never wrote such plays as Dekker's
Shoemakers' Holiday or Jonson's *Bartholomew Fair*.
Yet he loved the humors of simple country folk and
was never tired of introducing them into his plays
whether in comedy, as Dogberry and Verges in *Much
Ado* or in tragedy, as the grave-diggers in *Hamlet,* or the
clown who brings the asp to Cleopatra. And the language that Shakespeare puts into their mouths is vigorous, realistic, sometimes coarse, like that of the porter
in *Macbeth;* there is nothing affected or sentimental

about Shakespeare's treatment of common people. It took a German to transform the drunken porter into a pious old watchman chanting a morning hymn.

It is to his intimate knowledge of the common people that we may ascribe in part at least Shakespeare's partiality for broad jests. The Anglo-Saxon male is as a rule chaster in manners than in speech. There is nothing suggestive or veiled about these jests of Shakespeare's; many of them are, fortunately, lost to the average reader of today because of the change in the meaning of words. Some of them, no doubt, are interpolations in the text by a comic actor who once got a laugh by a "wisecrack" and handed it on to his successors in the part. But Shakespeare belonged to a free-spoken age and it is absurd to think of him as lowering himself to get a laugh from the yard when he and his noble friends probably enjoyed the joke as much as the groundlings.

It is another matter with a good deal of Shakespeare's language that offends æsthetic sensibilities of today. Dr. Johnson remarked that a pun had an irresistible attraction for Shakespeare; he indulges in puns at times in quite serious, even tragic passages, especially in his early plays. But the Elizabethans loved word-play of all sorts, and a pun to them was not necessarily comic. Shakespeare was certainly not aiming at a laugh when he made Lady Macbeth pun on "gild" and "guilt." The fact is that the power, the range, the versatility of the English language was only being discovered in Shakespeare's day and poets, scholars, wits, and courtiers indulged themselves to their hearts' content in taking liberties with their mother tongue. It is to this passion for playing with words that we must ascribe the so-called "conceits" that cluster in the early plays of Shakespeare. Once more, however, Shakespeare is not writing down to his audience, but writing what he and his audience, especially the better part of it, both alike enjoyed.

The songs and musical effects of Shakespeare's plays were written and composed to delight and entertain his audience. The English people before the Puritan revolution were famous singers. At a gentleman's house the music books were brought out after dinner as regularly as cards and bridge-tables would be now, and guests were expected to join the family in singing complicated part-songs. Foreign visitors to Elizabethan theatres were sure to comment on the beauty of the music they heard there. This music, of course, was instrumental as well as vocal, for most Elizabethans played one instrument or another. Citterns hung in every barber shop for the amusement of the waiting customers.

Shakespeare's plays are full of references to the various instruments of his day, the lute, the recorder, the viol de gamba. His kings come on the stage to flourishes, and trumpets announce the entrance of an army. Music is used to wake a sleeper, to lament the dead, to minister, as in *Lear,* to a mind diseased. All this is in perfect accord with the practice of Shakespeare's day, and here as elsewhere Shakesepare shows himself a true Elizabethan.

A word must be said in closing about the poetry of Shakespeare's plays. We wonder sometimes how the groundlings who packed the yard of the Globe could appreciate or even listen patiently to his poetic plays. It has been suggested that his poetry was for the gentlemen and scholars of the boxes as his clowns and combats were for the groundlings. But this, again, is to misunderstand the Elizabethan audience. In the first place it was by old tradition that the drama was written in verse; the miracle plays are composed in rhymed

stanzaic metres; the early farces and interludes in the
seven-foot doggerel of which traces still remain in some
of Shakespeare's early plays; blank verse had been introduced into tragedy by the authors of *Gorboduc* early
in Elizabeth's reign and had in Shakespeare's time come
to be the recognized medium for dramatic expression.
The Elizabethan age has been called "a nest of singing
birds," and while this phrase was meant to apply to the
lyric poets of the day, it might almost as well charac-
terize the Elizabethan people. They all sang; they all
loved poetry of a sort as well as music; the most popular printed works were the broadcast ballads in which
contemporary events of all sorts were versified and set
to popular tunes. And if this was the case with the
common people it was still more so with the better
classes. Gentlemen rhymed as naturally and as easily
as they sung. The proper way to court a lady was by
writing sonnets to her beauty. Orlando was simply following a fashion of the day when he festooned the trees
of Arden with poems in praise of Rosalind. We must
imagine, then, the Elizabethan audience listening, not
merely patiently, but with delight to the long tirades, the
high-flown speeches, the lyrical interludes of Shakespeare's plays. The Elizabethans read less and listened
more than we do to-day. They appreciated at its full
value the sonorous beauty of such a line as

> The multitudinous seas incarnadine.

They picked up to use, or to misuse, as the numerous
malapropisms in Shakespeare's comedies show, strange
new words that sounded well even if their sense was not
quite clear. And this delight in poetry was, so to speak,
grist to Shakespeare's mill. He could indulge his poetic
fancy to the limit, and sometimes in his early plays, it
outran his dramatic powers, knowing that it was ad-

dressed to a sympathetic audience. It was for his hearers at the Theatre and at the Globe that Shakespeare
wrote Mercutio's description of Queen Mab, the lyric
love-making of Romeo and Juliet, the soliloquies of
Hamlet, and the tragic outbursts of King Lear. All that
is changed today. Our playwrights, even when dealing
with tragic themes, are driven by the convention of realism to write common-place words and "language such
as men do use," to express even intense emotion in
colloquial speech. There has been perhaps quite as
much loss as gain.

Properly to appreciate the influence of the audience
upon Shakespeare we must always remember that Shakespeare was himself "of his age" as well as "for all
time," a true Elizabethan. What seem to us faults and
flaws in his works are not there because he consciously
wrote down to his audience, but because in taste and
tone and temper he was one with them. He wrote to
please his hearers and in so doing pleased himself. His
friend and critic Ben Jonson with a fine scorn for his
hearers wrote to please himself, to gratify his own
severe and limited critical standards. As a result Jonson failed to win his audience. Shakespeare was not
ignorant of these standards; he probably heard of them
often enough from Ben at their meetings in the Mermaid
Tavern. He could have observed the unities if he wished;
he did so, in fact, in *The Tempest*. Had he written for
an audience of scholars and critics he would have written
plays of another sort, perhaps such plays as his Hamlet,
scholar and critic, praises, when he speaks of one that
was "caviare to the general; but . . . an excellent play
. . . as wholesome as sweet and by very much more
handsome than fine." We can be thankful that he did
not. When we consider the work of Shakespeare as a
whole, its breadth, its infinite variety, its broad humor,

its unrestrained expression of emotion, its unparalleled poetic utterance, we may give some measure of thanks to the audience for which he wrote, which, like the actors who performed his plays and the stage upon which they were represented, contributed to make them what they are.

CHAPTER IX

THE NEW DRAMA

WHEN Shakespeare came to London, he found the acting drama in a vigorous and flourishing condition. It was in the hands of the professional actors protected by the court and supported by a growing popular demand. Playhouses had been built for regular dramatic performances and a group of young poet-playwrights was busily engaged with furnishing the actors with dramas. Their work must have been new and immensely interesting to Shakespeare who during his youth in the country can have seen little or nothing of the new drama which this group was creating. His prentice years as actor and playwright from 1588 to 1593 coincided with a wonderful advance in every line of dramatic activity and we cannot fully understand his own work, especially his early plays, unless we realize to some extent the nature of the new drama which was then taking shape.

Elizabethan drama is essentially an outgrowth of the religious drama of the Middle Ages, and it is well to remember that this drama was by no means extinct in Shakespeare's day. Miracle plays were acted at Coventry as late at 1584, and we have a record of a religious play in London eight or nine years after Shakespeare's death. Now the outstanding characteristic of this old drama was its frank and homely realism; it strove to represent events and characters of the sacred story in terms of simple everyday English life. This realism

101

struck at times a grim and almost savage note; the play-wright of the Passion did not spare Christ a buffet or a pang of pain. On the other hand it might turn into broad farce. When Mrs. Noah boxed her husband's ears, we may be sure that the audience was moved to laughter not by the wit of the words but by the humor of the situation. The characters, too, are real and English; the shepherds of the *Secunda Pastorum* are real shepherds grumbling about the weather and concerned about their sheep. All that there is of dramatic value in the miracle plays comes from the naïve, sincere, and convincing realism. Their technique, simplicity itself, consisted in representing the whole story on the stage.

This homely realism, long accepted as essential in popular drama, was transmitted in an unbroken channel from the miracle plays through the moralities and interludes of the early sixteenth century to the new drama of Shakespeare's day. It was a keen sense of its value as a drawing-card that led Shakespeare's company to call their great spectacular play of *Henry VIII, All Is True*. Titles like the *True Tragedy* and the *True History*, abound in Elizabethan drama. So strong, indeed, was the popular demand for realism, so ready to response of the playwrights, that we may fix on this note of realism as the distinguishing mark of one aspect of Elizabethan drama, the native and popular.

In early popular comedy this realism produced a series of lively humorous scenes and incidents rather than complete and well-made plays. The interest of closely complicated and neatly solved intrigue is almost entirely lacking. At best we get a series of dramatized incidents. Such comic scenes often appear at intervals in serious plays. They continue the tradition of the comic interpolations in the miracle plays and beget the convention of the so-called "comic relief," character-

istic of Elizabethan as compared with classical drama.
The characters of these scenes are drawn almost exclusively from the lower classes; the fun consists in showing them in absurd situations, as when the Vice in *Cambyses,* masquerading as a warrior, with a pot for a
helmet and a rake for a spear, is chased off the stage
by an old woman with a broom. The humor of early
popular comedy was essentially physical, the humor of
scuffles, kicks, and pots of water on unsuspecting heads.
The popular nature of such scenes and their lasting
appeal is shown not only by their constant appearance
in later Elizabethan drama—even in the works of
Shakespeare—but by their persistence through the farce
and fiction of later centuries down to the comic strips
and comic films of the present day.

The language of this popular comedy was, of course,
plain everyday English. There is a marked absence
of the witty, pointed dialogue, of the gay word-play, so
frequent in the later comedy. On the contrary there is
an over-plus of profanity, a "humor of filth," sinking
at times to gross obscenity. The dialogue is for the most
part composed in doggerel rhymed verse, and except for
occasional songs, there is nothing of the heightening
effect of poetry. The note of romance, more particularly what we call the "love interest," is conspicuously
absent. It would almost seem as if the old playwrights
felt this topic to be taboo.

Of early popular tragedy there is little to be said for
the simple reason that there was very little of it. The
old tradition of a realistic presentation of tragic scenes
from the Bible had died out and for a considerable
period nothing came in to take its place. The crowd
preferred boisterous farce to the falls of princes and
clamored for the appearance on the stage of the Devil
and the Fool. So far as they took an interest in tragic

themes, they demanded realism. A tragedy to be popular must present a true story in convincing fashion. The few specimens of early popular tragedy that remain from the time before Kyd and Marlowe might almost be called histories rather than tragedies proper. They fall into two classes: histories of private and of public life. In the first class we find such lost plays as *Murderous Michael* and *The Cruelty of a Step-Mother* presented at Court in 1578 and 1579. Such plays were the direct ancestors of the Elizabethan domestic tragedy like *Arden of Feversham* and *A Woman Killed With Kindness,* plays that bear witness to the popularity of such realism in the very heyday of the romantic drama.

The histories of public life strike the same note. The English chronicle play, to be sure, seems hardly to have appeared before Shakespeare came to London. It sprang into sudden life along with the outburst of patriotic enthusiasm that marked the years just before and after the defeat of the Spanish Armada in 1588. But before this time there were plays dealing with historical events which continue the technique of the miracle plays and anticipate that of the chronicles, that is a simple succession of scenes in their natural order of time. Those that remain to us deal with themes drawn from classical sources; but their apparent aim is to present an ancient story in as familiar and realistic a style as possible. In *Horestes* a murderer is very properly "hanged from a ladder;" a stage-direction in *Cambyses* reads: "Smite him in the neck with a sword to signify death." These plays are also marked as products of the popular drama by the presence of the Vice and of allegorical figures from the old moralities.

At the opposite pole from this native and popular drama lay another which may be called the classical and academic. It was one of the results of Renaissance humanism and began to appear about the middle of the sixteenth century. Springing from the study of the classical drama in the grammar schools, it was reinforced by the critical dicta of Aristotle and Horace as interpreted by Renaissance commentators. It flourished almost exclusively in such institutions as the grammar schools, the universities, and the Inns of Court where it produced a group of plays designed for cultured audiences. Apparently none of these plays ever attempted to compete on the public stage with the drama in the native tradition. Yet the influence of this academic drama was felt in both comedy and tragedy and it introduced into both elements that had permanent effect in the development of Elizabethan drama.

In comedy the models for this academic drama were the plays of Plautus and Terence, and the Italian comedies of the fifteenth and sixteenth centuries, themselves an imitation and elaboration of the Latin dramatists. Perhaps the most important gift of these models to English playwrights was a sense of the significance of plot. From the Latins and their Italian followers English comedy now took over involved intrigues and deft solutions. The division of a play into acts and scenes, adopted from the classical models, assisted the English playwright in an orderly development of the plot. Along with this came the adoption into English comedy of a number of stock characters from the classic models: the worldly wise father, the roistering son, the wily servant, the braggart, and the pedant. Commonplace as these types seem to us, they were a real enrichment of the stock figures of native English comedy, where the Devil and the Vice, plus a pair of rustics, had long been almost the sole representatives of the comic spirit.

In diction as well as in construction and characterization this new comedy represented a great advance over

the old. For the doggerel rhyme and coarse language
of the native comedy it substituted little by little a
polished prose, heightened by witty repartee, and word-
play. This too was an imitation of the diction of the
Latin playwrights and the academic character of the
new comedy is shown by the fact that most of the specimens that remain are the work of school-masters, university students, and Inns of Court men, written for
private performance. It was not until the time of Lyly
and his followers in the 1580's that the new comedy
appeared upon the public stage. Yet in spite of its
academic origin this comedy retained a distinctly English atmosphere, laying its scenes in England and drawing its characters from English life. The little masterpiece of *Ralph Roister Doister* is perhaps the best
example of this blending of the classic and native
comedy.

In tragedy the influence of classical studies was at
first rather different. Whereas in comedy the classic
models exerted an immediate and beneficent effect upon
the drama, in tragedy we find only a slavish imitation
which for a long period seems totally divorced from the
native tradition. The reason lies in the gulf which separated popular practice from the classical theory of
tragedy. The first consisted in action realistically presented; the second pushed action as far as possible off
the stage, reported it by messenger, and stressed primarily the emotions of the *dramatis personae*. The
popular practice enlivened a tragic theme with interpolations of "comical mirth;" classical theory rigidly
excluded comic scenes and characters from the tragic
stage. Popular tragedy either presented familiar English characters as in the murder plays, or attempted to
bring distant scenes and characters home to the audience by giving them a familiar English dress. Classical

tragedy, on the other hand, chose its themes by preference from the remote legendary or mythological past and threw about them an atmosphere of unreality, of stately aloofness. The ideal was, in Kyd's phrase—

> *Tragoedia cothurnata,* fitting kings,
> Containing matter and not common things.

Where such differences existed there was little chance of a direct influence of the classic model on populai practice, and classical tragedy in English remained for nearly a generation, from the first translation of Seneca in 1559 to *The Misfortunes of Arthur* in 1587, in academic isolation.

The first translation of a Senecan play into English marks the starting point of classical tragedy in English. It was Seneca, not the Greek dramatists, who during the Renaissance served as the pattern of classic tragedy on the Continent as well as in England. This was due, primarily, to the Renaissance mastery of Latin and comparative ignorance of Greek, but also to the fact that the tone and temper of Seneca, "the most modern of the classics and the most romantic of the ancients," were more in accord with the spirit of the Renaissance than were those of the Greek dramatists. There is something cosmopolitan, universal, one might say, in Seneca's discarding the local color and national tradition of his borrowed Greek themes in order to emphasize the tragedy of individual characters, and this treatment appealed with special force to the Renaissance belief in the supreme importance of the individual.

Certain characteristics of Seneca's work exerted a profound influence upon Elizabethan drama. Most obvious of these is his partiality for sensational themes; all his plays deal with adultery, incest, murder, and revenge. Yet Seneca's main interest lies not in the sensa tional action, but in its reaction upon the emotions of his characters. They are all self-conscious and introspective, and Seneca, crude as much of his work seems to us, is in fact a psychological dramatist. Moreover the technique of Seneca is simple and regular. His plays are divided into the standard five acts; he avoids epic detail in his plot, and concentrates upon the crisis of the action. His rather formal method of construction was much admired in the Renaissance, and many of his dramatic devices: the moralizing chorus, the messenger, the confidant, the ghost crying for revenge, passed over into Elizabethan drama. Finally, Seneca's diction evoked at that time an enthusiastic response which seems almost inexplicable to us. We find him verbose, bombastic, singularly deficient in true dramatic utterance. The Renaissance, however, loved language for its own sake and saw in the elaborate tirades of Seneca the perfect model of dramatic eloquence. Sidney could find no higher praise of the diction of *Gorboduc* than to speak of it as "climbing to the height of Seneca his style."

Seneca's fashion of moralizing comment, also—comment couched in terse and epigrammatic Latin—appealed especially to an age which held that the first function of tragedy was moral and didactic. The *sententiae,* or moral maxims, of Seneca appear again and again in the ethical commonplaces and moral "tags" of Elizabethan drama.

Perhaps the most important contribution of the Senecan school to Elizabethan drama was the adoption of blank verse as the medium of dramatic dialogue. This metre introduced into English poetry by Surrey in his translation of Virgil (published 1557) was employed by the authors of *Gorboduc* (1563) and the success of that play brought about a recognition of this metre as a standard form for tragedy. Simple, flexible, yet dignified, it was recognized at once as far superior to the popular rhymed doggerel, approximating in some degree at least the stately measures of classical tragedy.

There is nothing to show any influence of this Senecan school upon popular drama until the great dramatic outburst of the 1580's. The authors of the new tragedy, Peele, Greene, Marlowe, and Kyd were classical scholars, and it is in their work that we note for the first time a fusion of classical and popular strains.

Even before Shakespeare came to London another tendency had begun to show itself in Elizabethan drama. This may best be described as the romantic impulse. It differs in choice of theme, method of treatment, and manner of expression, alike from native tradition and from classical convention. It is marked by the romantic love of the strange and the mysterious. Instead of representing on the stage familiar scenes and characters of real life, it takes wing to distant lands and times, introduces knights, ladies, and emperors of the East, shifts the scene from England to Cathay or Arcady, and seeks above all to touch and kindle the imagination. It has the romantic love of the supernatural; it employs the devices of the old romances of chivalry, magicians, enchantments, and strange transformations, and it adds to these the fairies, witches, and ghosts of popular superstition. The ghost, to be sure, appears in Senecan tragedy, but there is a vast difference between the ghost of Tantalus in Seneca's *Thyestes* and the "perturbed spirit" that stalks across the stage in *Hamlet*. The first is a mere piece of machinery to set the plot in action; the second, fulfills the same purpose and is, so far, Senecan, but brings with him in addition a chill breath from the other world that gives the true romantic thrill.

Along with this desire for the strange and supernatural there begins to appear in the new drama the romantic passion for beauty. There is little sense of the beautiful in the old popular drama or in the imitations of Seneca, but the new tendency beginning with faltering accents swells gradually into the haunting music of Marlowe and of Shakespeare. It is in Marlowe's *Tamburlaine,* the first English tragedy inspired by this new force, that we get the supreme expression of this passion. Moved beyond his wont by the sorrow and loveliness of his mistress Tamburlaine exclaims:

> What is beauty, saith my sufferings, then?
> If all the pens that ever poets held
> Had fed the feeling of their masters' thoughts
> And every sweetness that inspir'd their hearts,
> Their minds and muses on admired themes;
> If all the heavenly quintessence they still
> From their immortal flowers of poesy,
> Wherein, as in a mirror, we perceive
> The highest reaches of a human wit;
> If these had made one poem's period,
> And all combined in beauty's worthiness,
> Yet should there hover in their restless heads
> One thought, one grace, one wonder, at the least,
> Which into words no virtue can digest.

A beauty ineffable, beyond all words, was what the romantic poet-dramatists were striving to express.

The development of this new tendency coincides with the amazing outburst of poetry that followed the appearance of Spenser's *Shepheards Calendar* in 1579. Before that date the popular drama was written for the most part in halting rhymed doggerel. After it we catch more and more clearly that "full-mouthed utterance of the early gods" which distinguishes Elizabethan drama from all that went before or followed it in English. The playwrights were quick to learn their art of speech from the poets.

This passion for beauty has all the range and richness of the Renaissance; it finds its food in the world of nature and in the works of man, but most of all in man himself, in his thoughts, his desires, and his emotions. In comedy it attaches itself particularly to the theme of love, a theme absent alike from popular and from classical comedy. In the former it is markedly avoided; in the latter it is often treated with a certain Latin cynicism. It remained for the new romantic comedy to treat this theme at once as a source of mirth and as a thing of beauty. It is a sign of the growing freedom of the Renaissance spirit in Elizabethan England that with the development of the drama the theme that had been shunned by the old mediæval tradition came forward in ever-growing grace and beauty until it reached its climax in the romantic comedies of Shakespeare.

Of the first beginnings of romantic tragedy it is impossible to speak precisely because of the scanty material that has survived. In fact it is only by an extension of the term "tragedy," to cover all serious plays, that we can speak of romantic tragedy as existing at all before the time of Kyd and Marlowe. The first plays of this type seem to have been dramatized romances, stories of strange adventure on land and sea. Plays founded on old tales of chivalry seem to have been particularly popular at Court in the 1570's.

As time went on and the spirit of the Renaissance made itself felt in the drama there is a notable enlargement of the field. Playwrights began to turn for their themes to the tragic stories of the Italian *novelle*. The interest of these tales centres upon individuals and the chief interest of the tragedy based on them tends to concentrate upon the struggle of the individual against the hostile forces of environment or of fate. The characteristic note of the new romantic tragedy is its appeal to sympathy and pity. The old histories and murder plays were satisfied to present an interesting action; the classical tragedies to arouse admiration and horror; but the new tragedy presents the protagonist in a sympathetic light and evokes pity for his fate. Shakespearean tragedy is essentially one of individual character and appeals perhaps more strongly than any other work of man to our human sense of pity, and Shakespearean tragedy springs directly from the romantic drama of his predecessors.

The fusion of these diverse elements, the traditional realistic, the conventional classic, and the new romantic into the fully developed Elizabethan drama was the work of a group of dramatists often known as the "university playwrights." Beginning their attack on the London stage somewhere in the early 1580's they carried it by storm and held the boards for ten years or so until the early 1590's when one by one they dropped out. Shakespeare's debt to them was very great; two or three are in a very special sense his models and masters. They did not, indeed, constitute a school with a formula for the creation of a new type of drama. Each of them was an individual genius and contributed something of his own to the stage; there is a vast difference between the courtly comedies of Lyly and the heroic plays of Marlowe. Yet essentially there is a similarity between them that goes far to unify their work. They were all born poets, makers, inventors; not one of them was content to follow the beaten path. They were all artists in words consciously engaged in devising for the drama a better medium of utterance than it had heretofore possessed. They were all imbued with the spirit of romance, seekers after the strange and lovers of beauty. Furthermore they had all enjoyed a sound classical education which gave them a command of classic sources, an acquaintance with classic models, and an admiration for the polished dialogue of comedy and the stately speech of tragedy in the classical masterpieces. They were, however, loving students rather than slavish imitators of the classics; they borrowed freely from their models, but their borrowings were for the purpose of improving and enriching the popular drama rather than for transforming it into an imitation of the classic.

The explanation of their free handling of the revered classic models may be found in another common bond which unites the members of this group. They were all professional playwrights writing for the public stage at a time when this career offered a man of letters the quickest and the surest reward. But this reward was only to be obtained if their plays were successful upon the stage, and of success or failure the London audience was the final arbiter. To gain their livelihood these playwrights would have been forced even against their will to yield in large measure to the demands of the public. Yet it is more than doubtful if there was any conscious yielding on their part. These men were themselves members of the public for which they wrote; they were men about town, gay Bohemians, haunters of taverns, not cloistered pedants nor refined courtiers. They shared the tastes of their public, but they guided, purified, and elevated these tastes until at last they trained an audience ready to receive and applaud the masterpieces of Shakespeare.

Of this group the work of four men was so individual, their contribution to Elizabethan drama and to the plays of Shakespeare so important that they deserve a brief consideration. John Lyly (1554?-1606), the first and oldest of them, was the creator of a new type of comedy. An Oxford graduate, he became famous in 1579 by his prose novel *Euphues*. The story of this book is a mere peg on which to hang a series of discourses on education, polite behavior, and courtly love. The brilliant, witty, and highly affected style of *Euphues* made a deep impression on the society of the day and actually set a fashion of speech in courtly circles. Sometime in the mid-1580's Lyly turned to the theatre and began writing plays for the Children of Paul's, plays which were first produced in public and later presented at court.

Lyly's plays, as their titles, *Endimion, Sapho, Midas,* show, deal with classic themes, but the characters in these plays are transformed from figures of the classic world into Elizabethan gentlemen and ladies. All the plays deal with love, but it is a graceful, courtly, passionless love more concerned with apt turn of speech than with attainment. Lyly can construct a deft plot; one of his later plays *Mother Bombie* presents an extremely complicated intrigue after the fashion of Plautus, but his main gift to English comedy was that of dialogue. For the rhymed metres of popular drama he substituted the brilliant balanced manner of speech that *Euphues* had made popular. He rejected altogether the knockabout farce and foul language of the old comedy and taught his hearers to delight in clever repartee and word-play. It is not too much to say that Lyly is the first English dramatist to have some notion of high comedy. Since his plays were presented by children he introduced as a stock character the impudent page who mocked his master and exchanged gay jests with the ladies of the play. Lyly's plays were all the rage in the best circles when Shakespeare came to town and though Shakespeare never adopted the full-fledged euphuistic style—he even ridicules it in the mouth of Falstaff

(*I K. H. IV.* II, iv, 4, 449ff.)—he learned from Lyly
the trick of fluent graceful speech, the value of polished
prose in comedy, and took over, as in *Love's Labour's
Lost,* some of Lyly's characteristic figures, as the braggart soldier and the mocking page.

The influence of Robert Greene (1558-1592) upon
later drama was less direct and visible than Lyly's, but,
perhaps, more profound. A brilliant and versatile man
of letters with something of the mocking-bird's facility
of imitation, Greene began his career by writing a series
of love stories in Lyly's euphuistic prose. He closed it
with a group of pamphlets revealing the sordid side of
underworld life in Elizabethan London and another
confessing the sins of his own wayward career. In the
meantime he had been a popular and prolific writer for
the stage. Some of his plays, no doubt, have been lost;
two of them are imitations of Marlowe's heroic vein, so
extravagant in style that one imagines Greene compos-
ing them with his tongue in his cheek. His real contribution to English comedy rests upon two plays, *Friar
Bacon and Friar Bungay* (ca. 1589) and *James IV*
(ca. 1591). The first of these tells the story of a
famous English magician, Friar Bacon. The novel element, however, and the lasting appeal of the play is
not in the doings of the wizard but in the love-story
of Margaret, the fair Maid of Fressingfield, beloved
by the Prince of Wales, herself in love with Lacy the
Prince's friend. When Lacy courts her for the Prince
she woos and wins him for herself, is apparently rejected by him later, and is finally re-united to him on
the threshold of a convent in one of the most delightful
scenes of Elizabethan comedy. Back and forth through
the scenes of magic and love-story wander two characters dear to the audience of the day, Ralph the Court
Fool, and Miles, Friar Bacon's blundering servant, a

development of the mischief-making Vice, who is finally carried off to hell upon a devil's back.

James IV, perhaps Greene's last, and in many ways his best play, was published in 1594 after his death under the title of *The Scottish History of James IV Slain at Flodden,* probably to exploit the contemporary popularity of the chronicle play. It has, however, no basis in history, but is a clever dramatization of an Italian story of romantic love. Greene shifts the scene to Scotland, shows us a Scottish king turning from Dorothea, his chaste and loving wife, to pursue Ida, a fair lady of the court. The queen escapes the murderer who has been hired to despatch her, assumes male disguise, and finally reconciles her penitent husband to her angry father, the king of England.

Greene's contribution to the new comedy is three-fold. He knew better than any of his predecessors how to tell an interesting story in dramatic form; his friend, Nashe, called him a "master of his craft" in plotting plays. And he set these stories in a homely realistic British background while at the same time breathing into them the spirit of romance, a fusion which was to be eminently characteristic of later Elizabethan comedy. Finally, Greene was the first of English playwrights to deal with the theme of romantic love and to centre it about the figures of real, charming, and lovely women. There are no characters in English drama before Greene that can compare with his Margaret, Ida, and Dorothea. It would be absurd to say that Greene taught Shakespeare how to create such characters as Portia, Rosalind, and Imogen, but it is perhaps reasonable to suppose that the success of Greene's plays suggested to Shakespeare the possibility of bringing lovely and beloved women upon the stage whether in their own dress, or like Dorothea and his own Rosalind and Viola in doublet and hose. Greene hated the upstart Shakespeare but the young Shakespeare was not too proud to learn all that he could even from an enemy.

As Lyly and Greene were Shakespeare's forerunners in comedy Kyd and Marlowe open the road for him in tragedy. Of Kyd (1558-1594), the elder of the two, little is known, though much is conjectured. Only one play can be certainly ascribed to him, but that play, *The Spanish Tragedy* (ca. 1584), was the most popular and influential tragedy upon the public stage before Shakespeare came to London, and was revived and revised over and over again during his lifetime. Its success was due to the fact that it represented the fusion of Senecan and popular elements in a play aimed at the London public. It is the story of a father's revenge for his murdered son, a revenge long delayed, in which the father hovers on the brink of madness, and finally accomplished in spite of obstacles and counter-intrigues in a general massacre that heaps the stage with corpses. We have here the Senecan ghost, the Senecan sensationalism, the stately though rather stiff and frigid Senecan blank verse. On the other hand Kyd knew his public too well to keep the action off the stage in Senecan fashion. There is no such thrilling scene in pre-Shakespearean drama as that in which the old father called from his bed at night discovers the body of his murdered son hanging in the arbor where only an hour before the youth had been courting his princely mistress. Kyd was no great master of characterization; the people in his plays resemble somewhat the figures of archaic sculpture; but he tried not altogether without success to make them real and lifelike. The intriguing villain, Lorenzo, in this play is the first of a long line of Machiavellian plotters which culminates in Shakespeare's Iago.

In addition to *The Spanish Tragedy* Kyd wrote, we

have good reason, though no definite proof, to believe₂ the lost play of *Hamlet* on which Shakespeare's masterpiece is founded. If he also wrote, as some critics hold, *Arden of Feversham* he broke fresh ground in the realistic domestic tragedy as well as in the drama of intrigue and revenge. Briefly Kyd's contribution to English tragedy can be summed up in a few words. He gave it a dignity and power unknown before by infusing it with Senecan elements; he was the first of English tragic writers to have some mastery of plotting and intrigue; and his keen sense of the value of a dramatic situation was something new in English literature and was caught up, exploited and brought to perfection by Shakespeare himself in his recast of the lost *Hamlet*.

Christopher Marlowe (1564-1593) the youngest, was also the greatest of these predecessors of Shakespeare, greatest in his influence on the evolving drama, and greatest in his transforming power of poetry. A Cambridge scholar he left the university in 1584 apparently to undertake some secret service work for the Government. He received his M. A. degree at Cambridge in 1587 and in the same year produced his epoch-making play of *Tamburlaine* upon the London stage with the great actor Alleyn in the title-rôle. The next six years of his short life were crowded with dramatic and poetic composition. He wrote five plays that we know of (*Tamburlaine, Dr. Faustus, The Jew of Malta, Edward II,* and *The Massacre at Paris*), possibly took part in several others, translated parts of Ovid and Lucan into English verse, and left unfinished the lovely erotic poem, *Hero and Leander*. He seems to have been closely associated with the group of poets and scholars that gathered round Sir Walter Raleigh where he must have read parts of *The Faerie Queene* in manuscript and caught something of the music of Spenser's poetry. He shared too in the popular suspicion of Raleigh's unconventional circle, and was accused, justly or not, of blasphemy and atheism. He was in fact under bond to answer such charges before the Privy Council when he was killed in a tavern brawl. The story that he was killed in a fight over a low woman is a slander invented by Puritan enemies of poetry and drama; there seems reason to suspect that he was put out of the way by a gang of rascals who feared him.

Marlowe's contribution to Elizabethan tragedy may be summed up in three words: Passion, Power, and Poetry. Himself a reckless passionate nature he transformed the cold and stiff tragedy of the Senecan school into a fiery presentation of human passion, the passion for power, for knowledge, and for wealth. Furthermore he embodied these passions in superhuman figures, the Scythian Shepherd "scourging kingdoms with his conquering sword," Dr. Faustus selling his soul to hell to obtain a knowledge that shall make him master of the world, Barabas the Jew gloating over the gold and jewels that give him

> Infinite riches in a little room.

With a single exception the plays of Marlowe are one-star plays and this concentration of interest in the single figure of a great protagonist was one of the secrets of his art which he handed down to the young Shakespeare. The single exception to this rule is his historical play *Edward II* and here too Marlowe was an innovator of genius. Instead of simply reciting in dramatic form the events of a king's reign in chronological order, he so selected, arranged, and altered the facts of history as to transform the chronicle play into a tragedy, foreshadowing such Shakespearean plays as *King John, Richard III,* and *Richard II*. His greatest gift, how-

WILLIAM SHAKESPEARE

ever, to the drama was his transformation of the stiff monotonous blank verse written by Kyd and his predecessors into the most perfect vehicle for dramatic utterance that English literature has known. It is not too much to say that Marlowe is the first great English poet to write drama and the effect of his dramatic poetry upon his contemporaries and successors was overpowering. It is interesting to recall the fact that the young Shakespeare must have heard the music of Marlowe's mighty line for the first time after he came to London, that he was fascinated by it and set himself, as we see in his early plays, to imitate it and then to study its powers and possibilities until he came to write such poetry as Marlowe himself never dreamed of. We do not know whether Shakespeare ever met Marlowe face to face; we do know that he admired and followed him and that of all his contemporaries it is Marlowe alone whom Shakespeare honors by allusion and quotation. When Phoebe in *As You Like It* says

> Dead shepherd, now I find thy saw of might,
> Whoever loved that loved not at first sight

the dead shepherd is no other than Christopher Marlowe and the "saw" a quotation from *Hero and Leander*.

Marlowe was cut off in his prime. What he might have accomplished had he lived out his life like Shakespeare no one can say. Certain limitations of his genius are apparent; he had little sense of humor, none of Shakespeare's interest in the whimsicalities of common folk. We cannot imagine him ever creating such a character as Dogberry or writing the grave-diggers' scene in *Hamlet*. He had nothing of Shakespeare's sincere patriotism; a Renaissance individualist, his desire of the impossible leaped over the bounds of country. Finally he lacked Shakespeare's profound sense of the moral

order of the universe and of man's life in this universe
of law. Marlowe is a rebel against order and convention;
his sympathy goes out to rebels against and tramplers
upon the established order, to such a conqueror as Tamburlaine, to such a defier of God's law as Faustus, even
to the desperate revengeful Jew. Marlowe would never
have become a Shakespeare, but it is not too much to say
that his influence upon the young Shakespeare was
greater than that of any other poet or playwright and
that without Marlowe there would never have been the
William Shakespeare whom we know.

CHAPTER X

SHAKESPEARE'S DEVELOPMENT

Part I

It is plain from what has been said that Shakespeare knew little or nothing of the new drama before he came to London. Nor is there any reason to suppose that he sprang into sudden prominence as a dramatist. Marlowe did so with his first play, but Marlowe was a more precocious genius than Shakespeare and at his death left a body of work far superior to anything that his contemporary Shakespeare had yet achieved. There is good reason to believe that Shakespeare slowly formed himself as a playwright gaining experience as an actor and in the hard school of experience. It is possible in fact to trace his development from somewhat hesitant beginnings to supreme mastery of his art; but to do this we must have a fairly definite knowledge of the chronological order of his plays.

This knowledge has been made possible by the untiring labor of Shakespearean scholars for a century or more. Nothing can be gained from the arrangement of his plays in the first Folio. The editors of that work grouped the plays in classes: Comedies, Histories, and Tragedies. They opened the volume with *The Tempest,* Shakespeare's latest play and one which had never yet been printed, probably in order to stimulate a possible purchaser. They arranged the Histories in the order of their historic time, beginning with *King John* and ending with *Henry VIII.* They inserted *Troilus and Cressida* between the Histories and the Tragedies, uncertain perhaps to which class it belonged; we group it today with the so-called "bitter comedies." There seems to be no reason at all for the Folio's order of the Tragedies which begins with the late *Coriolanus,* follows it with *Titus Andronicus,* certainly very early work, and ends with *Cymbeline* which we would not call a tragedy.

Scholarly research, however, has given us three kinds of evidence which help to fix with some degree of precision the date of composition of Shakespeare's plays and so to arrange them in approximately chronological order. Approximately only, for while we can be sure that *The Tempest* is a late play and the *Comedy of Errors* an early one, it is by no means certain that such a table as that printed on pp. 249 *ff.* is accurate as regards either the year or the position of any particular play. These three kinds of evidence are known as the external, the internal-external, and the internal. The first of these is the most important and the most satisfactory. It consists of references to Shakespeare's plays by his contemporaries, dates of performances at Court, and the entry of a play in the Stationers' Register for subsequent publication. Thus Francis Meres in his *Palladis Tamia,* entered for publication on September 7, 1598, speaks of Shakespeare with highest praise and lists a dozen of his dramas as examples of his work. It is of course apparent that all the plays he names had been produced on the stage, few of them had been published, when Meres wrote. Conversely, since he seems to have been well acquainted with the stage of his day it is at least probable that with one exception Shakespeare had not written any other plays than those of this list before the summer of 1598. The exception is the historic trilogy of Henry VI, already discussed (p. 46). Another piece of evidence of this kind is found in the mention by a member of the Middle Temple of a performance of "a play called *Twelve Night*" at a feast in that Inn of Court on February 2, 1602. The Stationers' Register lists sixteen plays by Shakespeare entered for publication in his lifetime beginning with *Titus Andronicus* in 1594 and ending with *Pericles* in 1608. This evidence, however, which only establishes a date before which a play was written does not cover all the dramas; there is no external evidence at all for *The Taming of the Shrew, All's Well, Coriolanus,* and *Timon of Athens;* and for a number of other plays it is quite uncertain. For these, then, we must depend on evidence of another sort.

Internal-external evidence is furnished by allusions in the plays themselves to events which can be historically dated. The most striking of these is the allusion in one of the choruses of *Henry V* to the campaign of Essex in Ireland and to the confident expectation of his return in triumph. Now Essex set out on this campaign in March, 1599, and returned in anything but triumph (see p. 49) in September. It is plain, therefore, that the chorus, and presumably the play of which it is a part must have been written in the summer of 1599. Few pieces of evidence of this sort, however, are so definite as this. There seems to be an allusion in *Midsummer Night's Dream* to the rainy summer of 1594; in *King Lear* to the eclipses of sun and moon in 1605; in *Macbeth* to the "equivocation" charged against a Jesuit connected with the Gunpowder Plot. The epilogue to *2 King Henry IV* promises another play to follow which can be identified with *Henry V*. Here belong also the known dates of sources such as North's *Plutarch,* from which Shakespeare drew his material. All these, however, fix only an initial date and show that the play in which they occur was written after the event alluded to; how long after they do not show, although it seems safe to assume that it would not be long after since allusions of this sort to be understood by the audience would naturally be to recent events. On the whole there is not a large body of such evidence; Shakespeare does not seem to have been in the habit of indulging in topical allusions.

Internal evidence is that derived from the plays themselves, from their subjects, method of treatment, weakness or mastery of dramatic technique, and in particular from the style, the use of language, the employment of prose, the amount of rhyme, and more especially the development in the way of free expression of the prevailing blank verse. This so-called metrical evidence will be discussed later (p. 240); it is sufficient to say here that by combining this internal with the other types of evidence we can at least arrange Shakespeare's plays in periods. It is plain, for example, that the histories, except *Henry VIII,* follow one another through what we call the first and second periods of Shakespeare's career and come to a close with *Henry V;* that the "joyous comedies" belong together about the turn of the century, 1599-1600, and that a long succession of tragedies stretches from *Julius Cæsar* in 1599 to *Coriolanus,* ca. 1608. Within these periods, however, and interrupting the succession of such groups we find plays of quite another type; the grim tragedy of *Titus Andronicus* (1593-94) falls within the period of the early comedies, and the "bitter comedy" *Measure for Measure* (ca. 1604) interrupts the succession of the tragedies. We must not think of these "periods" of Shakespeare's work as water-tight compartments sharply cut off from one another in which he confined himself to writing only plays of a certain type. They are more like the seasons of the year which melt almost imperceptibly into one another, where in spring we may get a day that recalls winter weather and another that foretells the approach of summer. Yet by a study of these periods and of the plays now by general assent assigned to them it is possible to get a fairly accurate view of Shakespeare's development as a dramatist.

It is usual to divide Shakespeare's work into four periods: the first of apprenticeship ending about 1594, the second of mastery of comedy and history, 1594-160C the third that of the tragedies and of the "bitter comₑ dies," 1599-1608, and the last, that of the "romances" or tragi-comedies, 1608-1613. It is unsafe to ascribe the changes in theme as some critics have done to changes in Shakespeare's outlook on life; various causes may have influenced him to shift, for example, from history in *Henry V* to tragedy in *Julius Cæsar,* or from tragedy in *Coriolanus* to tragi-comedy in *Cymbeline.* Yet it is by no means impossible as we follow the development of Shakespeare's art to see also a broadening, deepening, and finally a ripening of his conception of human life and his judgment of men's acts and motives.

It is often said that Shakespeare's earliest work wa. confined to patching up and revising plays by other dramatists. There is little evidence for this and it seems rather unlikely that an apprentice in the art should be asked to revise plays that had already won success upon the stage. We can be certain, however, that the trilogy of *Henry VI* belongs to this early period. The first part was staged by Lord Strange's Men in the spring of 1592. It was immensely successful, particularly because of the scenes which showed the English hero Talbot fighting and dying heroically in the wars in France. Some of these scenes were undoubtedly written by Shakespeare either in collaboration with other authors—Peele and Greene are suggested—or to replace older work. The finest scene of the play, which represent the origin of the Red and the White Rose quarrel, is also his, but seems to have been written later, perhaps about 1598 when the play was revised to bring it into organic connection with the later parts and with *Henry V*. This play was printed for the first time in the Folio, 1623.

The second and third parts of *Henry VI* were originally a two-part play dealing with the Wars of the Roses. They were on the stage in 1592 as is shown by Greene's parody of a line occurring in the third part in his attack of Shakespeare already mentioned. They were published under the titles of the *First Part of the Contention* (1594) and the *True Tragedy of Richard Duke of York* (1595) in an abbreviated and corrupt form on the break-up of the company, Pembroke's, by which they were first performed. There seems some reason to believe that they were the work of Marlowe, perhaps with the assistance of Peele, that they came into the hands of Shakespeare's company, and that their present form, as it appears in the Folio, represents Shakespeare's revision of the lost original. Another theory holds that these two parts are early and original work by Shakespeare alone. If so, he was clearly working under the influence of Marlowe. The inclusion of all three parts in the Folio shows that they were considered by the editors as in their final form the work of Shakespeare. The omission of any mention of them by Meres in his well-known list may be due to the fact that they were withdrawn from the stage during his residence in London in the mid-1590's.

Another play of this early period, *Titus Andronicus*, has been the subject of much debate. It is a Senecan tragedy of closely woven intrigue in the manner of Kyd and apparently very popular on the Elizabethan stage. That in its present form it represents the work or at least the revision of Shakespeare is as certain as anything can be. It is not only included in the Folio, but is mentioned by Meres in 1598. Its early history, however, is most obscure. A play on the subject of Titus and the Goths was on the stage as early as 1592 as is shown by an allusion in *A Knack to Know a Knave,* a play of that year. In the winter of 1594 Sussex's Men produced a play called by the illiterate Henslowe *Titus & Ondronicus.* He marked it *ne* which is supposed to mean either a new play or, as in this case, a revision. When the theatres were again closed by the plague, Henslowe sold the play to a printer who brought out a copy of it in this year, 1594. Of this edition, the first of Shakespeare's plays to be printed, only one copy, that in the Folger Library at Washington, still survives. It does not bear his name on the title-page. Later the play passed into the hands of Shakespeare's company and was played by them on various occasions.

Perhaps the simplest explanation of these facts is to assume that an unknown writer, possibly Peele, traces of whose hand abound in *Titus,* was the original author, that Henslowe secured the acting rights and in the plague season of 1593-94 called on the young dramatist Shakespeare, who had recently achieved great success by his poem *Venus and Adonis* (1593) to touch up the play so that it could be produced with a flourish of trumpets as *ne.* It is certain that Shakespeare was in London in 1593-94 busy on his *Lucrece.* He was probably glad to earn an honest penny in a time of deep depression for actors and playwrights by doing an odd job of this sort. Traces of Shakespeare's revising hand are fairly evident in the play [1]; but he apparently left

[1] See the edition of this play in the new *Cambridge Shakespeare,* 1948.

the original framework untouched. Such an explanation
agrees with a tradition dating from 1687 that Shakespeare "only gave some master touches to one or two
of the principal parts" and it relieves Shakespeare of
the responsibility of the crude horrors with which this
play abounds.

It is sometimes asserted that *Romeo and Juliet* must
have been written as early as 1591 because of an allusion in that play to an earthquake which occurred eleven
years before, 1580. If so, it attracted little attention at
the time and must have been thoroughly reworked some
years later. It may best be considered with the plays
of Shakespeare's second period.

It was in the field of comedy that the young Shakespeare learned the technique of his craft, and a trio of
comedies of this early period, *The Comedy of Errors,
Two Gentlemen of Verona,* and *Love's Labour's Lost,*
show him at work experimenting in different types of
comedy and practicing construction, characterization,
and dramatic expression. Of these three the *Errors*
probably comes first. In fact there is some reason to
believe it Shakespeare's first unaided and original play.
The interesting suggestion has been made that he may
have drafted it while still a country school-master, but
if so he revised it later from beginning to end, for the
play is written in Marlovian blank verse which Shakespeare would not have been able to imitate before he
came to London. Traces of the old-fashioned doggerel
still remain in the dialogue and we are probably not far
wrong in dating it ca. 1590. We first hear of a performance during the Christmas Revels at Gray's Inn in
1594, but it was certainly on the boards long before that
time; in fact it was probably selected as a play for the
Revels because of its fame as a fun-maker.

The *Errors* is a good example of a common Elizabethan practice, the adaptation of classical comedy to the contemporary stage. It is founded upon the *Menaechmi* of Plautus, an amusing comedy dealing with the adventures and mishaps of two indistinguishable twin brothers. In the Plautine play there is only one pair of twins; in Shakespeare's there are two, twin servants as well as twin masters, which, of course, makes the comic confusion more confounded. For this duplication Shakespeare probably drew on another Plautine play the *Amphitryon.*

These classical comedies gave Shakespeare what he needed most at this time, a well-knit plot, ingeniously developed, and neatly solved: the final rally of all the characters and the solution of the mistaken identities in the last scene is a little masterpiece of construction. Yet Shakespeare in this play did much more than imitate or even adapt a classical comedy. The atmosphere of the play, the citizens' houses, the old inns, the merchants doing business on the streets, all is genuinely and realistically Elizabethan England. Moreover Shakespeare sets this scene against a romantic background drawn from the well-known story of *Apollonius of Tyre,* a tale of the separation of a family by shipwreck, of a father's wanderings in search of a lost wife and child, and of the final happy reunion of the family. To this he adds the shadow of tragedy, so often found in his later comedies, by presenting the father, Ægeon, in the first scene under sentence of death, saved at the very end by his recognition as the father of the twins. Finally Shakespeare adds the "love-interest" demanded in a popular play by providing the shrewish wife of one twin with an amiable sister with whom the other twin promptly falls in love.

We look in vain in the *Comedy of Errors* for the

characterization and the poetry in which Shakespeare was later to excel. It is essentially an ingenious piece of dramatic construction, far more complex and amusing than its source and lifted above the realm of farce by added touches of love-making and romance.

The *Two Gentlemen of Verona* is a somewhat less successful attempt at a form in which Shakespeare was later to become pre-eminent, romantic comedy dealing primarily with the theme of love. The rather slight story of two lovers, one constant, the other fickle, of a lady disguised as a page following her faithless lover, of love's crosses and misadventures, crowned at last with a happy ending is somewhat artificial for modern taste, but very much in the fashion of Elizabethan courtly love. Especially shocking to our ideas is the scene where the true lover Valentine actually hands over to his faithless but now repentant friend his own beloved Sylvia upon whom that friend has just laid violent hands. Yet this very action is part of the Renaissance creed which rated friendship between man and man far above love between man and woman. Shakespeare himself was once a believer in this creed, traces of which appear again and again in his sonnets—see especially numbers forty and forty-two. He never again allowed himself to end a play in such an unsatisfactory and hurried fashion as he did here, and this huddling up of the conclusion is one of the signs of his immaturity. When he had Plautus to guide him he could manage a capital denouement; working on his own he was less successful. Yet there are certain features in which this play shows an advance upon the *Comedy of Errors*. It pays more attention to characterization; the lovers are well discriminated, Julia, the forsaken lady, anticipates some of the most charming of Shakespeare's later heroines, and the two comic servants, especially Launce with his dog, are capital bits of realistic comedy. The special charm of the play, however, is its poetry. Here in a tale of love the young poet-playwright lets himself go to his heart's content and fills his scenes with passages of lyric beauty. One of the first and loveliest of Shakespeare's songs "Who is Sylvia?" appears here as a serenade. All in all while the *Two Gentlemen of Verona* is a poorer stage play than the *Comedy of Errors* it is a play of more promise and points more directly to later triumphs in romantic comedy.

In *Love's Labour's Lost* Shakespeare attempted this time with brilliant success a new type of comedy, one of personal and social satire. The play has come down to us in a revision prepared for presentation at court in the Christmas season of 1597. Signs of this revision are apparent in the text, particularly in Biron's long speech, IV, iii, 289-365 and it is probable that much of the play was carefully rewritten. At any rate it shows a marked advance, if not in construction at least in its outlook on life, over the *Two Gentlemen*. In that play Shakespeare accepted the conventions of courtly love and friendship without question; in this he ridicules the social follies of the day. More especially he laughs at the Elizabethan extravagance of language, at the Renaissance parade of learning, and even at the fashions of courtly love. There is some reason to believe that it was written for a private performance in the plague year of 1593 and that some of the comic characters, Armado, Holofernes, Moth, are caricatures of well-known people of that day. This personal satire is lost to us; what is not lost is Shakespeare's fine strong com-

mon sense. This is embodied in the chief character Biron,
the first and one of the best of Shakespeare's witty
gentlemen, into whom, no doubt, Shakespeare has put a
great deal of himself. It is Biron who recognizes the
folly of the vow taken by the king and his comrades to
live a life of seclusion devoted to study and to abjure
the society of women. It is he who exposes the perjury
of his fellows when they yield to the charms of the
princess and her ladies and, when his own passion for
one of them is revealed, he defends in a burst of eloquence love as the source and fountain of poetry, beauty,
and true wisdom. The moral of the whole action is
plain enough: men cannot live without women and if
they wish to win their loves they must woo them with
simple sincerity. The play is a courtly comedy something in the style of Lyly as is shown by the artificial
grouping of the characters, the king and his three lords
balanced against the princess and her three ladies. There
is little of Lyly's characteristic euphuism, but there is
all of Lyly's delight in word-play, puns, conceits, and
far-fetched images. It is written for the most part in
rhyme, sometimes in artful rhyme-schemes such as alter-
nates and sonnets. Yet around all this courtly extravagance of speech Shakespeare has thrown an atmosphere
of rural England. The scene, supposedly in Navarre, is
really somewhere in the English country side. The
country parson, school-master, and clown are figures
such as Shakespeare knew at home and the fanciful and
artificial play ends with a lovely song of spring and
winter redolent of the breath of Shakespeare's England.
All in all when allowances are made for topical allusions lost to us today and for confusions caused by
the revision *Love's Labour's Lost* remains the most
original and the most delightful of Shakespeare's early
comedies.

Part II

There is nothing to show that any one of Shakespeare's plays except those already discussed was written before 1594. The great plague of 1593-94 closed the theatres for many months in those years and Shakespeare spent a good part of his time in the composition of two long poems, *Venus and Adonis* and *Lucrece* (see below, p. 184 ff). He may also have been at work on one or more plays in view of the reopening of the theatres. Certainly with this reopening in the summer of 1594 he resumes his work as a playwright and for the next six years is extremely busy turning out play after play in quick succession.

This second period is the time of his great histories and most brilliant comedies, but these come toward the end of the period. It opens with a group of plays that link it with his earlier work. Of these we may first discuss the early histories.

It is perhaps well to begin with *King John* (ca. 1596), in some ways the least interesting, as it is the least original of Shakespeare's histories. It is a rewriting of an old chronicle play, *The Troublesome Reign of King John,* published in two parts in 1591, but certainly written some years earlier, possibly by Peele. Shakespeare's skill as a playwright is shown by the manner in which he condensed the two parts into one, selecting, omitting, and enlarging as he sees fit; his independence appears by the fact that while he keeps in the main the scenario of his source he disdains to take over any of the dialogue.

Like the other chronicle plays of the day *King John* appeals to the enthusiastic patriotism of the Elizabethan audience. Following old tradition Shakespeare repre-

sents John as a valiant defender of England against
France and more especially against the arrogant claims
of the Pope, a "sure-fire" hit in Elizabethan days.
Yet Shakespeare knew history too well to make King
John a hero. As a matter of fact he appears in this play
as the villainous murderer, in intent if not in fact, of
his little nephew. The true hero of the play is Falcon-
bridge, the bastard son of Richard Cœur de Lion, who
avenges his father's death, leads the royal army against
foreign invaders and domestic rebels, and rallies the
nobles of England around John's innocent successor with
the proud words:

> Now these her princes are come home again,
> Come the three corners of the world in arms,
> And we shall shock them. Nought shall make us rue,
> If England to itself do rest but true.

There are two interesting omissions in this play; there
is no mention of the great event of John's reign the
granting of the Magna Carta; it would not have been
prudent, perhaps not even safe, for Shakespeare to show
a body of rebellious nobles wresting by force a charter
from their king. The second is the excision of an amusing but scandalous scene in his source attacking the
morals of nuns and friars; Shakespeare never stoops to
win a laugh by abusing his mother's church.

The play is written in rather formal Marlovian blank
verse; there is no prose, and little rhyme. Shakespeare
is following in the footsteps of Marlowe in his treatment of English history in tragic fashion.

This is even more apparent in the next of the chronicle plays, *Richard III*, probably staged soon after the
opening of the theatres in 1594 and possibly written a
little earlier. It picks up the thread of English history
where Marlowe, if it was he who wrote the *Henry VI*

plays *II* and *III* in their first form, had dropped it, and carries the story on to the end of the Wars of the Roses. More than this it centers all the action in Marlowe's own manner about a single figure, Richard Crookback. This character had been sketched by Marlowe in *3 King Henry VI,* but Shakespeare develops, refines, and varies the hero-villain until while still recognizable as one of Marlowe's supermen of the Renaissance, Shakespeare's Richard is more real, more human, and more effective on the stage than any character in Marlowe's plays. Here certainly the disciple has surpassed his master. Six editions of this play were published before 1623. We could ask for no better evidence of its contemporary popularity and we know that the part of Richard was one of Burbage's most successful rôles. From Shakespeare's day until the present the play has held the stage, largely because of the magnificent opportunity it offers for a star in the part of Richard. It must be confessed, however, that the acting version has as a rule been Colley Cibber's revision, (1700), rather than Shakespeare's own play.

Like *King John, Richard III* is written in Marlovian blank verse; there is no better example of Shakespeare's adaptation of Marlowe's style than the opening soliloquy of the play. The verse is rhetorical and declamatory rather than lyrical, and the long tirades and choral lamentations are reminiscent of Senecan influence. On the whole it is a play for the stage rather than for the lover of Shakespeare's poetry.

There is one feature of this play, however, that marks it as characteristically Shakespeare's and represents a distinct advance over Marlowe's and his own earlier work. This is his interpretation in dramatic form of history. To Shakespeare the internecine Wars of the Roses was a period to be looked back upon with horror.

He represents this period as culminating in the "caco-demon," Richard, who after trampling on the Red Rose turns in his mad pursuit of power against his own family. Richard rises by slaughter to the throne, only to become a prey to the stings of conscience, to be out-witted and betrayed by his subjects, and finally slain in battle by the founder of the House of Tudor who unites the Roses and brings peace to England. The concep-tion of the Nemesis that pursues the hero-villain, the hatred of civil strife, and the sincere belief in the great-ness and unity of England under the Tudors, all this is Shakespeare's contribution to the tragic story of Richard's rise and fall.

By common consent *Richard II* is dated in or near 1595. It is certainly later than *Richard III* and shows Shakespeare diverging still further from the school of Marlowe. There is to be sure a certain resemblance between it and Marlowe's *Edward II*. Both plays deal with the tragical fall of a weak but lovable king; but while Marlowe tells the story of the whole reign, Shake-speare concentrates on the last years, the crisis and col-lapse of Richard. Compared with Marlowe's simple and straightforward presentation of his protagonist, Shake-speare's portrayal of Richard shows a more penetrating and subtler psychology. Edward is overthrown by an outside power, the rebellious barons; Richard is a vic-tim of his own character, his self-indulgence, his rash-ness, his blindness to the realities of life, and Shake-speare brings out at once the weakness and the charm of Richard by contrasting him with the hard realist, Bolingbroke. It is hardly too much to say that this play foreshadows, however faultily, the later and greater tragedies of Shakespeare.

In the matter of style, too, *Richard II* shows a sense of conscious freedom in the young dramatist. Shake-

speare abandons the rhetorical blank verse of Marlowe
for a more fluent metre. There is a greater proportion
of rhyme in this play than in any of the earlier histories
and even the blank verse often has a lyric lilt. Shakespeare indulges in this play, too often for one's taste,
in puns, in word-play and conceits. In short, one feels
in reading *Richard II* that the poet has graduated from
the school of Marlowe and is now his own master. It
is not as good an acting play as *Richard III* but it is
more Shakespearean.

The one tragedy of this period, *Romeo and Juliet,*
may be dated fairly definitely in its present form in
1596. An unauthorized edition, Q1, appeared in 1597;
an authoritative edition, Q2, "corrected and augmented"
two years later. Like *Richard II* with which it has many
points of resemblance *Romeo and Juliet* shows Shakespeare striking out for himself, this time in the field of
tragedy. He turns his back on Seneca and the Senecan
convention of horrors, and writes the first tragedy in
English literature to deal with the theme of romantic
love. *Romeo and Juliet* is the work of a poet-playwright
who has found a plot into which he can throw all his
power and his passion. At times indeed it seems as if
the passion of the poet got the better of the playwright's
power as when Shakespeare stops the action to let
Mercutio recite the well-known verses on Queen Mab.
Yet one has only to compare Shakespeare's play with
its source, a long narrative poem by Arthur Brooke
(1562) to see how skillfully he adapted the story to the
stage. In characterization, too, *Romeo and Juliet* shows
an advance over Shakespeare's earlier work; Romeo is
at first a sentimentalist like Richard II, but he is
ennobled by his love and rises above himself as Richard

never does. Juliet is the first and in some ways the most appealing of Shakespeare's tragic heroines; the nurse is his first complete triumph in the realistic presentation of a comic character. Yet the real charm of the play lies neither in its construction nor in its characterization but in its poetry. The theme of young love, pure, passionate, and ill-fated, is given, dramatic form with a lyric beauty that is unmatched elsewhere in English literature. *Romeo and Juliet* lacks the depth, the power, the tragic intensity, of the great plays of the third period, and it may well be that Shakespeare, no doubt his own severest critic, felt he was not yet ready to deal competently with great tragic themes. At any rate in spite of the instant success of *Romeo and Juliet* upon the stage and with all lovers of poetry, he turned his back on tragedy and set himself to write a long series of comedies and to complete his group of English histories.

The first comedy of this period, *A Midsummer Night's Dream,* (ca. 1595), is Shakespeare's first complete success in the field of romantic comedy. It is a little masterpiece of plot construction; the various threads drawn from diverse sources are deftly woven together into a most delightful pattern. The "enveloping action," the wedding festival of Theseus and Hippolyta, comes from Plutarch by way of Chaucer; the story of the lovers probably from a lost Italian source; Oberon, the fairy king, had appeared in Greene's *James IV;* Puck is a well-known character in English folklore, and Bottom with his crew of rude mechanicals represents Shakespeare's laughing observation of amateur performances in English country towns. It is interesting to note how skillfully Shakespeare has blended in the play the classical, the realistic, and the romantic elements of Elizabethan drama. The setting, Athens, and the main characters are classical in name at least; but more important is the complicated intrigue and the deft solution of an artfully entangled plot. This is a technique that Shakespeare learned from his classic masters, but he has surpassed them in this play. It seems almost needless to call attention to the homely realism of the scenes in which Bottom plays a part. This is genuine English stuff and it is interesting to note that when the theatres were closed these scenes were made into a "droll" and played by touring actors in English towns and villages. In Oberon, Titania, and the magic herbs we have pure matter of romance and nowhere in literature is there such a union and comic contrast of romance and realism as in the scene where Titania falls in love with Bottom crowned with the ass's head.

The style is a delightful blending of blank verse and rhyme; the blank verse itself, like much of *Romeo and Juliet,* has a lyrical note, and the frequent songs and rhymed speeches of the fairies add to the musical effect. The Bottom scenes are written in vigorous prose which Shakespeare was coming to realize as the true vehicle for realistic comedy. Had Shakespeare written nothing else his fame as a master of English romantic comedy would have been assured; but he was to go on to even greater work.

The *Merchant of Venice* (ca. 1596-97), again represents an advance in Shakespeare's art and a deepening of his outlook on life. *A Midsummer Night's Dream* is a comedy of fancy; the *Merchant* is a rather serious study of certain aspects of human life, of love and marriage, of the use and abuse of wealth. The idea of a play whose chief character should be a wicked Jew may have been suggested to Shakespeare by the revival in 1594 of Marlowe's *Jew of Malta,* a revival provoked by the outburst of the anti-Semitism that accompanied the execution in that year of the Queen's Jewish physician for alleged high treason. Yet Shakespeare's Shylock is a very different character from Marlowe's Jew, at once more dramatically effective and more truly human than the monster Barabas.

The main plot, the bond entered into by a merchant in order that his young friend may woo and win the lady of Belmont, the forfeiture of the bond, and the delivery of the merchant by the lady disguised as a lawyer, along with the intrigue of the rings, goes back to an Italian *novella* of the fourteenth century. The theme of the caskets, Shakespeare's clever substitution for the somewhat indelicate fashion in which the lover of the *novella* wins the lady, comes from a collection of moral tales, the *Gesta Romanorum.* The Jew's fair daughter who loves a Christian has a counterpart in Marlowe's play. These diverse elements have been combined into a harmonious whole by masterly plot construction. Especially ingenious is the manner in which the tragic threat of the court scene is averted by the wit and wisdom of Portia, and in the last act tragedy is pushed quite into the background by the romance of the lovers and the merry business of the rings in the moonlit garden of Belmont. Actors starring in the part of Shylock who have rung down the curtain with his exit from the courtroom have quite misunderstood the significance of Shakespeare's play.

It is not so much in construction however as in characterization that Shakespeare shows his developing mastery. Shylock is in some ways the most complete,

rounded, and convincing character that he had yet created; the motivation of his action, the blending of greed,
racial antipathy, and personal revenge is admirably rendered. And Shylock's part in the play is admirably
balanced by that of Portia, the perfect picture of a
great lady of the Renaissance. Shakespeare's transformation of the siren of the *novella* into the heroine of
this play is one of his masterpieces of character creation. There is less gay fancy and riotous fun in the
Merchant than in the earlier comedies, but this lack is
more than atoned for by the grave beauty of the verse,
the moral earnestness of the central casket scene, and
the natural magic of the opening lines of the last act.

It must have been shortly after the *Merchant of
Venice* that Shakespeare took up the revision and com-
pletion of the trilogy which crowns his series of histories, *Henry IV*, parts *I* and *II,* and *Henry V*. There
is some reason to believe that the *Henry IV* plays were
written earlier, probably soon after *Richard II,* 1595;
it is certain that the fat knight who figures in them was
originally called Sir John Oldcastle. The presentation
on the stage of the historic Sir John, as a "villainous
abominable misleader of youth" naturally provoked an
indirect descendant, Lord Cobham, then holding the high
office of Lord Chamberlain, and he insisted on a re-
baptism of the character. Shakespeare yielded, apolo-
gized, indeed, in the epilogue to the second part, and
substituted the name of Falstaff, apparently a corruption of Fastolfe, also a historic character who had left
no descendant able to enter protest. There is a consensus of opinion that the revised form of the two parts
dates in the year 1597-8 and *Henry V* in 1599.

In these plays Shakespeare shakes off definitely and
completely the influence of Marlowe. He reverts in fact
to an older type of chronicle play where comic scenes

are interspersed in the serious matter of history. Following an old tradition which told of the riotous youth of Prince Hal and represented Oldcastle as his companion, Shakespeare created the glorious comic figure which we know as Falstaff. He carries him triumphantly through the first part, and shows his gradual degeneration in the second which closes with his rejection by his old friend, the newly crowned king. It seems plain from the epilogue to the second part that Shakespeare's first intention was to carry him on into the play of *Henry V*, but he thought better of it, feeling no doubt that such a character would be out of place in the epic-heroic play of Henry's war in France. And so all we have of Falstaff in *Henry V* is the humorous-pathetic account of his death-bed babbling of green fields and his passage to "Arthur's bosom."

The serious matter of these plays deals with the last great monarch of medieval England, "the mirror of all Christian kings," Henry V. He is first mentioned in *Richard II* as a wild young reprobate, a thorn in his father's side. We see him in the first part of *Henry IV* as a haunter of taverns and a companion of rioters and purse-takers, yet able to rise to heroic heights at the call of duty. In the second part we see less of him till near the end when he is reconciled with his father on the old king's death-bed, and assumes the crown. The play that bears his name is rather dramatized history than drama proper and is composed of a series of scenes showing Henry as the perfect king, taking wise counsel with his lords, crushing domestic treason, winning the crowning victory of the English wars in France, and finally completing his conquest by wooing and winning Katherine. the French princess. The note of love of country, of pride in England's past, which rings through all the histories of Shakespeare rises to what has been called "a chant of patriotic triumph" in *Henry V*. The enthusiastic nationalism which evokes this note was waning sadly in the last troubled years of Elizabeth's reign and Shakespeare must have felt that he had done all that could be done with the chronicle play and that it was time to turn to other fields. The period of Shakespeare's tragedies follows hard upon the closing of the series of his histories, but before we turn to them we still have a group of comedies to consider.

Shakespeare seems to have found time during his work on the Henry trilogy to write a couple of farce comedies. The first of these, *The Taming of the Shrew,* must be dated at least as late as 1598 since it is not included in Meres' list. It is a rewriting by Shakespeare, apparently with the help of a collaborator, of an old play, *The Taming of a Shrew,* published in 1594. The induction and the scenes dealing with Petruchio and Katherine are Shakespeare's and in his best vein of lively comedy; he follows the scenario of his source fairly closely but completely rewrites the dialogue. The underplot, dealing with the wooing of the shrew's gentle sister, is the work of the collaborator, who, perhaps on Shakespeare's suggestion, lifted the plot from Gascoigne's prose comedy, *The Supposes,* and turned it into such tame flat verse that it seems impossible that Shakespeare could have written it at any time of his life. Yet the two plots are so well woven together than we must assume that Shakespeare planned and directed the whole work. It is an interesting fact that the old play has an epilogue in which the drunken tinker is laid asleep by the ale-house where he had been discovered in the Induction, awakes to fancy that the play he has seen was a dream, and goes home to tame his own shrewish wife. Such an ending seems almost necessary and the absence of anything corresponding to it in Shakespeare's play is hard to explain. Possibly the manuscript from which the Folio version was printed—there is no earlier text—had lost the last leaf or two in which some such scene was written.

The Taming of the Shrew is not a great play; it is probably a work dashed off in haste by Shakespeare; but it bears witness to his skill in construction, to his sense of fun and farcical situation and, in the Induction, to his loving reminiscence of the country side about Stratford.

An old tradition tells us that Queen Elizabeth was so delighted with the character of Falstaff that she commanded Shakespeare to write another play about him and to show him in love. It is also said that he wrote the play she ordered, *The Merry Wives of Windsor,* in fourteen days. We need not take this last statement literally, but there is good reason to believe that the play was written at top speed for a performance before the Queen. It may be safely dated late in 1599 after *Henry V* and may be regarded as Shakespeare's apology to Elizabeth for having failed to keep his promise and introduce Sir John in that play.

To show Falstaff in love was beyond the power even of Shakespeare; Falstaff as Shakespeare knew him and drew him in the *Henry IV* plays was incapable of the tender passion. To comply with the royal command, however, he stooped to show his comic hero engaged in amorous pursuit of two merry but honest English wives who confederate together to pretend love to him, arrange to get him ducked in the Thames, well-beaten by a jealous husband, and finally exposed to the derision of the entire company. This is not the old Sir John, master

of every situation in which he finds himself, and indeed
there is little of the true Falstaff in the character who
bears his name in *The Merry Wives* except his exuber-
ant language.

The Merry Wives is the one example in Shakespeare's
work of bourgeois comedy, written in the realistic satiri-
cal mood which was becoming popular toward the end
of the century. Jonson's *Every Man In* and *Every Man
out of his Humour,* both performed by Shakespeare's
company, had opened this vein with marked success, and
it seems quite likely that Shakespeare writing under
pressure tried his hand for once at this type of play.
There is no touch of his romantic imagination in it; the
slender story of the love of Fenton and Mistress Anne
is pushed quite into the background; the fairies of the
last scene are not real fairies but children in disguise.
Half a dozen characters, the Welsh Parson and the
French Doctor, Corporal Nym, taken over from *Henry V,*
and above all the jealous Ford are "humour characters"
of the Jonson school. This may be one of the reasons
why the play has always been successful on the stage;
a "humour character" is an excellent part for an actor,
and the combination and contrast of "humours" in this
play along with the lively well-planned farcical action
gives *The Merry Wives* a dash and vigor that is irresistible on the stage. No one would rank the play, however, among Shakespeare's best comedies: it is a hasty
experiment triumphantly carried off, but never repeated.
The next comedies that we have to consider are in quite
another vein.

A trio of plays sometimes called the Jovous Comedies
concludes this period; these are in the order of composition: *Much Ado about Nothing, As You Like It,* and
Twelfth Night. The first of these, *Much Ado,* can be
dated fairly accurately. It is not mentioned by Meres

in 1598, and Kemp who played the part of Dogberry left the company about the middle of 1599; the play therefore was probably written between the autumn of 1598 and the summer of 1599.

Much Ado is in some ways Shakespeare's comic masterpiece. Founded upon an Italian tale of a slandered lady deserted by her lover and at last reunited to him, it incorporates a bit of genuine English realism in the Dogberry-Verges scenes and adds to this combination the two characters by whom the play really lives, those of Benedick and Beatrice. There is no source known for this couple, nor need one be sought; they are Shakespeare's creation, or rather his re-creation in more perfect form of the reluctant witty lovers of *Love's Labour's Lost*. Their story is technically the sub-plot, but it is by far the most interesting part of the play and Shakespeare has in fact rearranged the incidents of the main plot so as to bring these lovers together. There is nothing in the Italian tale to compare with the dramatically effective scene in which Claudio, the nominal hero of the play, renounces his bride at the altar and Benedick and Beatrice unite to revenge and vindicate her.

There is less fine poetry in this play than in most of Shakespeare's comedies. On the other hand the comic scenes, whether the stupidities of Dogberry and his mates or the wit-combats of the lovers, are written in his very best prose. It has always been successful on the stage. Just before the closing of the theatres in 1642 a contemporary writer tells us that an appearance of Benedick and Beatrice was sure to pack the house, and most of the famous actors and actresses since Garrick's day have starred in these rôles.

As You Like It (probably early 1600), the second of this group, differs as much from its predecessor as one romantic comedy can from another. *Much Ado* is one of the best built of Shakespeare's comedies; *As You Like It* one of the most loosely constructed. Its charm, and it is one of the most delightful of Shakespeare's plays, lies largely in the woodland atmosphere in which the greater part of the action is laid, and not a little in the group of lovable people who meet and make love, or laugh at love's follies under the greenwood tree. It is an adaptation for the stage of a popular romance of the day, Lodge's *Rosalynde* (1590). Lodge's book is a pastoral romance of the type that Sidney's *Arcadia* had introduced into English literature, and Shakespeare's play is in some sense a pastoral drama. Yet Shakespeare, now full master of his art, is by no means inclined to accept the artificialities and false sentiment of the pastoral. Indeed he ridicules them in the figures of Silvius and Phoebe, the despairing lover and the cold shepherdess of the pastoral. Over against these unreal characters he places such realistic figures as Audrey and William and opposes to their conventional amours the very human love-affair of Orlando and Rosalind. Touchstone's wooing of the rustic Audrey is a frank burlesque of romantic love.

Apart from the atmosphere, largely created by the woodland scenes and the lovely lyrics with which the play abounds, *As You Like It* lives by its characters. Rosalind is to many lovers of Shakespeare the most charming, as in some ways the most modern of his heroines. Touchstone, the first part Shakespeare wrote for his new "fellow" Armin, is the wittiest of his court fools; Jacques, a humour character, is Shakespeare's por-

trait of the "malcontent" or melancholy cynic, a figure
not uncommon in both Elizabethan life and literature
as the century drew to an end; and both Touchstone and
Jacques are Shakespeare's inventions; there is no trace
of them in his source. We may well excuse the careless
plotting of the play and its huddled and conventional
conclusion for the sake of its poetry and its delightful
characters.

Twelfth Night, late in 1600, the last of the trio is
in some ways the most nearly perfect of the three. Less
poetical than *As You Like It,* less witty than *Much Ado,*
it is a perfect blend of romance and realism. The main
plot, the story of the twin brother and sister, with the
business of love at cross purposes and mistaken identity,
goes back ultimately to an Italian play which had been
retold in English prose some twenty years before *Twelfth
Night* was written. Shakespeare takes this plot, sets it in
Illyria for the purpose of romantic distance, although his
Illyria is hardly distinguishable from Elizabethan England, and to keep it from degenerating into mere intrigue or mawkish sentiment surrounds it with background figures of English life, the steward, the jester,
the hard-drinking cousin, the foolish suitor, such as
might be found in any noble house in England. The
romantic plot deals with love in its varied forms, the
fanciful sentiment of the Duke, the sudden passion of
Olivia, the true and tender passion of Viola. The comic
realism turns about the trick played on the presump-
tuous steward, Malvolio. Perhaps no comedy of Shakespeare exhibits so clearly his mastery of his craft as the
way in which he interweaves and complicates these plots
and brings them at last together in a most natural and
happy solution.

The characterization, too, represents Shakespeare at
his best. The characters are not sacrificed to the plot

as some of them are in *Much Ado* nor is the plot a mere
background for the characters as in *As You Like It*.
Viola is perhaps the most lovable of Shakespeare's
heroines; Sir Toby, a figure of the family of Falstaff, is
nicely adjusted to his surroundings; Sir Andrew is the
most hopeless simpleton that Shakespeare ever drew;
and Malvolio the perfect picture of the overweening
Jack in office. All in all, *Twelfth Night* with its blend
of mirth and beauty is Shakespeare's supreme creation
in high romantic comedy.

A brief review of this period will show both the character of Shakespeare's work and his great advance in
independence and mastery in these crowded years. In
his chronicle plays he begins as a disciple of Marlowe,
excels his master in *Richard III*, and carries this genre
to its highest pitch in the Henry trilogy. In comedy he
achieves the first of his masterpieces, *A Midsummer
Night's Dream*, his first serious drama, *The Merchant
of Venice*, and toward the close his supreme trio of
romantic comedies. History and comedy occupy his
attention during this period. The tragedy of *Romeo and
Juliet*, though enough in itself to make Shakespeare
immortal, is the only play of this type between 1594
and 1599.

Part III

The third period is essentially the period of the great
tragedies, but it includes a trio of plays usually known
as the Bitter Comedies which may first be considered.
The first of these, *All's Well that Ends Well*, is generally thought to be a revision (ca. 1602-3) of an earlier
comedy, possibly the *Love's Labour's Won* of Meres'

list. It has come down to us in one text, that of the
Folio, a text so corrupt and at times so obscure as to
suggest that it was printed from a manuscript where
passages had been crossed out and re-written until it
was a puzzle to the compositor, as it has been to later
editors. Internal evidence, especially the amount of
rhyme and the varying style of the blank verse in different parts of the play, go far to support the theory of a
revision.

The source of *All's Well* is a story of Boccaccio (*Decameron,* iii, 9) which Shakespeare probably read in an
English translation, Painter's *Palace of Pleasure,* 1566.
In Boccaccio the story is told to illustrate the constancy
in love and the cunning practice by which a woman of
comparatively low birth wins a reluctant noble husband.
It must have been the character of the woman, Helena
in Shakespeare's play, which attracted him to the theme,
for there is little else in the story likely to have appealed
to him. To exalt her he degrades the ostensible hero,
Bertram, even below the corresponding character in the
novella and the simple and effective ending of the tale
is altered in the play to a tissue of lies, charges and
counter-charges that leave a most unpleasant impression
on the modern reader. There is none of the laughing
humour of Shakespeare's earlier comedies; the Clown is a
dull jester, not to be compared with Touchstone or Feste,
and Parolles a poor specimen of the *miles gloriosus.* The
breath of romance that blows through the earlier comedies has given place to a grave and often bitter wisdom.
There seems no better explanation of this strange play
than the hypothesis that it is a careless early comedy
re-written at a time when Shakespeare's heart was not
in his work.

Troilus and Cressida may be dated with some degree
of accuracy in 1602. It was entered in the Stationers'

Register Feb. 7, 1603 "as it is acted by my Lord Chamberlain's men." A clear allusion to Jonson's *Poetaster* acted in 1601 sets the earliest date. The play was not published until 1609 in which year two editions suddenly appeared. The second contains what is found in no other play of Shakespeare's, an epistle to the reader urging him to buy the book and remarking that this play was "never stal'd with the stage, never clapperclawed with the palms of the vulgar." If this means anything it means that the play had never been acted, which seems to contradict both the original entry and the statement on the title-page of the first edition that it had been acted at the Globe. It seems certain that the quartos of 1609 were unauthorized; the epistle intimates that "the grand possessors," i.e. Shakespeare's company, would have prevented its publication if they could. Possibly the publishers got hold of a transcript of the play made for a friend of the author after a private performance at Court or one of the Inns of Court.

The play is a strange compound of old and new. It tells the story of the siege of Troy from the point of view of medieval historians and romancers who without exception took the Trojan side against the Greeks; it retells the story of the love of Troilus told long before by Chaucer in perfect form, but here by Shakespeare in the later tradition which had degraded Cressida into a synonym for inconstancy in love; it takes the character of Thersites from Chapman's unfinished translation of Homer and converts him into the most foul-mouthed rogue in all Shakespeare's plays. All in all a strange and mystifying play. So far as the love-story goes it is a comedy of disillusion. Troilus is as true a lover as Romeo, but he loves a wanton and inconstant Cressida instead of a Juliet. On the other hand some of the speeches especially those of Ulysses are in Shakespeare's gravest and most thoughtful vein. It is supposed to be a play for the study rather than the stage, but a performance by the Players in New York in 1932 showed an undreamed-of theatrical effectiveness. Possibly the puzzling nature of the play might be explained by the hypothesis that Shakespeare was called on by his company to write a Siege of Troy play to compete with one that was being performed at a rival theatre and that the poet whose mind and heart were busy with his tragedies wrote something that he thought would fill the bill.[1]

Measure for Measure was played at Court on December 26, 1604, and was almost certainly written some time earlier that year when the theatres were opened after the Great Plague of 1603-4. A possible revision for the court performance may account for the difficulties and inconsistencies in the one text preserved, that of the Folio. Like the two preceding plays it is nominally a comedy, but it deals with a tragic theme violently wrested to bring about a happy ending. As Sir Walter Raleigh says, if Shakespeare's fellows asked him for a comedy in his tragic period they got *Measure for Measure*. The source is a tedious two-part play, *Promos and Cassandra*, 1578, by George Whetstone which in turn goes back to an Italian *novella*. The Italian story, based apparently upon some historical incident, tells how a deputy of the Emperor condemned to death a young gentleman for having outraged a virgin. The culprit's sister pleaded for his life and the deputy offered to spare him if the sister would become his mistress. She refused, but finally yielding to her brother's entreaty, consented to sacrifice her honor to save his life. The deputy, however, had her brother executed

---

[1] Interesting and suggestive interpretations of this play are given by Wilson Knight in *The Wheel of Fire* and by R. W. Chambers in *Man's Unconquerable Mind*.

and sent her the dead body. The lady took her case to
the Emperor who first ordered the deputy to marry her
and then condemned him to suffer death. The lady now
begs for the life of her new-made husband which is
granted by the Emperor and the story concludes by
saying that they lived happily together. Whetstone
altered the story by saving the brother's life who
escapes from prison and comes forward at the end to
second his sister's plea for her husband's pardon. Shakespeare went a step further in ameliorating the tragic
theme and spared his heroine the necessity of sacrificing
her honor. To effect this he substitutes for her at the
rendezvous another woman, the former betrothed of the
judge who mistakes her for the sister. It is plain that
Shakespeare simply lifted this device from his own
All's Well where the substitution of the virgin wife for
a lady guiltily desired by the husband is an integral and
essential part of the story. It is not so here and the
comic device of mistaken identity makes possible a conventional happy ending. It seems as if after the climax
of the play when the heroine indignantly repels her
brother's plea for life a comedy of intrigue has been
super-imposed on what had begun as a tragedy; certainly the great scenes of the play are in the earlier, the
tragic part. Why Shakespeare did this no one can say;
we may guess that when he decided to spare Isabella,
he felt bound to provide a way for her escape and
adopted the easiest solution. The conclusion in which
Angelo is spared to marry his betrothed and Isabella is
asked in marriage by the Duke has seldom satisfied
lovers of Shakespeare and believers in justice. Yet the
play is full of poetry, contains a group of realistic
humorous characters, and shows in every scene Shakespeare's profound knowledge of human nature and his

genial sympathy with all sorts and conditions of men.[1]

The long roll of the great tragedies opens with *Julius Cæsar*. This play was certainly on the stage in the autumn of 1599, the year of *Henry V*. It is a link-play between the histories and the tragedies, based upon a famous episode, the murder of Cæsar, in Roman history, yet dealing with it in tragic fashion. It has none of the bitterness of the later tragedies, and the grave beauty of the verse is rather that of the second period than of Shakespeare's later style. All this goes to show that the periods of Shakespeare's work are not rigidly defined, but melt imperceptibly one into another. Two at least of Shakespeare's finest comedies follow *Julius Cæsar*.

The direct source of the play was Plutarch's *Lives* in the English translation of Sir Thomas North, 1579, one of Shakespeare's favorite books. Plutarch supplied him not only with the historical facts, but also with an admirable presentation of the leading characters. Sometimes, indeed, Shakespeare turns the very words of North's prose version into his own verse. Yet this is not to say that *Julius Cæsar* lacks originality. Shakespeare selects, arranges, and emphasizes his material; the famous oration by Antony is not found in Plutarch at all, and his suppression of a whole series of events between the death of Cæsar and the battle of Philippi gives a speed and unity to the play that is lacking in the source.

The essential unity of the play is due to the fact that it revolves about the murder of Cæsar and the revenge exacted for his death. Yet Cæsar is not the hero of the play; on the contrary Shakespeare has some-

[1] A suggestive and stimulating appreciation of this play occurs in Knight's *The Wheel of Fire*.

times been blamed for depicting the greatest man of
ancient times as an arrogant, superstitious, and physi-
cally feeble despot. He drew some of these traits from
his source, but he also followed a Renaissance tradition which depressed the character of Cæsar to exalt
that of Brutus. Yet Shakespeare was not unaware of
the greatness of "the mightiest Julius" and the last acts
of the play show his spirit still powerful and "ranging
for revenge."

The true tragic hero of the play is Brutus and it is
in his treatment of this figure that Shakespeare shows
his developing power and his gradual approach to the
protagonists of the later tragedies. Romeo in Shakespeare's first original tragedy is a victim of fate, a "star-
crossed lover." Brutus, like Hamlet whom he much resembles, is a victim of his own character. A philosopher,
an idealist, he is incapable of seeing things as they are.
He undertakes a great action, the freeing of Rome from
a tyrant without realizing the true situation or the probable consequences of the deed. He makes mistake after
mistake and finally falls upon his sword a beaten man.
Yet his high sense of honor, and his sweetness of temper
are such that he never forfeits our sympathy. This was
to become Shakespeare's practice in his characterization
of his later tragic heroes, even of such a far from honorable murderer as Macbeth.

In *Hamlet* (1600), the second of the great tragedies, Shakespeare definitely abandoned the field of history and devoted all his energies to the reconstruction
of a tragic theme. A reconstruction, for strange as it
may seem *Hamlet,* Shakespeare's best known play, is
not an original creation.

An old play on the subject was on the stage some time in the 1580's; Shakespeare's company played a *Hamlet* in 1594 and again in 1596. Some years later about the time that revenge plays came into fashion again Shakespeare undertook to revise this old play. We know that a version bearing his name was on the stage in 1600, since a contemporary writing toward the close of that year says that "Shakespeare's *Lucrece* and his tragedy of *Hamlet Prince of Denmark* have it in them to please the wiser sort." The writer, Gabriel Harvey, must have seen the play or heard of it from a friend for no version of it had yet appeared in print. In 1603 a printed version was offered for sale to the London public. This is known as the first Quarto, a "stolen and surreptitious" copy. It was advertised with a flourish as written by Shakespeare and played by the King's Men, but it was as a matter of fact an impudent fraud. It seems to rest on the old play partly revised by Shakespeare, along with passages corresponding word for word with his latest revision, these being acting parts spoken by the hired man who perpetrated the theft, and finally on what the thief could remember of parts spoken by his fellow actors. It is hard to believe that such a hodge-podge as this was ever played on the stage.

Shakespeare and his fellows must have been shocked by such an outrage and took prompt pains to set it right. In the plague year of 1603-4 when Shakespeare had time on his hands he set himself to a final revision of the play which was published in 1604. This is the second Quarto "enlarged" the title-page states "to almost as much again as it was, according to the true and perfect copy." Except for a good many errors in printing and a few deliberate omissions this is the play as Shakespeare conceived it. A third text, that of the Folio, represents the acting version shortened for representation. Modern editions represent a fusion of the second Quarto and the Folio text.

The story of Hamlet goes back to the Viking age in Denmark. It was first written down by Saxo Grammaticus toward the close of the twelfth century, translated from Saxo's Latin into French about 1582 and shortly after dramatized for the Elizabethan stage, quite possibly by Kyd. The old play is lost but we can form some idea of it from a German play *Der Bestraffte Brudermord (Fratricide Punished)* which probably represents an abbreviated and corrupt form of the old play carried to Germany by English actors.

If we can reconstruct the old play from the German version and from what we know of Kyd's method, we shall see that he materially altered the story to fit it for the English stage. He introduced the Ghost crying for revenge—a genuine Senecan note—and in so doing deprived Hamlet of the obvious reason for his feigned madness—self-preservation. Instead of the open slaughter of the old king as in the story Kyd devised a secret murder by poison; he used the device of a play within a play as in his *Spanish Tragedy* to force a betrayal of the murderer's guilt; and finally he ended the play by a general massacre in which the hero and his enemies perish together.

Something, at least, like this must have been the outline of the play as it came to Shakespeare's hands. His transformation of the Senecan play of revenge for blood into the *Hamlet* that we know is one of the miracles of genius. He was bound to keep in the main the familiar action and indeed he found it, as the world has found it since, immensely effective on the stage. What he did was to re-create the character of the protagonist. Shakespeare's Hamlet is quite another person than the hero of the old saga or the straightforward revenger of the lost play. He is perhaps the most complex character that Shakespeare ever drew, a prince of the Renaissance, "courtier, soldier, scholar," a disillusioned idealist, a contemplative rather than an active man. It is worth noting that about 1600 Shakespeare had turned away from such men of action as Bolingbroke and Prince Hal and was interesting himself in such characters as the melancholy Jacques, the pessimistic Duke of *Measure for Measure,* and the worldly wise Ulysses. Hamlet is his supreme creation of this type and into the character of Hamlet Shakespeare has put more of himself than into any other figure in all his work. To sum up briefly, others had told the story; Shakespeare created the character of Hamlet, and by this creation solved the dramatic problem that confronted him. It is because Hamlet is what he is that he delays his revenge until the last moment; it is because Hamlet is what he is that the play is perennially effective on the stage—there is no other such rôle in dramatic literature for a great actor—and perennially fascinating in the study.

Othello was played at Court on Nov. 1, 1604, and there can be little doubt that it was written earlier in that year. It follows directly upon *Hamlet* and there is no greater proof of Shakespeare's versatility and independence of formula than the contrast between these plays. *Hamlet* deals in Senecan fashion with the tragic falls of kings and princes; *Othello* is almost a domestic tragedy; no kingdom nor noble house is involved in the catastrophe that overwhelms the Moor and his wife. In *Hamlet* Shakespeare was bound to follow lines already laid down in a popular play; in *Othello* his source was an Italian *novella*. Shakespeare apparently felt himself at liberty to handle this story, probably unknown to

most of his audience, in the freest fashion. The original
is a brutal tale of sexual jealousy. The raw material of
tragedy Shakespeare found there, the chief characters
and the main events of his play. His task was to transform a straggling narrative into a compact drama and
to lift a sordid story into the realm of high tragedy.
This he accomplished with amazing success; no one can
realize Shakespeare's magical power of turning dull
metal into gold who has not read the original story.
Here as nowhere else in this period he relied upon his
own power of invention and this did not fail him.

Othello is in many ways Shakespeare's masterpiece of
construction in the realm of tragedy. The magnificent
opening act which brings the situation at once before us
and stirs our sympathy for the characters is practically
his own invention, and serves as a sort of prologue to
the play. After the shift of the scene from Venice to
Cyprus the action begins in earnest and rushes on in
headlong haste to the final and terrible catastrophe.
Here, too, Shakespeare discarded the long drawn-out
conclusion of the *novella* and invented a solution—Emilia's loyalty to her murdered mistress and her denunciation of her husband—which dispels the fog of treach-
ery and slander in which the hero had wandered. The
action is single as it is swift; there is no double plot as
in *Lear;* no postponement of the deed to be done as in
Hamlet. There are no comic scenes, the poor part of the
Clown, probably forced on Shakespeare to make a rôle
for Armin may be disregarded, and the play is distinguished by unity of tone as by unity of action.

Of all Shakespeare's tragedies *Othello* is the most
realistic; it lacks the element of the supernatural and
the mysterious. Yet Shakespeare has transfigured the
characters of his source even as he transformed the
story. Othello himself is perhaps the most admirable of

Shakespeare's tragic heroes, a noble soldier betrayed by the friend he trusted, who after his fall regains our sympathy when he confesses his crime and executes judgment upon himself. Iago is the incarnation of selfish and cynical malignity. It is no doubt significant that Shakespeare gave this mercenary soldier a Spanish name. It was easy for an Elizabethan audience familiar with the cruelties of the Spanish soldiery in the Low Countries and in Mexico to accept Iago as the perfect villain. Desdemona is the most wistful and pathetic of Shakespeare's tragic heroines, and the minor characters all fall naturally into their parts in the play.

The characters and events of *Othello* are the most real and credible in the whole range of Shakespeare's tragedies. Yet about this realistic play there breathes an air of romance. This in the main is due to the extraordinary charm of the poetry. Less profound and meditative than that of *Hamlet,* less impassioned than that of *Lear,* it is flexible enough to carry on easy colloquial conversation, but rises at times, especially in the speeches of Othello, to a singular power and beauty. Something of the romance of Italy and the Orient clings to the tragedy of the Moor of Venice.

King Lear was acted at Court December 26, 1606. It was probably written late in 1605 or early in 1606. It was published in 1608 with Shakespeare's name on the title-page, probably to assure the intending purchaser that this was the genuine play of the master and not another bearing practically the same name which had appeared a few years before. This quarto is one of the worst printing jobs ever turned out by an Elizabethan printer, yet it is invaluable to the student of Shakespeare since it contains about three hundred lines omitted in the Folio. The Folio text rests upon a manuscript probably revised and shortened for the performance at Court.

The immediate source of the play is the old play of *King Leir,* acted as early as 1594, but not printed till 1605. There is some evidence that Shakespeare had read this play, saw in it good usable material, and set himself to revise it for his stage as he had lately remade the story of Othello. The old play presents in rather pleasant tragi-comic form the legend of Lear and his daughters which was first told by Geoffrey of Monmouth in the twelfth century and had been retold by poets and historians ever since. Shakespeare seems to have known various versions of the legend and to have borrowed from them whatever he could use. His one great original stroke was the conversion of the legend into a stupendous tragedy.

King Lear differs from *Othello* as from the other great tragedies in that it contains an under-plot, the story of Gloster and his sons which runs parallel to and is interwoven in the story of Lear and his daughters. This story Shakespeare drew from the most popular romance of his day, Philip Sidney's *Arcadia.* Possibly Shakespeare felt that the legend of Lear alone lacked the element of dramatic action and might as in the old play degenerate into the merely pathetic. By interweaving the Gloster plot he introduced an element of intrigue and counter-action that heightened the interest, and the wicked son of this story becomes the unwitting agent of the ruin of the wicked daughters. Moreover by the duplication of an instance of a child's ingratitude and cruelty he adds credibility to the old tale—one such instance might be exceptional, two are far more convincing—and before we finish *Lear* we feel ourselves transported into a world torn by strife between the powers of good and evil.

Shakespeare gained the effect he wanted by this use of the sub-plot but he lost something as well. *Lear* lacks the unity and concentration of *Othello* which precedes or *Macbeth* which follows it. The action especially toward the close is excessively complicated; the play in its first form was too long for presentation and was heavily cut even in Shakespeare's day. It was driven from the stage for over a century by the sentimental adaptation of Tate (1681) and is rarely produced in the modern theatre. In fact it has become a commonplace of criticism to say that *Lear* is a great dramatic poem but not a great play. This is a superficial error. The play was acted with success on Shakespeare's stage; that it cannot be presented on the "picture-frame" stage is hardly Shakespeare's fault. It remains for some modern producer capable of exploiting all the resources of the twentieth-century theatre to restore to the stage this most tremendous of Shakespeare's tragedies.

There is something symbolic, awe-inspiring, in *King Lear*. Shakespeare alone of all those who had handled the theme perceived its tragic quality, and in his hands it takes on a universal significance; it becomes a world war on a heroic scale between Evil naked and unashamed and Good, suffering, enduring, and sustaining. In the end the leading figures of the two parties perish in a common catastrophe, an offence against "poetic justice" which has shocked old-fashioned critics, but the storm of evil has blown over and a new world is left purified. Yet symbolic as the play, taken as a whole, seems to be, the characters are real and human. Lear is not a symbol but a king, a father, and a man "more sinned against than sinning." Kent is something more than the faithful servant; Cordelia than the loving daughter. In some ways the most interesting figure is that of the Fool, introduced into high tragedy by Shakespeare in defiance of classical decorum, whose shrewd comments furnish an ironic chorus to the tragic action. All in all it is not too much to say that the play of *King Lear* is the most magnificent example of Shakespeare's tragic genius.

Timon of Athens (ca. 1606) is one of the most puzzling plays in the Shakespeare canon. It first appeared in print in the Folio and there is no evidence that it was ever performed. The elaborate stage-directions, however, show that the play was prepared for a performance and we may guess that it was played a few times, proved a failure, and was withdrawn from the stage. The reason for its failure is plain enough; the play as we have it is, by common consent, only in part the work of Shakespeare. Of the two theories to account for this, (a) that Shakespeare revised the work of an inferior playwright, (b) that Shakespeare left some fragmentary scenes of a play on Timon which were patched up for presentation by an inferior hand, the second seems the more acceptable. It is hard to believe that Shakespeare at the very height of his power turned over to his fellows a revised play so incoherent, inconsistent, and unplayable as this. On the other hand we may well believe that his fellows finding among his papers some splendid dramatic scenes felt warranted in having them patched up by one of their working playwrights, perhaps by Middleton, who as we shall see (p. 166) certainly touched up *Macbeth*. At any rate Heminges and Condell felt that there was enough of Shakespeare's work in the play to warrant their including it in the Folio where it appeared in print for the first time. The text is so bad as to suggest that it was printed from a much revised manuscript.

There is no external evidence to fix the date of *Timon*. Internal evidence of metre, style, and temper connects it rather closely with *King Lear*. Perhaps the best guess that we can make is that Shakespeare shortly after his tremendous effort on *Lear* began to write another play in something of the same style, planning to provide Burbage with the rôle of a misanthrope as eloquent in his curses as Lear in his ravings. After writing certain scattered scenes—his hand is plainer in the last acts than in the beginning—he laid it aside. Perhaps he was weary of the task; possibly he realized as he worked on it the undramatic nature of the Timon story. It is an interesting fact that several playwrights at different times in different countries have tried to dramatize this theme and that not one of them has made a good play out of it. For once Shakespeare seems to have erred in his choice of a subject; but he was wise enough to see his mistake and abandon his unfinished work.

The chief source of *Timon* is Plutarch's *Life of Antony*. Some hints were caught also from Lucian's dialogue, *Timon the Misanthrope*, which Shakespeare may have read in translation. An old play written ca. 1600 but not printed till the last century contains the incident of the mock banquet which occurs in no other version of the story. Shakespeare may have seen this play, or even heard of it, and lifted from it this effective bit of business.

It contains some passages of magnificent poetry as the great curse (IV, 1) or Timon's farewell to the world:

> Come not to me again: but say to Athens,
> Timon hath made his everlasting mansion
> Upon the beached verge of the salt flood;
> Who once a day with his embossed froth
> The turbulent surge shall cover.

It would be an interesting task for the young student of Shakespeare to read through this play and mark the passages in which he seems to catch the unmistakable voice of the master of dramatic poetry.[1]

Macbeth can be dated with some degree of certainty in 1606. The subject may have been suggested to Shakespeare by a show presented to King James at Oxford, August 27, 1605, in which three youths dressed as sybils recited some Latin verses containing the old prophecy that Banquo's descendants should be kings. As James claimed descent from Banquo he was naturally gratified by this performance. It has even been suggested, though without any proof, that the letter James is said to have written Shakespeare contained a request that the poet write a play on this subject.

The text has come down to us only in the Folio version. It is the shortest of all Shakespeare's plays except the *Comedy of Errors* and the confusion and corruption of the text shows that it was printed from a manuscript that had been cut and revised. Unfortunately it was shortened in order to interpolate some spectacular and musical effects; the songs in III, 5 and IV, 1 and a couple of speeches by the first witch in this last scene along with the dance of the witches are interpolations. They are probably the work of Middleton who was writing for Shakespeare's company before the publication of the Folio. The songs in question, mentioned by title in *Macbeth,* appear in full in Middleton's play *The Witch.*

The source of *Macbeth* is Holinshed's *Chronicle* familiar to Shakespeare from the time of his English history plays. Holinshed's account contains the story of the prophecy of the witches to Macbeth and Banquo and various other incidents which Shakespeare uses in the play. For the actual murder of Duncan, however, he

---

[1] For a full discussion of the problem of this play see my article in the publications of the British Shakespeare Association, 1923.

turned over a few pages of Holinshed and read the tale
of the murder of King Duff by Donwald, a story far
more to his purpose than the true account of Duncan's
death, since Duncan was killed in battle by Macbeth,
whereas Duff was murdered in his sleep by his host and
subject acting on the instigation of his wife. It is proof
of Shakespeare's now complete freedom of treatment
that he should have dared to depart so far from historical fact. He would hardly have felt free to do so
at an earlier period.

The "supernatural soliciting" of the witches is part
of the old story, but Shakespeare has made it an essential feature of the play; the first scene in which the
witches prepare to meet Macbeth is his own invention,
as is Macbeth's visit to them in the caldron scene. Original with Shakespeare also is the great scene in which
the ghost of Banquo rises to appal his murderer at the
royal feast. Shakespeare no doubt knew that a play
about witches, ghosts and prophecies would please his
royal master, but he had more in mind than that. *Macbeth* is essentially the tragedy of a man who wittingly
does evil, sells himself to the devil whose servants and
representatives are the witches of the play, suffers the
agonies of remorse without repentance, and meets his
just fate at the hands of the man he had most wronged.
The supernatural element is the very atmosphere that
pervades *Macbeth* and lends the play its characteristic
tone and color.

One gets the impression that *Macbeth* was written
in headlong haste by Shakespeare. It shows no such
marks of careful revision as does *Hamlet,* nor such evidence of planned construction as *Othello.* The great
scenes are in Shakespeare's most splendid style; others
scattered through the play are tame and colorless; the
long dialogue between Macduff and Malcolm in the

fourth act taken almost literally from Holinshed is so
dull that one wonders why it was not cut by the first
reviser as in all modern performances. The metre shows
signs of experimentation with blank verse looking forward to the license Shakespeare allowed himself with
this form in later plays. *Macbeth* is the last of the great
tragedies, but one feels in reading it after the others
that Shakespeare was beginning to weaken; the mental
and emotional strain under which he had labored for
the past five or six years must have been more than
any mortal could endure. We shall see in his later plays
that he turned away from tragedy, as about 1599 he
had turned away from history; his best work in the tragic
field was already done.

Antony and Cleopatra was entered in the Stationers'
Register on May 10, 1608, but did not appear in print
until its inclusion in the Folio, 1623. There is reason to
believe that it was written in 1606 or early in the following year.

There is but one source for the play, Plutarch's *Life
of Antony* in North's translation. Shakespeare follows
his source more closely than in his former Roman play
Julius Cæsar. Not only does he at times adopt the very
words of North, but the scenario itself, the arrangement
and succession of scenes, particularly in the last acts,
follows the order of the source. Yet Shakespeare is not
slavishly dramatizing a history; again and again when
he is versifying North's prose he adds a phrase of his
own which glorifies the passage.

In form *Antony and Cleopatra* is a chronicle play.
Shakespeare's reversion to this older type of drama
shows, we may believe, his inability or unwillingness to
concentrate as he had been doing on the harder tasks

of tragedy. The play is a magnificent panorama of struggle for power in the Roman world and adds to this the struggle between ambition and love in the breast of one of the two masters of that world. Yet one scene, almost demanded by the theme, that in which Antony should make the tragic decision to return to Cleopatra, Shakespeare never troubled to compose. In his broad treatment with its shifting scenes he gains an effect unparalleled in any other dramatic version of this theme. Shakespeare's Antony is a heroic figure, though not exactly a noble character, and his fall and death followed by the death of the woman who caused his fall lift a chronicle play into the realm of tragedy.

In the matter of characterization Shakespeare concentrated in this play upon these two figures. Apart from them with the exception of Enobarbus, a realist whose ironic commentary recalls at times that of King Lear's Fool, and the clown of the last act, one of Shakespeare's homely country folk introduced rather incongruously into Cleopatra's palace, there is hardly a fully realized man or woman among the many characters who crowd the stage. Here as in the matter of construction we seem to feel a slackening of Shakespeare's powers as a playwright.

The peculiar glory of *Antony and Cleopatra* is its poetry. It is as if Shakespeare renouncing for a time the harder labor of the constructive dramatist had given full rein to the course of his poetic genius. Coleridge characterized it perfectly when he spoke of the "happy valiancy" of the style. Moreover this flow of poetry in *Antony and Cleopatra* is not lyrical as in earlier plays; there is no interruption of the action for the insertion of a little poem as in *Romeo and Juliet;* it is strictly adapted to the dramatic dialogue. It is not too much to say that the verse of *Romeo and Juliet,* like the passion of the lovers, is that of youth; the poetry of *Antony and Cleopatra,* like the passion that dominates its hero, is that of the grown man. It is the veil of poetry, sensuous, glowing, highly figurative, and truly dramatic, which Shakespeare throws over the story of Antony and his mistress that adds glamour and romance to the tale and makes us believe for a moment that for such a love as theirs the world was indeed well lost.

Coriolanus certainly follows *Antony and Cleopatra* and may be dated late in 1608 or early in 1609. It was printed for the first time in the Folio, 1623. Here too Shakespeare found the source of this play in North's *Plutarch* and as in *Antony and Cleopatra* he followed his source closely, more than once simply versifying the prose of the original. On the other hand he deals more freely with the matter of his source, suppressing, condensing, and arranging to suit his dramatic aims; certain scenes such as those in which the hero reluctantly seeks the "voices" of the people, or withstands the pressure of his family and friends to humble himself to the populace, are Shakespeare's addition to the story. Certain characters, especially that of Menenius, are practically Shakespeare's creation.

There are some aspects of *Coriolanus* that resemble the chronicle play. In the first act there are the alarums and excursions, single combats and pitched battles, of the old histories; but after this prologue Shakespeare sets himself resolutely to molding the narrative into strict dramatic form. He does this by centering the whole action about the person of his hero and by revealing in scene after scene how the character of Coriolanus brings about his inevitable fall. The play has too often been interpreted from a modern point of view and used as a text to proclaim Shakespeare's hatred of democracy. Of democracy in the modern sense of the word Shakespeare could by the nature of things have no conception and therefore could not hate it. As a matter of fact the play might quite as well be interpreted as a dramatic denunciation of the aristocratic temper. Coriolanus is a thorough aristocrat, brave, proud, insolent, incapable of flattery, but capable under pressure, as aristocrats have been since his day, of turning his arms against his country. Like Antony he is a heroic figure, but he is the least amiable of Shakespeare's heroes. He shares with Lear an ungovernable temper, but unlike Lear never learns the folly of his rage, and at the very end it is a last outburst of well-nigh insane anger that precipitates the catastrophe.

Unlike *Antony and Cleopatra* there is little of Shakespeare's finest poetry in this play; he seems here to be subordinating poetic expression to strict and even severe dramatic treatment; rhetoric and eloquence take the place of fancy and imagination. None of Shakespeare's tragedies lacks so completely his characteristic breathings of romance; the atmosphere is realistic, and, except as relieved by touches of humour, cold and hard. *Coriolanus* is Shakespeare's farewell to tragedy; the tragic temper, the sympathy with the tragic hero, the poetic rendering of the tragic theme, are perceptibly waning in this fine play. The time had come for Shakespeare to turn to other fields.

A brief summary of this period may serve to show something of the development of Shakespeare's power as a tragic poet. The bitter comedies of the early years of this period may be disregarded here; they serve only to show how far his mind had swung away from the joyous mirth and gay romance of the earlier work. The series of the tragedies begins calmly and gravely with

Julius Cæsar. This play, almost as much history as tragedy, is followed by *Hamlet,* Shakespeare's most complex and subtle drama, but one where he was definitely limited by the conditions under which he worked. In *Othello* he attains his full height as a master of his art, in construction, in characterization, and in dramatic expression. *Lear,* less nearly perfect perhaps than *Othello,* is yet a greater work, more universal, more significant, more magnificently tragic. This is the mountain peak. The fragmentary *Timon* shows already something like a collapse; ground is regained in the feverish and unequal tragedy of *Macbeth* and then the end approaches. *Antony and Cleopatra* and *Coriolanus* close the period, neither of them for all their beauty, eloquence and power a match for the earlier plays, and with *Pericles* we see the transition to the tragi-comedies of the final period.

PART IV

Pericles, Prince of Tyre (ca. 1607-8) is the play that links the tragic period to that of the comedies. Its date is uncertain. A play called *Pericles* was entered in the Stationers' Register on May 20, 1608. This may be Shakespeare's play but it is more probably an old one of the same name.

It is quite certain that the *Pericles* now included in the Shakespeare canon is his rewriting in part, and only in part, of an older play, possibly by George Wilkins a very minor playwright of the day. In 1608 Wilkins published a prose version of the story, which was advertised as "the true history of the play as it was lately presented." Possibly the explanation is that Wilkins wrote a play with this title for Shakespeare's company, that Shakespeare saw that something more could be made of the theme than the bungling Wilkins had accomplished and so consented to touch it up. He let the first two acts stand almost unchanged, grew interested as he went on, and from the beginning of the third act practically rewrote the whole, though he retained some of the old choruses and dumb shows.

Whether Wilkins was pleased or not we cannot say, but as the play was immensely successful he tried to turn an honest penny by publishing what we should call a "novelized" version. The publisher who had entered *Pericles* in 1608 never printed his version, but in 1609 another bookseller got hold of a "stolen and surreptitious" copy and straightway printed it. It sold so well that he got out a second edition in the same year; a third appeared in 1611, and others followed. The play was not included in the first Folio; probably the editors thought Shakespeare's part in it was too slight to warrant ascribing it to him. It was added to the third Folio, 1664, along with six other plays none of which have any claim to Shakespearean authorship. Later editors alternately accepted or rejected it. Tennyson once said to a scholar who questioned whether Shakespeare wrote any of it: "Oh that won't do. He wrote all the part relating to the birth and recovery of Marina and the recovery of Thaisa," and Tennyson's verdict is now generally accepted.

The source of *Pericles* is the mediæval legend of *Apollonius of Tyre,* a legend which took on fresh life in the Renaissance with its delight in tales of voyages, shipwrecks, and adventure. The great popularity of the play shows the revived taste of the theatre-going public for romantic drama as the vogue of realistic comedy began to wane. Shakespeare's revision of *Pericles* was his first experiment in this genre and his success may have been one of the reasons that impelled him to devote the few years remaining of his working life to romantic tragi-comedy.

Pericles is a poor enough play; Shakespeare's revision left the absurd meandering construction unchanged. Yet it contains some lovely poetry and the recognition scene between father and daughter (V, i) points in both style and temper to the best work of his last period.

Cymbeline (1609-10) opens the last period of Shakespeare's work. It is a romantic tale dramatized in loose and careless form, dealing in part with the theme of marital jealousy which in *Othello* had furnished matter for tragedy, but handling it in such fashion as to bring about a happy ending. This play resembles Beaumont and Fletcher's *Philaster* and the suggestion has been made that Shakespeare was following a fashion set by these young playwrights. This suggestion has been considered above (p. 60) and need not be discussed here. There is only one text of *Cymbeline,* that of the Folio.

There is a double source for *Cymbeline,* the story of the wager laid by Postumus and its well-nigh fatal consequences, and the pseudo-historic matter of the wars of the Britains and the Romans. The first of these comes from a tale in the *Decameron* (ii, 9) which itself goes back to a French original, the *Roman de la Violette.* The second comes from Holinshed's account of the legendary kings of early Britain. Shakespeare has cleverly woven these two threads together by making the slandered lady the daughter of a British king and using a British victory over the Romans to bring about the revelation of her innocence. Hints from various other sources have been picked up and worked into the play which interests mainly by its lively and varying action, its surprises, and, indeed, its sensationalism. Like all the plays of this period *Cymbeline* contains a good deal of the spectacular. We have not only scenes at court and pitched battles, but in the last act a masque-like spectacle—"Jupiter descends in thunder and lightning, sitting upon an eagle; he throws a thunderbolt"—which must have taxed the resources of the Globe and Black-friars.

Cymbeline is not one of the best of Shakespeare's plays, but it contains one of his most lovely characters, Imogen, the perfect wife. It has always been a favorite with poets; Swinburne closes his *Study of Shakespeare* with an impassioned eulogy of this his favorite play, and Tennyson died with his copy of Shakespeare open at a page of *Cymbeline.*

The Winter's Tale can be dated fairly accurately. It was originally licensed by Sir George Buc who became Master of the Revels in August, 1610, and it was played at Court on November 5, 1611. Somewhere between these dates it must lie, probably early in 1611, since the dance of satyrs in Act IV seems an imitation of such a dance in Jonson's *Masque of Oberon,* performed at Court, January 1, 1611, and Forman saw it at the Globe, May 15, 1611. The only text is that of the Folio.

The source of this play is Robert Greene's pastoral novel *Pandosto* (1588) reprinted in 1607 as *Dorastus and Fawnia.* This later edition may have come into Shakespeare's hands some time in his last period and suggested to him the composition of a romantic pastoral drama. Shakespeare deals very freely with his source, altering names, changing scenes, and particularly eliminating the death of the slandered queen and the suicide of her remorseful husband. Such tragic incidents he felt were out of keeping with the tone of the play that he was planning. He did not, however, disdain to delight his audience by having a bear chase a minor character and—off-stage—tear him to pieces.

The Winter's Tale is, perhaps, Shakespeare's master-piece of tragi-comedy. It lacks unity of action, to be sure; there is a gap of sixteen years between the third and the fourth acts, and in the last two the interest shifts from Hermione, supposed dead, to her daughter, Perdita. But the play has all the characteristics of tragi-comedy: intrigue, disguise, suspense, and surprise, and all most dexterously handled. Fault has been found with the causeless jealousy of the king but to have given him grounds for his suspicion would have been to write *Othello* over again. Leontes is jealous for no other reason than to start the action and his outbreak of jealousy in the second scene starts it with a rush to the complete surprise of the reader or spectator. In the midst of the delightful scene of the shepherd's festival the revelation of the disguised Polixenes and his de-nunciation of his son's love for the fair shepherdess give another startling change of tone. The last and best surprise of all is at the very end when the statue of the dead queen comes to life and Hermione descends to embrace her penitent husband and to bless her restored daughter. This scene is wholly Shakespeare's invention; and of its superb effect upon the stage those can testify who have had the good fortune to see the beautiful Mary Anderson in the rôle of Hermione.

Fine characterization, as a rule, is not expected in tragi-comedy where the plot governs the characters; but in this play Shakespeare lavishes his skill upon such figures as the noble queen, the faithful shrew Paulina, the old shepherd, and above all upon Autolycus, the most delightful rogue in literature. One feels that Shakespeare was happy when he wrote *The Winter's Tale;* perhaps part of his happiness came from his return to Stratford. Rural sights and sounds, country folk and country customs, give a pleasant background of realism to a romantic tragi-comedy.

The Tempest cannot have been written before the autumn of 1610 and may date early in 1611. It was performed at Court on November first of that year. It was printed for the first time in the Folio.

The theme of a shipwreck on an enchanted island was certainly suggested to Shakespeare by a series of events that had aroused great interest in London. In June of 1609 a fleet set sail from England for the new colony of Virginia. It was scattered by a storm and the flagship was wrecked on a reef off Bermuda. The crew reached shore safely and spent the winter in what was then known as "the Isle of Devils." They built two small ships and in May, 1610, sailed across to Virginia. In England they had been given up for lost and the news of their escape was hailed with joy. Several accounts of the shipwreck and of the islands appeared late in 1610 which Shakespeare certainly used, as he also seems to have used a manuscript account not printed till after his death. Kipling has made the interesting if fanciful suggestion that Shakespeare got his information from a drunken sailor of the shipwrecked crew whom he later introduced into the play as Stephano who swam to shore upon a butt of sack.

No direct source has been found for the main plot of the exiled duke turned magician who gets his enemies into his power by magic only to forgive them, and who marries off his daughter to his chief enemy's son. Shakespeare may have picked up hints for this story from various sources; he has woven them very artfully into a background suggested by the Bermuda voyage.

The Tempest is a unique play; there is nothing quite like it in all the rest of Shakespeare's work. The character of Prospero, especially in his farewell to his art, so strongly suggests the poet-dramatist about to retire from the stage that the whole play has been interpreted as an allegory. This is far from likely though the temptation to read between the lines is strong indeed. It has been called a masque adapted for the stage, but it is rather a play which includes a formal marriage masque. Alone among Shakespeare's plays it preserves the unities of time—the action lasts about four hours—and place—after the first scene the action is all on the island. It is as if Shakespeare after defying the unities in *The Winter's Tale* amused himself by showing Jonson and other classical critics that he too could obey the classic rules.

Essentially *The Tempest* is what we would call "a good show." It has enough of incident to interest the spectator, with a charming love-story, with characters good and bad, serious and comic, and with plenty of spectacle in the way of songs, dances, hunting dogs, and "quaint devices." The poetry, the serene wisdom, are Shakespeare's additions to the "show," but such glorious addition as to outweigh at least in a reader's mind all else in the play. It is a drama of forgiveness, of reconciliation and of peace, a beautiful sunset after the storms of the tragic period.

There are two other plays of this period that are only in part by Shakespeare. The first of these is the spectacular historical pageant, *Henry VIII* (1613). It is included in the Folio and was long accepted as Shake-

speare's own unassisted work. Recent scholarship has
proved beyond all reasonable doubt that about half the
play was written by Fletcher, at this time succeeding
Shakespeare as the chief dramatist for the King's Men.
The evidence is internal and rests upon Fletcher's unmistakable stylistic and metrical idiosyncrasies. A comparison of one of his scenes, II, i, for instance, with a
Shakespearean scene, II, iv, will show such a difference
in diction, rhythm, and treatment of the blank verse as
to convince any unprejudiced reader that the scenes are
by two authors, and any reader acquainted with Fletcher's style that he is one of them.

Scholars are now generally agreed that Shakespeare
wrote I, i, ii; II, iii, iv; III, ii, ll.1-203; and V, i.
Shakespeare starts most of the various themes in this
loosely constructed play and Fletcher finishes them. This
division, it may be noted gives Fletcher some of the best
known scenes of the play including Wolsey's famous
farewell to greatness, III, ii, ll. 350–372. It has been
remarked that if Fletcher wrote the scenes ascribed to
him in this play he did better work here than anywhere
else. This is quite possible, for he was writing under the
influence of Shakespeare and no doubt anxious to put
his best foot forward as Shakespeare's successor with
the company.

Henry VIII cannot be judged by comparison with
any of the earlier histories; strictly speaking it is less
a drama than a succession of scenes dealing with striking events in the king's reign interspersed with a great
deal of spectacle. This may be due in part to the manner of the collaboration, in part to the desire of the
company to stage a magnificent pageant, for which
they charged the high admission price of one shilling
(Prologue l. 12). Probably the company begged
Shakespeare now residing at Stratford to furnish them

with a play of this sort, and he consented to write certain scenes, allowing Fletcher to finish it off. The one character that is his throughout is that of Queen Katherine and Dr. Johnson's comment "Shakespeare's genius comes in and goes out with Katherine" still holds good.

As a brilliant stage spectacle with several good acting parts *Henry VIII* has held the stage intermittently from Shakespeare's day down to the time of Irving and Beerbohm Tree; but we can learn little from it as to Shakespeare's art or the point to which it had developed by 1613.

The second of these plays, *The Two Noble Kinsmen* (1613) has a curious history. It was not included in the Folio and did not appear in print until 1634, eighteen years after Shakespeare's death and nine years after that of Fletcher. Both these names appeared upon the title page of the first edition which advertises the play as "presented at the Blackfriars with great applause; written by the memorable worthies of their time; Mr. John Fletcher and Mr. William Shakespeare Gent." In spite of this title-page the play was long regarded as the work of Fletcher and was included in the second Folio (1679) of the Beaumont and Fletcher plays.

It was not until the time of the Romantic critics that voices were raised to defend Shakespeare's share in this play; both Lamb and Coleridge were certain that Shakespeare had a hand in it and for the last hundred years or so there has been a general agreement, though by no means unanimous, that the play represents a collaboration of Shakespeare and Fletcher. Certain scenes—the greater part of Act I, the first scene of Act III, and the magnificent invocations of Act V, i—are unmistakably Shakespeare's; others appear to be his only in part; throughout the play there seem to be signs of Fletcher as the last writer, welding scattered scenes together and writing little patches of his characteristic verse at the beginning and end of Shakespearean scenes. This may perhaps explain the exclusion of the play from the Folio; Fletcher then at the height of his popularity may have consented to surrender his claim to *Henry VIII* on condition that *The Two Noble Kinsmen* should be regarded as essentially his work.

The source of the play is Chaucer's *Knight's Tale*. On the whole the play follows its source rather closely, but, naturally, reshapes the narrative in dramatic form. In spite of some superb poetry by Shakespeare one can hardly say that the authors have improved upon their source. There is an evident intention to transform the tragic tale of Chaucer into a tragi-comedy in the later Elizabethan manner. In particular the death of Arcite and his farewell to Palemon, the climax of Chaucer's poem, is hastily glossed over in the play; the death of a main character was out of place in a tragi-comedy. Yet in spite of alterations, spectacular interpolations, muddled construction and confused characterization— all due, we may suppose to Fletcher—the play is pleasant reading and contains many lines of splendid poetry. One can only regret that Shakespeare was unable for one reason or another to complete a play which he evidently began in the best style of his final period.

A bitter controversy has raged in recent years over a play, more especially over one scene of a play, that bears the name of *Sir Thomas More*. It is one of the few original manuscripts of Elizabethan plays that are still preserved and was not printed till 1844. There is no reason to believe that it was ever played and rather good reason why it should not have been. The original author, Anthony Munday, was rash enough to introduce certain scenes dealing with a London riot provoked by

the insolence of alien residents. Elizabeth and her coun-
cillors were eager to promote the immigration of such
industrious craftsmen as French and Flemish Protest-
ants, and quick to suppress any threat directed against
them. Accordingly her Master of Revels, Edward Tilney
returned this play when it was sent to him for his
license with a sharp warning "Leave out the insurrec-
tion wholly and the cause thereof," besides marking
various passages for alteration. To have followed his
directions would have been to destroy the play, so it
was apparently laid aside for some years when a group
of writers was called on to revise and write new scenes
for it with the hope that this time it might pass the
censor.

One hand in the five that contributed the additions
has been identified on good authority with that of Shakespeare as preserved in his signatures. This hand contributed one scene so markedly superior in thought and
expression to the rest of the play that it was suspected
to be the work of Shakespeare long before a study of
the handwriting was undertaken. This scene deals with
the climax of the riot and contains More's address to
the rebels which persuades them to submit. It is hard
to believe that any Elizabethan author except Shakespeare was capable at once of such humorous sympathy
with an unruly mob and such vigorous insistence on
order and authority as this speech shows. If we accept
this scene as Shakespeare's, as most scholars are inclined
to do, we must imagine him lending a friendly hand to
a group of dramatists in an effort to achieve the impossible. For Tilney's orders were not complied with and
consequently the play remained unstaged. When it was
first written and when the additions were made is quite
uncertain. The style and metre of the Shakespearean

scene point to a date midway in his second period, ca. 1595-96.

Of the many plays ascribed at various times in whole or in part to Shakespeare there is, with possibly a single exception, none that deserves consideration. This exception, *Edward III*, contains a romantic episode of the wooing of the Countess of Salisbury by the young king, which has some slight resemblance to the style of Shakespeare in his first period, and contains a line,

Lilies that fester smell far worse than weeds,

that appears in one of his sonnets. But his sonnets, as we know, were circulating in manuscript at the time this play appeared, 1596, and it is not impossible that the unknown author simply lifted the line to adorn his play. On the whole the episode in question does not carry with it such conviction of Shakespeare's authorship as does the scene in *Sir Thomas More*.

The last plays mentioned need not be seriously considered in a study of the development of Shakespeare's art. In *Sir Thomas More*, indeed, we seem to catch a glimpse of his mind; in *Henry VIII* we see one of his strong yet pathetic characters; and in *The Two Noble Kinsmen* we find some lofty poetry. But Shakespeare's course as a playwright was run before he agreed to assist his young successor Fletcher in the composition of a couple of plays for the Globe. His last active years had been devoted to the writing, probably at his ease in Stratford and with a certain careless abandon, the delightful trio of his so-called romances.

CHAPTER XI

THE POEMS AND SONNETS

SHAKESPEARE was a poet before he became a playwright and there was a period in his life when he was better known as the author of his first long poem than of any of his plays. Except for the *Sonnets* his poems are little read nowadays, but no account of Shakespeare's work would be complete without a discussion of his two long narrative poems, so characteristic are they both of the writer and of his age.

Venus and Adonis was entered in the Stationers' Register on April 18, 1593, and published early in that year by Richard Field, like Shakespeare a Stratford boy, who had come to London and set up there as printer and publisher. The first edition is so carefully printed, so free from the errors that mar the early editions of the plays, that there is good reason to believe that Shakespeare read the proof himself, a thing we can be sure he never troubled to do for the plays. There was a good reason for this painstaking care; the poem was to be a gift to a noble lord, the young Earl of Southampton whose favor and patronage Shakespeare was seeking. In the dedication prefixed to the poem Shakespeare apologizes for dedicating his "unpolished lines" to his lordship, calls the poem "the first heir of my invention," and promises, if the work pleases his patron, to honor him "with some graver labour," a promise which he fulfilled a year later in his *Lucrece*.

184

The phrase "first heir of my invention" has sometimes
been understood to mean that this poem was the first
thing Shakespeare ever wrote, and a pleasant fancy has
suggested that he brought it up to town from Stratford.
This is most unlikely; *Venus and Adonis* is in the full
tide of the fashionable narrative and erotic poetry of the
day and full of hints from poems that Shakespeare could
have known only after he came to London. It was, however, the first of his writings to be given to the world,
and Shakespeare no doubt regarded his plays, especially
his early experimental plays, as matter for the stage
rather than for the press.

The poem was instantly and immensely successful; a
whole series of editions in quarto and octavo form followed the first; there were some sixteen issues before
1640. The references to *Venus and Adonis* in contemporary literature are constant; it became indeed a
sort of *vade mecum* for amorous young gentlemen and
wanton ladies.

The source of the story is found in Ovid's *Metamorphoses*. Ovid was evidently Shakespeare's favorite Latin
poet; he had studied him in school and re-read him not
only in the original but in Golding's translation (1567),
some lines from which he paraphrases in a famous speech
in *The Tempest* (V, i, 33-50). The two Latin lines prefixed as a motto to *Venus and Adonis* come from Ovid's
Amores. There is no trace in Ovid's version of the reluctant youth wooed by the goddess of love; but elsewhere in Ovid Shakespeare found a story of the
passionate wooing of a boy, Hermaphroditus, by a
nymph, Salmacis, which he skillfully blended with the
Adonis theme. Apparently he picked up suggestions for
this fusion from various contemporary poems which represented Adonis coldly rejecting the advances of Venus.
Here, as in his plays, it is not so much Shakespeare's

power of invention as his skill in combining and transforming his material that compels our admiration.

Venus and Adonis is written in iambic pentameter, rhyming *ababcc,* like the last six lines of a Shakespearean sonnet. This was a common verse form of the day; Spenser had used it in his *Shepheards Calendar,* and Lodge, the author of *Rosalynde,* in a long and rather incoherent erotic poem, *Glaucus and Scylla;* but no poet of the day, not even Spenser, handled it with such ease and grace or shaped it into such a form of beauty.

Like Marlowe's *Hero and Leander,* which Shakespeare must have read in manuscript, *Venus and Adonis* is a narrative poem. The story is well told with a beginning, middle, and end, but it is not the story that makes the poem. The dress in which Shakespeare has clothed the tale is, perhaps, more lovely than the tale itself and this dress is woven of various threads. We have first what one may call the landscape pieces, a landscape which is that of Shakespeare's England rather than of Greece or the Orient. This landscape is animated with English beasts and birds, the hunted hare, the hunting dogs, the grisly boar, the lark, the nightingale, and fragrant with English flowers. Upon this more or less realistic background are super-imposed the "discourses," the set speeches of Venus and her beloved. Here, too, Shakespeare is writing quite in the fashion of the day, as Lyly did when he used the story of Euphues as a peg on which to hang long discourses of every sort. The set speech, the formal plea, for and against such a topic as love or friendship, seems strange and unreal to us. It was not so to Shakespeare, and it is impossible to deny the grace and eloquence of his "discourses." Finally and most important, we have what may be called the dominant theme of the poem, Beauty, the incarnation of Beauty in the beloved, and the desire to perpetuate beauty by the bodily union of two lovers. This is a characteristic Renaissance conception, but there is nothing like it in the various erotic poems of Shakespeare's day. It is a theme that he made his own and was to treat more fully with greater power and beauty in the *Sonnets*.

A book called *The Ravishment of Lucrece* was entered in the Stationers' Register on May 9, 1594 by Master Harrison who, a month later, bought from Field the copyright of *Venus and Adonis*. He engaged Field to print it and it appeared in 1594 under the simpler title of *Lucrece*. Field did a good printer's job with *Lucrece,* as he had done with the earlier poem, and once more we may believe that Shakespeare read the proof. The second poem, like the first, was dedicated to Southampton.

Lucrece was no doubt the "graver labour" which Shakespeare had promised his friend a year before. It never achieved the signal popularity of *Venus and Adonis,* but something like eight editions were published before 1640 and the wiser sort, as Harvey noted, were pleased to see that the young poet had abandoned erotic poetry to strike a deeper note.

The story of Lucretia, told in Ovid's *Fasti* in verse and in Livy's prose, was well known in the Middle Ages; Chaucer enrolled the heroine among the martyrs of love in his *Legend of Good Women.* All these versions were known to Shakespeare, who used them as he saw fit; from Livy he must have drawn the straightforward historical "Argument" prefixed to the poem.

Lucrece is written in iambic pentameter rhyming *ababbcc.* This is the so-called Rhyme Royal stanza; it should really be known as the Chaucerian, for the old poet had used it again and again, with special power and beauty in his *Troilus.* It had come down to Shakespeare with a tradition of dignity and distinction, a metre "very grave and stately," an Elizabethan critic called it. Shakespeare's contemporary, Samuel Daniel, had used it in his *Complaint of Rosamond* (1592), and it may be that the grave beauty of this work suggested to Shakespeare the use of this stanzaic form.

It is an interesting fact that Shakespeare was at work on this poem at the very time that he was engaged in revising *Titus Andronicus*. There are several points of resemblance between play and poem, particularly in the manner in which a veil of poetry is thrown over a tale of brutal outrage. It is possible, though of course not certain, that the rape of Lavinia in the play suggested to Shakespeare a narrative poem on the famous story of Lucretia.

Like *Venus and Adonis*, *Lucrece* purports to be a narrative poem, but the narrative is even less essential in this than in the earlier work. Shakespeare omits the interesting incidents of the rivalry between the husbands at camp as to the virtues of their wives at home, and the visit of the lords to Rome with the winning of the wager by Lucretia's husband. At the close of the poem, too, he hurries over the consequences of her suicide, the revolt of the people and the expulsion of the Tarquins. What interested him was not so much the story, but its emotional values, the struggle in the heart of Sextus between shame and lust, and the bitter anguish of Lucrece after the perpetration of the outrage. These are in their essence dramatic themes belonging rather to tragedy than to narrative poetry; and as we have already seen Shakespeare was not yet prepared to handle high themes of tragedy. The situation, the conflicting emotions of Sextus before the deed, are not unlike those of Macbeth before the murder of Duncan, but what a difference in the writer's grasp and power between the diffuse argu-

ment pro and con of Sextus and the brief soliloquy of
Macbeth, where every word goes home. *Lucrece* finds
fewer readers today than *Venus and Adonis*. To our
minds the poem drags interminably; to appreciate it
properly we should strive to put ourselves back in the
mood of the Renaissance reader and enjoy with him the
"conceits," the *sententiæ*, and the eloquence of the long
tirades. It is in these tirades, the long set speeches that
correspond to the "discourses" of *Venus and Adonis*
that the poet has expended all his strength, and they
abound in lovely single lines as in the apostrophe to
Time

> Thou ceaseless lackey to Eternity

who delights

> To feed oblivion with decay of things.

To enjoy *Lucrece* one should read the poem slowly, a
little at a time, with an eye open to catch and appreciate
at their worth Shakespeare's felicities of diction, felicities that often link it with his supreme lyrical expression
in the *Sonnets*.

On May 20, 1609, Thomas Thorpe, a not very repu-
table publisher, entered in the Stationers' Register a
book called "Shakespeares sonnettes." He published it
the same year, appending to the sonnets an elegiac poem,
The Lover's Complaint. We may disregard this last;
there is no warrant for ascribing it to Shakespeare
except the statement of an unscrupulous publisher.

The text is not too good; there are misprints and evident corruptions, enough to show that Shakespeare had
not authorized publication and read the proof as he had
done for the poems. There is reason to believe that
Thorpe secured various manuscripts in which Shake-

speare's sonnets were circulating, arranged them as best he could, and gave them to the world. The book was a "stolen and surreptitious copy"; but we may well be grateful to Thorpe, for without his enterprise we might never have known some of the loveliest sonnets in the English language.

Instead of a dedication by the poet to his patron, Thorpe wrote his own dedication in terms that have puzzled readers ever since: *To the onlie begetter of these insuing sonnets Mr. W. H. all happinesse and that eternity promised by our ever living poet wisheth the well-wishing adventurer in setting forth. T. T.* It is best to take the word "begetter" in the sense of inspirer, that is, the friend who was the inspiration of most of the sonnets. Evidently Thorpe knew, or thought he knew, the identity of the friend whom he addresses as Mr. W. H. and for whom he wishes the immortality of fame that the sonnets so often promise the friend. If Thorpe really knew, it seems a pity that he hid his knowledge behind the mysterious initials. Had he spoken out he would have saved the world of scholarship many volumes of weary controversy.

Thorpe's enterprise in securing and publishing the sonnets was not rewarded. It is interesting to note that while the poems were very successful, the volume of sonnets, so greatly superior as poetry, fell almost dead from the press. No second edition was called for until 1640 when they were included in the volume called *Poems Written by Wil. Shakespeare Gent.*, where they were fortified, so to speak, by the addition of other poems, including the well-known elegy on Shakespeare by the young John Milton. Little interest was shown in them during the late seventeenth and eighteenth century. Only when students of Shakespeare began to suspect that some passionate secret of his life was concealed in these poems did attention revert to them. Even down to the present there has been more discussion—for the most part futile—of the "mystery of the sonnets" than appreciation of the poetry they contain.

It is harder to date the *Sonnets* than it is to date one of Shakespeare's plays. In fact, it is impossible to fix on a year or two in which they were written, for the simple reason that they seem to have been written over a period of years, three at least, at various times. Probably they may be regarded as occasional verses or verse-letters sent from time to time by Shakespeare to his friend or to his mistress. Yet it is possible to set certain limits within which the greater part of them were in all likelihood composed.

A comparison of the sonnets with the poems and the plays goes to show a large number of correspondences in thought and expression between them and the poems and the plays up to 1594-95; a much smaller number with plays after 1596-97. This internal evidence is strengthened by what we know of the vogue of the sonnet, especially of the sonnet-sequence in the 1590's. In 1591 Sidney's *Astrophel and Stella,* which had been circulating in manuscript, got into print. Sidney's fame, the romantic story enshrined in this sequence, and the beauty of the poetry, gave the work an instant and great success. It set a fashion and all the poetasters and many of the poets of the day broke out in like fashion. Constable, Daniel, Drayton, all composed sonnet-sequences; Spenser's lovely *Amoretti* appeared in 1595. It would be strange if Shakespeare, always responsive to the fashions of the day, had himself not experimented in this form. In fact, we know that he did; his early plays, *Love's Labour's Lost* and *Romeo and Juliet,* contain sonnets, and in 1598 Meres spoke of "mellifluous and honey-tongued Shakespeare witness his . . . sugred sonnets among his private friends." Evidently by 1598 Shakespeare had not only begun to write sonnets but copies of his poems in this form were circulating among his friends, yet not so privately as to escape the notice of the inquiring Meres. It is safe to assume that most of the sonnets were composed somewhere between 1592 and 1596; some, it may be later; one indeed, number 107, has been thought to allude to the death of Elizabeth in 1603.

Shakespeare followed the fashion, but as usual he followed it in his own way. His sonnets are not a conventional sonnet-sequence; they bear no title, they are not for the most part addressed to a woman, but to a friend, and the conventional lament that mourns an unrequited love is altogether absent. Yet like other sequences of the time, notably those of Sidney and Spenser, Shakespeare's sonnets seem to spring from a personal experience and to imply, though not to tell, a story. Briefly the story seems to be this: the poet has a friend, young, beautiful, of high birth, whom he loves better than himself; he has also a mistress, the so-called Dark Lady, an accomplished and fascinating wanton who at once attracts and repels him; "Two loves I have," he writes in sonnet 144. The woman seduces the friend who betrays the poet, but after a brief period of alienation the poet forgives and rejoins his friend, assured, as a man of the Renaissance would be, that true friendship is a purer, loftier thing than woman's love. Some such story seems, indeed, to be implied, but there are many sonnets that have no relation to the story, and to think of Shakespeare's sonnets as written to immortalize such an experience, if such there was, is quite to misunderstand them.

Assuming that the sonnets imply such a story a natural question arises as to the identity of the friend and of the mistress. To this question various answers have been given. The friend has been identified with Southampton,

naturally enough considering the known relation between Shakespeare and his patron. But if the friend
was, as seems certain, Mr. W. H. of the dedication, he
cannot also be Henry Wriothesley, Earl of Southampton, and there are other reasons against this identification. Again, the friend has been found in William, Lord
Herbert, Earl of Pembroke, one of the brothers to whom
the First Folio was dedicated. This theory carried with
it the notion that the Dark Lady was Mary Fitton, one
of the Queen's maids of honor, with whom Herbert is
known to have carried on an intrigue. There are, however, very strong arguments against this theory which
is now abandoned by most scholars. It is no doubt wiser
to renounce any attempt at identification and think of
Mr. W. H. simply as a charming young gentleman of
good birth who was fortunate enough to win the almost
adoring friendship of the poet. As for the lady the less
said of her, perhaps, the better.

It is a relief to turn from such matters to the true, the
poetic values of the sonnets. They are written like most
sonnets of that age in the English form which Surrey
had invented as an equivalent to the Italian sonnet with
its division into the octave (eight lines) and sestet (six
lines). This English form consists of three quatrains
rhyming *abab, cdcd, efef,* and closing with a couplet.
This gives a progressive movement, repeating, illustrat-
ing, reinforcing the topic, and winding up with a sen-
tentious comment in the couplet. The English form may
lack the unity of the Italian with its interwoven rhymes
and the harmonious correspondence of the sestet to the
octave that precedes it. Indeed from the time of Milton
English poets for the most part have preferred the
Italian form. Yet in the hands of such a poet as Shakespeare the English form reveals undreamed of qualities
of beauty, grace, and dignity.

This is not to say that all the sonnets are of great
and equal value; on the contrary, many of them are
slight things, occasional verses, too often marred by the
Elizabethan fondness for strained conceits. But when
the poet is strongly moved he rises to very lofty heights
of thought and to such perfection of expression as is
matched, if matched at all, only in his own plays. What
moves him most and stirs him to such expression is the
Renaissance theme of Beauty, beauty revealed in the
person of his friend, beauty that irresistibly evokes love,
beauty warred upon by Time, love triumphing over the
wreckage of Time, and conferring immortality on the
beautiful beloved in enduring verse.

> Love's not Time's fool, though rosy lips and cheeks
> Within his bending sickle's compass come;
> Love alters not with his brief hours and weeks,
> But bears it out even to the edge of doom.
> If this be error and upon me proved,
> I never writ, nor no man ever loved.

It would be well for the young student to avoid a consecutive reading of the sonnets, especially if undertaken
in the vain hope of puzzling out the story. It would be
more profitable by far to select a few written in what
Tennyson called the deeper vein, read and re-read them,
get them by heart, and learn the truth of Shakespeare's
words when he spoke of

> Beauty making beautiful old rhyme.

In the great sonnets, as nowhere else in his works, we
may hear the voice of the supreme master of English
poetry opening his heart, revealing his profoundest
thoughts and most poignant emotions in accents surer of
immortality than the eternity promised to the beloved
friend.

3. Holy Trinity Church at Stratford-on-Avon, and (*below*) its Chancel. The Shakespeare monument is affixed to the left wall of the Chancel, and the grave lies below it just within the rail at the left.

4. The Courtyard of the White Hart Inn

Inn-yards such as this served for the presentation of plays by strolling actors before the first permanent playhouse was built, and greatly influenced the design of the first buildings planned specifically for theatrical performances.

The original White Hart Inn (mentioned by Shakespeare in *2 Henry VI*, Act IV, Scene viii) was burned down in the great Southwark fire of 1676. Its successor, pictured in the above print, stood on the original site until it was torn down in 1889.

7. THE HALL OF THE MIDDLE TEMPLE, LONDON

Shakespeare's *Twelfth Night* is known to have been performed here on
February 2 (Candlemas), 1602. This photograph was taken before the
Hall was damaged by enemy bombs in World War II.

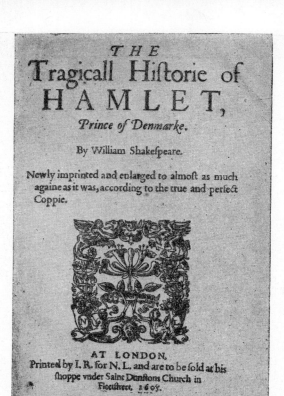

THE
Tragicall Historie of
HAMLET,
Prince of Denmarke.

By William Shakespeare.

Newly imprinted and enlarged to almost as much
againe as it was, according to the true and perfect
Coppie.

AT LONDON,
Printed by I. R. for N. L. and are to be sold at his
shoppe vnder Saint Dunstons Church in
Fleetstreet, 1605.

8. THE TITLE-PAGE OF THE SECOND "HAMLET" QUARTO (1604–5)

(*Below*) A diagram to illustrate the meaning of the words Folio and Quarto. In a Folio volume, each sheet of paper is folded once to make two leaves or four pages. In a Quarto volume, each is folded twice to make four leaves or eight pages. A Folio page is therefore about twice the size of a Quarto page.

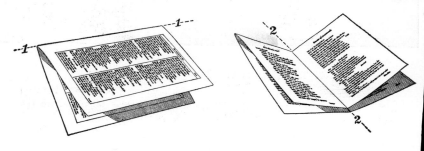

11. DAVID GARRICK (1717–1779)

was perhaps the greatest of all English actors. He is here shown
in the role of Macbeth, dressed in the uniform of a British officer
of his own time, with Mrs. Pritchard as Lady Macbeth.

12. Edwin Booth (1833–1893) as Hamlet.

13. ELLEN TERRY as Portia, and SIR HENRY IRVING as Shylock, in *The Merchant of Venice*.

14. EDWARD H. SOTHERN AND JULIA MARLOWE,
the most famous American stage partnership during the early part of the
present century, in *Romeo and Juliet,* Act I, Scene v: "If I profane with
my unworthiest hand . . ."

CHAPTER XII

THE TEXT OF SHAKESPEARE

THE student who reads a play of Shakespeare's in the usual school or college textbook probably thinks, if he thinks about the matter at all, that he is reading what Shakespeare wrote as certainly as if he were reading a modern play by Shaw or Eugene O'Neill. On the other hand, a student who opens a critical edition of Shakespeare, such as the Furness *Variorum,* is likely to be greatly puzzled by the multitude of readings in the textual notes with their references to quartos, folios, and modern emendations. The truth is that in no single play of Shakespeare's can we be quite sure that we are in every line reading the very words the poet wrote. And the reason for this lies in the methods of the publication of plays in Shakespeare's day, a method which was widely different from that followed by a dramatist of today. Mr. Shaw, for instance, when he was ready to publish a play contracted for its appearance with a publisher, sent him a neatly typed manuscript, received several sets of proof which he carefully corrected, and finally saw his work given to the world in a printed form as nearly accurate as human ingenuity and care can make it. Things were otherwise in Shakespeare's day.

In the first place throughout the greater part of Shakespeare's life plays were hardly regarded as literature in the true sense of the word. They were written to be produced on the stage, not for publication. "Comedies," said Marston, Shakespeare's contemporary play-wright, "are writ to be spoken, not read." It is true that in the early years of the seventeenth century, owing in part to the excellence of Shakespeare's own works, plays began to rise in estimation, and various authors, Chapman, Jonson, Heywood, and Massinger, began to send their plays to the press with dedications to prospective patrons. Shakespeare, however, never did so, and he was well on in his career before his name appeared on the title-page of any of his plays; *Love's Labour's Lost, Richard II,* and *Richard III* were all published in 1598, the year in which Meres proclaimed the excellence of Shakespeare as poet and playwright, as the work of Shakespeare. Evidently by this time his name had an advertising and commercial value.

The usual practice, as has already been said (page 69), was for a dramatist to sell his play outright to a company of actors. It then became their exclusive property; it was considered distinctly unethical for a writer to re-sell his play to a publisher. After securing a license for performance from the Master of the Revels, making the changes, if any, that he demanded, cutting the manuscript to a proper length for the two-hour limit, and equipping it with the necessary stage-directions, the company entrusted it to their bookkeeper, who had it bound up, often in an old bit of vellum, and carefully preserved it among the company's archives.

This final form was the so-called "book of the play," and as a rule the company was most reluctant to allow the publication of this their property. For this there were two reasons: rightly or wrongly they felt that if the public could read a play they would be less likely to come to the theatre to see it. A still stronger reason was that if a play were in print it would be difficult, if not impossible, to prevent another company from acting it in London or on the road. There were at that time no such stringent laws to prevent the infringement of stage copyright as exist today. Nevertheless the public which flocked to see plays on the stage was equally eager to read them in print and as always the demand created the supply. All through Shakespeare's lifetime his plays as well as those of his contemporaries kept appearing in print. Finally, in 1616, the year of Shakespeare's death, Jonson set the seal of his great reputation upon the practice of publication by collecting such of his plays as he was willing to own, seeing them through the press, and giving them to the world with the title of *The Works of Benjamin Jonson,* a title, by the way, which elicited a good deal of ridicule at the time, since mere plays were hardly considered to be "works."

There were various ways in which copy for setting up a play in print might come into a publisher's hands. These may be distinguished as legitimate and illegitimate methods. It was, of course, illegitimate for a publisher to print and sell a play without the consent of its owners the actors, but in the absence of copyright laws at that time the owners had no redress. A publisher bent on securing copy might send a stenographer to the theatre to take down the play in shorthand. We know enough of the systems of shorthand in use at that time to be sure that such a report would be very imperfect. In fact, Heywood, one of Shakespeare's contemporaries, remarks of a successful play of his own that

> "some by Stenography drew
> "The plot: put it in print: (scarce one word trew:)"

A similar practice would be to send a man or men repeatedly to a play to memorize and report as much of it as possible. This, too, would not be likely to get satisfactory results but would at least produce copy that could be palmed off on the public. Lastly, and this is a method from which we know that Shakespeare suffered, it was possible to bribe one of the hired men of the acting company to transcribe his own carefully written-out part, which would of course be an accurate reproduction of his rôle, and to eke this out by repeating from memory what he had heard his fellow actors recite in rehearsals or public performances. It seems fairly certain that the first editions of *Romeo and Juliet, The Merry Wives, Henry V,* and *Hamlet* rest upon copy obtained in this fashion. After the publication of the first quarto of *Hamlet,* Shakespeare no longer suffered from such piracy; it seems likely that his company detected and discharged the thief.

Such illegitimate methods, however, were exceptional. Most Elizabethan publishers were honest business men, and copy for the great majority of plays published in Shakespeare's lifetime was obtained in perfectly legitimate fashion. When a company broke up, for instance, as Pembroke's Men did in 1594, their play-books might be sold to publishers and the money divided among the needy actors. Similarly, when a company was in straits for money it might dispose of its play-books in this fashion. It is an interesting fact that during and immediately after the great plague years of 1593-94 and 1603-1604 an unusual number of plays issued from the press. Finally a company might consent, however reluctantly, to the publication of an authentic edition of one of their plays to supplant a "stolen and surreptitious" copy. It seems fairly certain that the second editions of *Romeo and Juliet,* and *Hamlet,* for instance, were printed from copy supplied by the actors and published to supplant the badly garbled reports of these plays in the first quartos; the second quarto of *Hamlet,* in fact, carries on the title-page the statement that it is enlarged to almost as much again as it was, *according to the true and perfect copy."* It has been suggested also that the first edition of *Lear* rests upon copy supplied the publisher to forestall the appearance of a stolen and garbled version like the first quarto *Hamlet,* which the actors had reason to believe was about to be published.

When an honest publisher got the manuscript of a play his first action was to pay the usual fee of 6d. and enter it on the Stationers' Register. This was the record kept by the corporation of printers and publishers, and an entry therein of intent to publish any book protected or was supposed to protect the entrant from infringement of his right by a fellow member of the corporation. Another purpose of such an entry was to prevent the illicit publication of a play. Roberts, who printed the play-bills for Shakespeare's company, was frequently employed to enter plays that they wished to withhold for the present from publication.

It was not necessary to make such an entry and it is an interesting fact that most stolen plays were published without an entry in the Register. Having thus secured his rights the publisher turned his copy over to a printer to compose for him. Now the art of printing and of book-making in general was at a rather low ebb in Elizabethan England and plays were cheap books—the usual selling price was 6d. Consequently the printing as a rule was hastily and rather carelessly done. We must remember also that if the compositor was setting up his form from a "book of the play," he was working on copy that had been cut, revised, altered, and emended on its passage from the author's hands to those of the licenser and back again to the prompter, who scribbled stage directions and actors' names in the margin. Even if there had been careful proof reading of the first impression, the result would probably have been far from accurate; but proof reading in an Elizabethan printing shop was notoriously careless. It was a rare exception for an author to read the proof of his plays as Jonson did for the publication of his folio edition. More often some one in the shop had a hasty glance at the sheets as they came from the press, corrected the more obvious blunders, and made the compositor correct his forms. By this time, however, a number of sheets had been struck off and instead of throwing them away and starting afresh, the old misprinted sheets were bound up indiscriminately with the new more or less corrected ones. As a result, it is unusual to find copies of the same edition of a play which correspond exactly. Of the first quarto of *Lear*, one of the worst jobs of printing turned out in Shakespeare's days, some nine or ten copies still survive and not a single one of these even approaches accuracy; every copy has some corrected and some uncorrected sheets, and no two of them correspond. It is not surprising, therefore, that the text of Elizabethan plays is far from representing accurately the words the author wrote.

Sixteen of Shakespeare's plays were published in quarto form during his lifetime and one more, *Othello*, six years after his death just before the appearance of the First Folio. These sixteen are now divided into two classes, the good and the bad quartos. The bad quartos are those which were published without the consent of the actors, copy for which had been obtained by one of the illegitimate methods described above. There are five, perhaps one should say six of these, namely *Romeo and Juliet*, *The Merry Wives*, *Henry V*, *Hamlet* and *Pericles*, to which we might add *Troilus and Cressida*, although this play was apparently printed from a fairly accurate transcript of Shakespeare's manuscript (cf. page 152 above). The other ten, or eleven, were honestly secured and, as a rule, present a text nearer to Shakespeare's original than that of the Folio version of the play. In fact, it is now known that certain plays in the Folio were printed directly from quarto editions; a word will be said of this hereafter. All these quartos good and bad, except those of *Lear, Troilus,* and *Pericles,* were published before 1603, that is, before Shakespeare's company became the King's Men; after that date they seem to have had influence enough with the Master of the Revels, who now claimed the right to license plays for publication as well as for the stage, to stop the printing of all but these three plays. All his other plays, some nineteen or twenty in number, remained in manuscript in the hands of the Company until 1623 when they appeared in the Folio.

The following table shows the dates of the quarto editions of Shakespeare's plays up to 1623, and also the comparative popularity of the plays.

Titus 1594, 1600, 1611
Richard II 1597, 1598, 1608, 1615
Richard III 1597, 1598, 1602, 1605, 1612, 1622
Romeo and Juliet .. 1597, 1599, 1609, one undated quarto
I Henry IV 1598, 1599, 1604, 1608, 1613, 1622
Love's Labour's Lost 1598
Merchant of Venice 1600, 1619
Henry V 1600, 1602, **1619**
Much Ado 1600
II Henry IV 1600
Midsummer Night's
  Dream 1600, 1619
Merry Wives 1602, 1619
Hamlet 1603, 1604, 1605, **1611**
Lear 1608, 1619
Troilus 1609
Pericles .... 1609 (two editions), 1611, 1619
Othello **1622**

The publication of Jonson's collected plays in the Folio of 1616 may have suggested the collection and publication of the plays of his even more famous contemporary, William Shakespeare, who died in that year. The idea seems to have occurred first about 1619 to an unscrupulous publisher, Thomas Pavier. He owned the copyrights of the corrupt version of *Henry V*, of the *Contention* and the *True Tragedy* (see page 127), of a murder play called *A Yorkshire Tragedy*, which he had published as the work of Shakespeare as far back as 1605, and of a chronicle play, *Sir John Oldcastle*, often confused with Shakespeare's *Henry IV*, where Falstaff, as we have seen, was originally called Oldcastle. In addition to these he picked up copies of the popular *Pericles*, of the *Merchant of Venice* and *A Midsummer Night's Dream*, both long out of print, and secured from the owners the right to reprint the corrupt *Merry Wives* and the one edition of *Lear*. These ten plays he apparently meant to publish in a single volume, offering them to the public as a collection of Shakespeare's plays. He had actually started the printing of the set in quarto form when he was forced to abandon his purpose. Possibly the Company got wind of his scheme and appealed to their patron, Shakespeare's friend, William Lord Herbert, then Lord Chamberlain. In May, 1619, Herbert wrote to the Stationers' Company forbidding the printing of any of the King's Men's plays without their consent. Pavier, however, was unwilling to lose the money he had already spent on the work and proceeded to issue these ten plays in quarto form separately, except for the two *Henry VI* plays, which appeared in one volume under the title of *The Whole Contention*, etc. To cover his traces he gave false dates to a number of the plays, to *Henry V*, that of 1608, to the *Merchant* and *A Midsummer Night's Dream*, 1600 (the date of the original quartos) with the lying statement that they were printed by J. Roberts, dead some years before. On the title page of his *Lear* he put the name of Butter, the original publisher, and the date 1608. *The Merry Wives* and *Pericles* he dated correctly, 1619. These copies he disposed of separately, but it is known that a number of them were bound up by purchasers into a collected volume, one specimen of which still exists in the Folger Library at Washington. Pavier's trickery and the false dates he placed on various volumes long caused great confusion to Shakespeare's bibliographers, but some clever bibliographical and typographical detective work about 1909 cleared up the whole matter. The various editions dated 1619 in the table on page 201 are those which Pavier published in that year, regardless of the date he set on the title pages.

It must have been shortly after the break-down of Pavier's plan of publication, possibly even in consequence of it, that two of Shakespeare's "fellows," Heminges and Condell, resolved to collect and publish all his plays. These two were at this time, 1620, the sole surviving members of the original Globe "housekeepers," special friends of Shakespeare to whom he had in his will left a handsome sum for the purchase of memorial rings. As old members of the Company they probably had little difficulty in securing permission to print from the "play-books" the hitherto unpublished plays, but to secure permission to reprint those already in existence in quarto form involved probably a good deal of bargaining with the owners of the copyrights. To secure these and to finance an expensive undertaking a partnership was formed by Jaggard, printer of play-bills for the King's Men, and Blount, a publisher of some standing who owned the copyrights to *Antony and Cleopatra* and *Pericles* though he had never published either. Later two other publishers, Smithwick and Aspley, who between them controlled the copyright of six plays, were added to the partnership, and the volume was finally printed at their joint expense.

On November 8, 1623, Blount and Jaggard entered in the Stationers' Register "Master William Shakspeers *Comedyes, Histories* and *Tragedyes,* soe manie of the said copies as are not formerly entred to other men vizt. Comedyes. The Tempest. The two gentlemen of Verona. Measure for Measure. The Comedy of Errors. As you like it. All's well that ends well. Twelfe Night. The winters tale. Histories. The thirde part of Henry ye sixt. Henry the eight. Tragedies. Coriolanus. Timon of Athens. Julius Cæsar. Mackbeth. Anthonie and Cleopatra. Cymbeline."

One or two comments on this list are necessary. The "thirde part of Henry the Sixt" refers to what we now know as the first part; the two *Contention* plays had been entered by Pavier in 1602 as the first and second part of *Henry VI*. It would have been more accurate to speak of the play now entered as a third play introductory to the other two. There is no mention in this list of *King John,* which had neither been entered nor published previously, but this play, as has been shown (page 134), was Shakespeare's re-writing of an old chronicle, and registration was probably considered unnecessary. *The Taming of the Shrew,* also omitted from this list, is a re-writing of *A Shrew* (see page 144) of which Smithwick, one of the Folio syndicate, owned the copyright.

The owners of *Troilus* made so much difficulty in releasing the copyright that it was at first intended to omit this play from the collection; it is not mentioned in the catalogue of plays prefixed to the volume and was apparently crowded in at the last moment between the His-

tories and the Tragedies. *Pericles,* although owned by
Blount, was omitted from the collection, as was the
collaborated play, *The Two Noble Kinsmen* (see pages
172 and 180).

The Folio was a rather pretentious volume. It included besides the plays, a short poem by Jonson on
the portrait; the well-known Droeshout portrait of
Shakespeare, possibly costumed for the part of Old
Knowell in Jonson's *Every Man In,* inserted on the title-
page after the statement that Shakespeare's Comedies,
Histories, and Tragedies are here "published according
to the true original copies"; an elaborate dedication to
"the most noble and incomparable pair of brethren,
William Earl of Pembroke and Philip Earl of Mont-
gomery," signed by Heminges and Condell; an epistle "to
the great variety of readers" also signed by Heminges
and Condell, but possibly written by Jonson; a long
poem "to the memory of my beloved, the author, Mr.
William Shakespeare and what he hath left us," by
Ben Jonson; a sonnet by Hugh Holland; an elegy by
L. Digges; and a short poem by an unknown I. M.
Then follows the list of actors' names already referred
to (page 65), a catalogue of several comedies, histories, and tragedies arranged in these three groups, and
the plays begin with *The Tempest.*

In the epistle to the readers, Shakespeare's friends
state that whereas the public had heretofore been abused
by "diverse stolen and surreptitious copies," even these
were now offered to view "cured and perfect." These
expressions were once thought to be a denunciation of
all editions published before the Folio, but it is more
likely that the reference was only to the "bad quartos."
Modern scholarship has, in fact, demonstrated that various quarto editions were actually sent to Jaggard's
printing shop to be used as copy for the Folio. Thus

Love's Labour's Lost, Romeo and Juliet, and *The Merchant of Venice* were reprinted in the Folio from quarto editions; *Richard II, A Midsummer Night's Dream, I Henry IV, Titus,* and *Much Ado* were printed from quarto copies which had been used in the theatre as prompt books and contained various corrections and marginal notes. For six other plays which had previously been published, *Richard III, II Henry IV, Hamlet, Lear, Troilus,* and *Othello,* Heminges and Condell preferred to rely upon the Company's "play-books," even when, as is the case with *Hamlet,* the quarto presented a fuller and presumably more accurate form. The bad quartos of *Henry V* and *Merry Wives* were naturally rejected, and here as with the twenty unpublished plays they drew upon the "play-books." It is very doubtful whether they actually sent the valuable "play-books" bearing the Master of the Revels license to the printing shop; more likely they arranged to have them transcribed and sent the transcripts to Jaggard. It has been suggested also that the original play-books were lost for certain plays, as we know that of *The Winter's Tale* was in August, 1623, before the Folio was printed and that copy was prepared by "assembling" the actors' parts and so reconstructing the play. The evidence for this view, however, is not very strong.

From what has been said it is plain that the Folio can no longer be regarded as presenting everywhere the exact words of Shakespeare, "absolute in their numbers, as he conceived them," to quote a phrase of the epistle. Shakespeare's fellows, no doubt, did their best, but they were not critical scholars nor expert editors; and the text of the Folio, once regarded with almost superstitious reverence, leaves much to be desired. There are many palpable misprints, some careless omissions of words, phrases and even whole lines. There are evident signs of editing in modernization of spelling and grammar and in a rather inconsistent purging the text of profanity.

When one turns, moreover, from the text to the stage-directions, to exits and entrances, and to division into acts and scenes, the Folio is quite unsatisfactory. It has taken the labor of Shakespearean scholars a couple of centuries and more to restore the text of Shakespeare to something approximately like the "true original," and there is still work to be done. Some account of these labors will be found in a later chapter.

A second Folio published in 1632, reprinted the first, corrected some obvious misprints, and introduced a number of fresh ones. No other edition appeared until Restoration times, when the Third Folio was issued in 1663. To a second issue of this edition in 1664 there were added a new group of plays; of these *Pericles,* appearing for the first time in a folio collection, alone has any claim to authenticity. The others, *The London Prodigal, Thomas Lord Cromwell, Sir John Oldcastle, The Puritan, A Yorkshire Tragedy,* and *Locrine,* are all spurious, and are no longer found in any edition of Shakespeare. The Fourth and last Folio was printed in 1685. No authority can be attached to any alterations in these later editions, as one folio simply reprints another, making some obvious corrections and introducing new errors. The work of actual editing begins with Rowe's edition in 1709.

CHAPTER XIII

EDITORS AND EDITIONS

THE student of today familiar with the text of Shake-speare in the current amended and annotated editions of his plays can have little or no conception of the difficulties which confronted readers of the poet at the close of the seventeenth century. The First Folio was, as has been said, a poor piece of work, abounding in misprints, confused and confusing punctuation, printing verse sometimes as prose and sometimes prose as verse. Every succeeding folio increased the difficulty and confusion by adding to the errors of the first until the text had become a veritable jungle of errors and obscurities. It is no wonder that even such a lover of Shakespeare and such a clear-sighted critic as Dryden complained at times of the difficulty of the poet's style. With the beginning of the eighteenth century the first attempt was made to render his work more generally intelligible. It is probable that the idea of an emended, legible, and popular edition to replace the expensive and unsatisfactory folios occurred first to a famous publisher of the day, the well-known Tonson. He engaged the services of Nicholas Rowe, a practicing and successful playwright, to edit the plays of Shakespeare.

Rowe's work of reform, published first in 1709, was partial and unsatisfactory. He based his text upon the Fourth Folio, the worst of the four, and as a natural result reproduced many of its errors, retaining also the

spurious plays which had been added to the text in 1664.
He did, however, consult some of the quartos and added
to the text passages wanting in all the folios, notably the
last soliloquy of Hamlet. His chief work apparently,
apart from the correction of obvious errors, was to give a
list of dramatis personæ for each play—only eight of
such lists appear in the folios—and to divide the plays
into acts and scenes. This division he carried out in
accordance with the stage practice of his day, a practice
quite different from that of the Elizabethans. In the
main Rowe's arrangement has prevailed to the present
day, often to the bewilderment of the reader as when he
split the beginning of the second act of *Romeo and Juliet*
into two scenes where Shakespeare evidently meant it to
run on without a break. To a second edition of the
plays, 1714, Rowe prefixed the first biography of Shakespeare.

Rowe's editions apparently whetted the public ap-
petite for a revised version of Shakespeare and about
1720 Tonson called on Pope, then at the height of his
fame as translator of the *Iliad,* to superintend the publication of a new edition. This appeared in a handsome
and expensive form in 1725. Pope discarded the seven
plays added to the third folio, excluding even *Pericles.*
In his preface he professed to have made a careful
collation of the old editions, to have put the various
readings in the margin, to have explained obsolete words
and in general to have "discharged the dull duty of an
editor" to the best of his judgment. Unfortunately
Pope's judgment as an editor was far below his genius
as a poet. He based his text in the main upon Rowe,
only occasionally consulted the original copies, constantly altered the text to suit his own conception of
propriety of language and regularity of metre, and worst
of all cut out many passages which he considered un-

worthy of Shakespeare, stigmatizing them as interpolations by the actors and relegating them to the foot of the page or omitting them without notice. It seems hardly credible, but it is true, that he treated one of Shakespeare's grandest lines in this fashion, degrading

"The multitudinous seas incarnadine"

to a footnote and misprinting it even there.

Much had been expected of Pope's work and although he made some ingenious conjectures and occasionally corrected a bit of mangled metre, there was a general sense of disappointment. This found a voice and very emphatic utterance in the year following the appearance of his edition.

In 1726 Lewis Theobald, a first-rate classical scholar, for years a student of Shakespeare and of Elizabethan literature, published a work entitled *Shakespeare Restored, or a specimen of the many errors as well committed as left unamended by Mr. Pope*. About two-thirds of the book was devoted to a rectification of the text of Hamlet; an appendix of some sixty pages contained emendations for most of the other plays. Perhaps the most famous of these was the correction of Mrs. Quickly's phrase in describing the death of Falstaff which was printed in the Folio: "his Nose was as sharpe as a Pen, and a table of greene fields." Pope, who had been puzzled by the last quite unintelligible words, explained them as a stage direction which had crept into the text; a table was wanted for a tavern scene, he said, and Greenfield, the property man, was directed to have one ready. Quite an ingenious guess; unfortunately there never was any such person as Greenfield and directions of this sort never occur in the middle of a scene. Theobald's emendation "and a (*i.e.* he) babbled of green fields" is so happy that one feels that if Shakespeare did not write the phrase he certainly should have done so. It has been universally received into the text. This is only one of some three hundred of Theobald's corrections and emendations which have been very generally accepted by later editors.

Pope naturally was furious at Theobald's exposure of his incompetence as an editor. He made Theobald, "piddling Tibbald" as he called him, the hero of his first version of the Dunciad, 1728, and was never weary of abusing him and crying down his work. Undismayed, however, Theobald proceeded to bring out his own edition in seven volumes in 1734. In spite of the fact that Theobald used Pope's text to print from—a mere con cession to convenience—it is with this edition that a real beginning was made of the slow process of correcting the text of Shakespeare. Pope fancied that he was deriding Theobald by calling him The Restorer. It is a title that Theobald might have been proud to claim and he deserves it better than any other editor of Shakespeare. Working as he did without the apparatus of dictionaries, concordances, reprints of old plays and rare books accessible to the student today, he accomplished wonders. Yet the cloud of misrepresentation raised around him by Pope and Pope's disciples was so thick that it is only in late years that his true merit has been recognized. This merit can be stated very briefly: Theobald brought to the restoration of the text of Shakespeare the same diligence in collation, the same wide reading in contemporary literature, and the same reasonable prudence in emendation which heretofore had been practiced in the restoration of a Greek or Latin text; in other words he treated Shakespeare as a true scholar of the Renaissance treated an old classic.

Passing over other eighteenth-century editions we come in 1765 to that of Dr. Johnson. Johnson did little to improve the text, but his explanations of difficult passages remain today among the most convincing of the many that crowd the pages of the *Variorum Shakespeare*. Johnson's contemporary, Capell, made the fullest and most scholarly collation of the various texts that had yet appeared. Unfortunately his clumsy style—Johnson declared that he "gabbled monstrously"—robbed his work of half its value.

Malone's edition, 1790, restored *Pericles* to the plays and added the poems and sonnets which an earlier editor had rejected because, he said, "the strongest Act of Parliament that could be framed would fail to compel readers into their service." Malone's special merit was his knowledge of Elizabethan life and literature; he inaugurated the study of the chronology of Shakespeare's plays, and his tireless researches in Shakespearean lore were included after his death in the so-called *Third Variorum* edited in 1821 by the younger James Boswell.

Few of the many nineteenth-century editions deserve special mention. Little by little the work of correcting and explaining the text of Shakespeare went forward. Knight's once popular editions, 1838-42 and 1842-44, showed a reversion to the letter-worship of the First Folio. J. P. Collier's, 1841-44, work was marked, or rather marred, by perversely ingenious guesses for some of which that erratic scholar sought support by marginal entries, undoubtedly forged, in a copy of F_2. Finally, 1863-66, the *Cambridge Shakespeare* edited by Clark, Glover, and Wright (revised 1891-93 by Wright) appeared with a complete *apparatus criticus* containing all the textual variations and the most significant conjectures of former editors. This edition long remained the standard; its text reprinted in the popular Globe edition and in the well-known *Temple* format, one play to one volume, became, so to speak, the *textus receptus* of Shakespeare.

The *New Variorum,* begun in 1871 by Dr. Howard
Furness, continued after his death by his son, now also
deceased, and still in progress in the hands of a commit-
tee of scholars, started with an eclectic text and later
diverged into a reprint of the First Folio. Like the *Cambridge* it contains a complete collation of variants, the
best emendations, and a vast number of explanatory
notes.

The best single volume texts of Shakespeare are the
Oxford, edited by W. J. Craig, and the American *Cambridge,* edited by W. A. Neilson. The text of this latter,
revised and reprinted in the popular *Tudor* edition, has
deservedly attained wide circulation in this country; it
forms the basis of the text offered in the present series.

For the serious student copies or facsimile reprints of
the folios, specifically of the First and of the various
quartos are a prime necessity. There is an accurate reprint of this folio by Booth, 1862-64; another by Halliwell-Phillips, 1876, reproduced in smaller and cheaper
form, unfortunately in such minute type as to be almost
illegible. The best reproduction is probably that of Sidney Lee, 1902. The *Shakespeare Quarto Facsimiles,*
1880-89, forty-one volumes supervised by Dr. Furnivall,
are indispensible, although at times not absolutely accurate. The prefaces to the various volumes contain very
valuable textual studies.

Of late years English scholars have devoted much
time and pains to bibliographical and paleographical
studies. A better knowledge of the ways of Elizabethan
printers and the peculiarities of Elizabethan handwriting
have suggested many plausible explanations of errors or
variants in the old texts. The definitive text of Shakespeare has not yet appeared. There is still room for such
an edition as Theobald would have given to the world
had he possessed the knowledge and the facilities within
easy reach of Shakespearean scholars today.

CHAPTER XIV

SHAKESPEAREAN CRITICISM

CRITICISM is not, as is too often thought, a process of fault-finding. It is rather a process of discrimination, of sifting faults from merits, of determining the permanent as opposed to the ephemeral in an author's work and of bringing to light beauties ignored by the casual reader. The progress of Shakespearean criticism, like that of the correction and elucidation of the text has been slow and gradual. Often it reveals the idiosyncracy of the critic and the prevailing critical standards of his age quite as much as it does the merits and defects of Shakespeare. Yet it is quite true to say that with a few negligible exceptions all critics of Shakespeare, whatever their personal prejudices, whatever the accepted critical dogmas of their age, have recognized his transcendent greatness. A brief review of the progress of Shakespearean criticism from his own time to our own will make this clear.

There was little or no criticism of Shakespeare in Elizabethan time. The triumphant success of his plays upon the stage found an echo in a chorus of praise from his contemporaries. Only Ben Jonson exercised a certain liberty of expression. When the players mentioned it as an honor to Shakespeare that in his writing, "he never blotted **a line," Jonson replied "would** that he had blotted a thousand—he flowed with that facility that sometimes it was necessary that he should be stopped."

This is genuine criticism. One of the characteristics of Shakespeare's art, like that of the Gothic workman in Ruskin's famous chapter, is the quality of redundance, "the uncalculating bestowal of the wealth of its labor." Yet in his well-known eulogy of Shakespeare prefixed to the First Folio Jonson is lavish of praise. Shakespeare, he says, not only surpassed his contemporaries—Jonson mentions by name Lyly, Kyd, and Marlowe,—but challenged comparison with all the work of "insolent Greece or haughty Rome." He goes on to praise not only Shakespeare's truth to nature but the "art" which turned and fashioned his "true-filed lines." And finally his emphatic declaration that Shakespeare "was not of an age, but for all time" was the truest prophecy ever made by a poet-critic of a brother poet.

No age had such difficulty in understanding and appreciating Shakespeare as that of the Restoration. This was due in part to the shocking condition of his text at that time, even more perhaps to changed theatrical conditions and to the prevalence of neo-classical dogmas, especially as applied to the drama. This lack of understanding found its full and final expression in the work of Thomas Rymer, *Tragedies of the Last Age*, 1678, and *Short View of Tragedy*, 1692-93. Rymer has been styled "the worst critic that ever lived," and if the first qualification of a critic is a sympathetic appreciation of his subject, Rymer's bad eminence can hardly be disputed. "There is more meaning and expression," he declares, "in the neighing of a horse or the growling of a mastiff than in Shakespeare's tragical flights." A soldier, he believes, should always be shown as frank and plain-dealing, therefore Shakespeare's Iago is an unnatural monster; "there never was in tragedy, comedy, or nature such a soldier as Iago." Othello is, in short, "a bloody farce." The cause of all this, Rymer, like later critics who have found fault with Shakespeare, discovers in the "illiterate audience, carpenters and cobblers" for whom Shakespeare wrote.

Rymer, however, does not represent his own age; he is the hyper-critic rebuked even by his contemporaries for his excess. A better mirror of Restoration criticism is found in the work of Dryden. He begins, *Essay of Dramatick Poesie,* 1668, by calling Shakespeare "the man who of all modern and perhaps ancient poets, had the largest and most comprehensive soul." That is high praise and its effect is not greatly diminished when Dryden complains of the irregularity of Shakespeare's plots or the extravagance of his diction. We must always remember that Dryden read Shakespeare in the uncorrected folio text and was rightly puzzled and often offended by what he read there. Moreover one of the tasks of the Restoration authors and critics was to purge literature of the characteristic Elizabethan license of excess. In the Restoration adaptations of Shakespeare for the contemporary stage it is interesting to note how often the authors, themselves poets as well as playwrights, shy off in alarm from some fine figurative phrase of Shakespeare's and water it down to a harmless mediocrity. Thus in D'Avenant's *Macbeth* such a magnificent outburst as the Lady's

"The raven himself is hoarse
That croaks the fatal entrance of Duncan
Under my battlements"

becomes

"There would be music in a raven's voice,
Which should but croak the entrance of the King
Under my battlements."

Yet Dryden admits that Shakespeare has often written

better than any poet in any language and that he excels
in characterization. "We English venerate Shakespeare,"
he declares "as the Greeks do Æschylus."

Pope, the typical Augustan, was a better critic than
an editor of Shakespeare. The preface to his edition is
a better piece of work than the edition itself. Like Dryden, he is open-eyed to what seem Shakespeare's faults,
his puns, his "conceits," his extravagance of language,
but he is less severe than Dryden in his reprobation;
at times attributes them to Shakespeare's condescension
to his audience, at times clears him of them by ascribing
them not to Shakespeare but to interpolations by the
actors. He justifies Shakespeare's violation of the
Aristotelian canons by asserting that to judge him by
those rules would be "like trying a man by the laws of
one country who acted under those of another"—a perfect defence, if indeed defence is needed. Shakespeare's chief excellence is his unequalled perception of
nature; his characters "like those in nature are infinitely
diversified—every single character in Shakespeare is as
much an individual as those in life itself." A poet himself Pope feels Shakespeare's power over the passions;
Shakespeare induces our tears and commands our laughter. In his edition he marked by stars and commas the
most "shining passages" and it is gratifying to note that
the most "correct" of English poets could respond to
the lament of Constance for her lost Arthur and to
Prospero's

> "We are such stuff
> As dreams are made on, and our little life
> Is rounded with a sleep."

His final conclusion is that Shakespeare is "justly and
universally elevated above all other dramatic writers."

Like Pope, Dr. Johnson, literary dictator of the suc-

ceeding age, composed a critical preface for his edition
of Shakespeare. It is interesting to note that he
considers that Shakespeare "may now begin to assume
the dignity of an ancient and claim the privilege of an
established fame." Johnson's approach to Shakespeare
has been called the method of common sense. The first
aim of a poet, he holds, must be to instruct by pleasing
and Shakespeare pleases because he holds up "a faithful
mirror of manners and of life." Johnson defends the
mingling of tragic and comic scenes in Shakespeare's
plays, a grave fault according to neo-classical standards,
because this "mingled drama" resembles life more nearly
than either pure tragedy or comedy. Addison's *Cato* has
long been recognized as the masterpiece of "regular"
tragedy in English, and Johnson praises its innumerable
beauties but adds, what is quite true, that its sentiments
"communicate no vibration to the heart" whereas *Othello*,
so bitterly denounced by Rymer, is "the offspring of
observation impregnated by genius." Johnson is less
sensitive than Pope to the poetic beauty of Shakespeare;
he denounces Shakespeare's fondness for word-play and
conceits; "a quibble," he says, "is the golden apple for
which he will always turn aside from his career or stoop
from his elevation." He prefers Shakespeare's comedies
to his tragedies since "in his tragic scenes there is always something wanting"—one wonders what the Doctor would have added to the death of Lear—whereas
"his comedy often surpasses expectation." In the main,
Johnson, himself primarily a moralist, applauds Shakespeare as a great, although unconscious, master of morals;
it is from Shakespeare's truth to general human nature
that "so much instruction is derived." The practical
commonsense attitude of Johnson to Shakespeare comes
out perhaps most clearly in his advice to the young
reader: "notes are often necessary, but they are neces-

sary evils. Let him that is yet unacquainted with the powers of Shakespeare, and who desires to feel the highest pleasure that the drama can give, read every play from the first scene to the last with utter negligence of all his commentators,—let him read on through brightness and obscurity,—let him preserve his comprehension of the dialogue and his interest in the fable (*i.e.* the story). And when the pleasures of novelty have ceased, let him attempt exactness, and read the commentators." This is advice which might well be printed today at the beginning of every school and college edition of a play of Shakespeare's.

The dawn of a new school of criticism, the romantic, is seen in Morgann's famous essay, 1777, on the character of Falstaff. Its thesis is that Falstaff was neither a coward nor a boaster, but a man of natural courage and alacrity of mind. The whole essay is an elaborate and ingenious paradox, impressionistic rather than judicial. Here is no weighing of Shakespeare's faults against Shakespeare's merits, but an attempt to glorify his creative power by displaying his mastery of character creation. The fault that permeates the essay is Morgann's tendency to consider Falstaff not as a figure in a play but a real character, and to argue from what he says and does and what is said of him to what Morgann calls his "internal character" as distinguished from the impression he makes upon the stage. Yet it was just this impression for which Shakespeare created the character. More and more the tendency grew in the romantic school to forget Shakespeare the dramatist and to think of him as a creator of real characters about whom one could argue as about characters in history.

The romantic school of criticism broke into full flower in the work of Coleridge, Hazlitt, and Lamb. Of these Coleridge is the greatest critic as he is the greatest poet

and philosopher. His criticism preserved in fragmentary
form from two series of lectures delivered in 1811-12
and in 1818 is indeed a blend of poetry and philosophy.
Like a true philosopher he seeks to find a unity in the
whole of Shakespeare's work and in each play that belongs to the body of that work. Like a true poet he is more
keenly sensitive to the beauty of Shakespeare's verse
than any preceding critic. He defends Shakespeare
against the old charge that he was an "irregular" genius
of vast powers, but little judgment. One feels indeed
in reading Coleridge on Shakespeare that the critic was
possessed with the conception that the object of his
worship was incapable of error. When something in
Shakespeare offended even Coleridge—as the speech of
the drunken porter in *Macbeth*—he was inclined to re-
ject it as an interpolation by the actors—a throw-back
to the method of Pope. With a growing tendency toward
a realistic historic criticism today it is only natural that
the extraordinary value of Coleridge's criticism should
be slighted or ignored; but it is impossible to read even
one of his studies of a play of Shakespeare's without
feeling that here was something wholly new, imaginative
interpretation of a great work of art, no mere weighing
of merits and defects. And much that Coleridge was the
first to say has become the commonplace of criticism
ever since.

Not much need be said of Lamb in this connection. His
Tales from Shakespeare, 1807, still a classic, is not
criticism, but a rendering into easy prose of the plots of
Shakespeare's plays. He was widely read in Elizabethan drama, and his *Specimen of English Dramatic
Poets,* an anthology of gems from Shakespeare's contemporaries accompanied by brief notes of genuine critical appreciation, did much to bring back forgotten
playwrights to the reading public. His fine essay *On*

the Tragedies of Shakespeare, 1810, is his one contribution to Shakespearean criticism. Lamb's point of view is that of the reader and lover of poetry; he holds that Shakespeare's plays are "less calculated for performance on a stage than those of almost any other dramatist whatever. Their distinguishing excellence is a reason why they should be so." This is, as Lamb admits, a paradox. It seems indeed an absurd one; the greatest dramatist of all time, whose plays have held the stage through successive changes of public taste in the centuries since his death, wrote, it would seem, plays unsuitable for acting. The truth is that Lamb's own keen delight in the poetry of Shakespeare left him incapable of realizing the potential dramatic power of the poetry he loved. To render it in public seemed to him to vulgarize it; "Hamlet," he says, "what does he suffer by being dragged forth to give lectures to the crowd—the shy, negligent, retiring Hamlet!" Evidently Hamlet is to Lamb a real person, not a character created by Shakespeare for the sole purpose of being represented in action on the stage.

Hazlitt, whose main body of Shakespearean criticism is preserved in his *Characters of Shakespeare's Plays,* 1817, is in some ways a more useful, as he is a more practical critic than either Lamb or Coleridge. Like them he is an enthusiastic worshipper of Shakespeare and is frank to confess it. "An overstrained enthusiasm is more pardonable with respect to Shakespeare," he says, "than the want of it; for our admiration cannot easily surpass his genius." Like them he is a lover of poetry; he anticipates Arnold in his belief in the high moral value of poetry: "Poetry is an interesting study, for this reason, that it relates to whatever is most interesting in human life. Whoever therefore has a contempt for poetry, has a contempt for himself and humanity." Ac-

cordingly the pages of his studies of Shakespeare's
characters are packed with quotations chosen for their
poetic beauty and dramatic fitness. Yet Hazlitt, though
a devotee of the acted drama and an expert dramatic
critic, felt like Lamb that Shakespeare was better in the
closet than in the theatre; "poetry and the stage do not
agree well together." He is not always consistent in
this; he praises Mrs. Siddons's performance of Lady
Macbeth: "She was tragedy personified," and calls Kean
"this celebrated actor and able commentator on Shakespeare (actors are the best commentators on the poets)."
Like a true Romantic he denounced Johnson's "judicial"
criticism of Shakespeare. "Johnson," he says, "was
neither a poet nor a judge of poetry"—his "powers of
reasoning overlaid his critical susceptibility." It is just
this "susceptibility" to the beauty and the grandeur of
Shakespeare's poetry that gives to Hazlitt's criticism its
peculiar charm, that "gusto" which characterizes all his
best prose, and in his criticism as in his other essays,
Hazlitt contrives to impart something of his own delight
to the reader of his work. "For the reader of today who
wishes to read the plays of Shakespeare with unadul-
terated enjoyment—Hazlitt is a sure guide," says a
writer who knows and loves his Hazlitt better than
most of us.[1]

The note struck by the Romantics echoes through the
nineteenth century until it culminates in the ecstatic
rhapsody of Swinburne, *A Study of Shakespeare,* 1880.
Criticism in the old sense ceased; for it we have admiration, applause, almost adoration. A more sober appreciation appears in such a writer as Dowden, *Shakespeare
—His Mind and Art,* 1875, where the attempt is made to
reveal Shakespeare's personality and his attitude toward

[1] W. D. Howe, *Cambridge History of English Literature,*
Vol. xii, p. 186.

the great problems of human life through a study of his plays. Something of the same sort, combined with a subtler psychological analysis of Shakespeare's characters, is found in Bradley's admirable *Shakespearean Tragedy,* 1904. Here after a philosophic æsthetic lecture on the *Substance of Tragedy* there follows an illuminating discussion of construction in Shakespeare's tragedies. This might lead one to believe that Bradley meant to deal with Shakespeare primarily as a dramatist, but the four lectures which follow on the four great tragedies are in the main character studies, often indeed of the most interesting and suggestive sort, but with too little consideration of their prime purpose, that of presentation on the stage. To this book there must be added to complete Bradley's criticism of Shakespeare his lectures on *Antony and Cleopatra, Shakespeare the Man,* and *Shakespeare's Theatre and Audience,* in *Oxford Lectures on Poetry,* 1909, and his study of *Coriolanus (British Academy,* 1912).

A natural and necessary reaction from romantic criticism began to appear as far back as the German Rümelin's onslaught on the Shakespeare presented by German professors of æsthetics, *Shakespearean Studies,* 1874. It it current today in such work as Schücking's *Character Problems in Shakespeare's Plays,* 1919, and in the work of Professor Stoll ranging from *Shakespeare Studies,* 1911, to *Art and Artifice in Shakespeare,* 1933. In both of these we find a return to the critical attitude of the eighteenth century with, be it said, a great and striking difference.

Unbounded admiration for the genius of Shakespeare has been replaced by a recognition, at times even an insistance upon, his faults. But these faults are no longer perceived by an application of classical critical standards but rather by what one may call the historic method.

Schücking points out with real acumen that Shakespeare's technique is that of Shakespeare's day when modern drama was just emerging from medievalism. He sees Shakespeare combining an extraordinary insight into human nature with an almost naïve technique in the conduct of his plot and an inconsistency in character portrayal. Stoll, who has done real service in forcing a re-examination of romantic eulogies, lays stress on the theatrical conventions of Shakespeare's day; he sees in Falstaff the traditional *miles gloriosus,* in Hamlet the conventional revenger of the tragedy of blood. Both critics denounce the excess of psychological analysis in romantic criticism, and insist that Shakespeare wrote with more regard for the immediate impression of each scene than with an eye to a unified conception of the whole play. One feels at times in reading their work that one is listening to the voice of advocates, of prosecutors even, rather than of judges; their reaction against the indiscriminate eulogy of earlier writers carries them at times to excess. Yet their criticism serves as a valuable corrective to much that has been written in the last hundred years.

Some of the most stimulating contemporary criticism has been written by Granville-Barker (*From Henry V to Hamlet—British Academy,* 1925, *Prefaces to Shakespeare,* 1946–7, *Shakespeare's Dramatic Art* in the *Companion to Shakespeare Studies,* 1934). Himself, like Shakespeare, both actor and dramatist, Granville-Barker comes to a study of the plays with other qualifications than those of the academic critic. His special merit is his insistance on the perfect adaptation of Shakespeare's plays to the theatre for which Shakespeare wrote, on the excellence of Shakespeare's dramatic art, on the fact that Shakespeare wrote "not merely plays in poetic form, but something that is essentially and fundamentally poetic drama." It should follow, he holds, in opposition to most romantic critics, that only in the theatre can Shakespeare's plays come to their full life. Only in an ideal theatre perhaps and under the direction of an ideal manager, but Granville-Barker's plea for the actor's part in the interpretation of Shakespeare carries with it profound significance.[1]

[1] The foregoing sketch of Shakespearean criticism is necessarily limited to the history of that genre in English. The student who cares to inform himself as to the work of French and German critics of Shakespeare is referred to the account of Shakespeare's reception on the Continent in J. G. Robertson's chapter in the *Cambridge History of English Literature,* **Volume v, Chapter 12.**

CHAPTER XV

SHAKESPEARE ON THE STAGE

So much has been said and written about Shakespeare's plays as literature that it is sometimes forgotten by the student of his work that he was a supremely successful playwright. Of all the brilliant group of dramatists of his day he alone survives in the twentieth century, and there never has been a time in the history of the English-speaking stage when some, at least, of his plays in one form or other were not being presented to the public.

Shakespeare's success was early attained and endured without a break till the closing of the theatres in 1642. From the time that he is known as a member of the Chamberlain's Company, 1594, until the death of Elizabeth, 1603, there is an unbroken succession of plays presented by that organization at Court during the Christmas festivities. Probably most of the plays presented were Shakespeare's; we know certainly that *Love's Labour's Lost* and *Merry Wives* were acted before the Queen and it is to be presumed that other and better plays had the same honor. Royal favor continued and increased during the reign of James. We find the King's Men presenting ten, twelve, and thirteen plays at Court during the holiday season. Once more we may assume that many of these were Shakespeare's. *King Lear* was played at Court in 1606, *The Tempest* and *Winter's Tale* in 1611. Among the many plays presented during the festivities in honor of the Princess Elizabeth's marriage we find listed *Much Ado, The Tempest, Winter's Tale, I King Henry IV, Othello,* and *Julius Cæsar.* Later, in 1618, *Twelfth Night,* in 1619-20 *Hamlet, Two Noble Kinsmen,* and *II King Henry IV* were played at court.

. With the accession of Charles I, 1625, there seems to have been some falling off, but we hear of Court performances of *Richard III, Taming of the Shrew* and *Cymbeline* in 1633-34, and of *Hamlet, Othello* and *Julius Cæsar* in 1636.

Meanwhile the popularity of Shakespeare's plays on the public stage continued undiminished by the rise to favor of new writers. Their drawing power was such that a rival company playing at the Red Bull attempted in 1627 to produce them there; Shakespeare's old friend, Heminges, had to hurry to the Master of Revels and fee him with £5 to secure a prohibition of such a trespass. As late as 1640 Leonard Digges in a copy of verses prefixed to the edition of Shakespeare's *Poems* in that year asserted that it was Shakespeare's plays which kept the King's Men alive, that performances of *King Henry IV,* of *Much Ado,* and of *Twelfth Night* packed the house at Blackfriars when revivals of Jonson's *Volpone* and the *Alchemist* were so scantily attended that the receipts barely covered the cost of production. We can check performances of at least twenty-two of Shakespeare's plays before the closing of the theatres.

During the interregnum, 1642-1660, the Puritan rule forbade the performance of all plays, Shakespeare's or others. We hear of some private and illegal representations of Beaumont and Fletcher plays in this period, but of Shakespeare we have only records of a few "drolls," comic scenes adapted from his plays, such as those of Bottom in *A Midsummer Night's Dream* and the Grave-diggers in *Hamlet* which seem to have been played at town and country wakes and fairs. With the Restoration and the reopening of the theatres Shakespeare promptly returned to the stage.

In the first year of Charles II's reign Davenant and Killigrew were granted the sole right to form companies of actors, lease or build theatres, and produce plays. Some rough division of Shakespeare's plays was made between them. Killigrew secured *Othello, Julius Cæsar, Henry IV* and a couple of comedies; Davenant seems to have had the acting rights of most of the rest. Killigrew was responsible for one most important innovation, the substitution of women actors for the Elizabethan boys. The long roll of famous Shakespearean actresses begins on the Restoration stage with Mrs. Betterton, the lovely Bracegirdle, and the lively Barry. Contemporary records show that the Beaumont and Fletcher plays were more popular with Restoration audiences than those of Shakespeare. Yet Pepys in the ten years covered by his diary attended forty-one performances of twelve of Shakespeare's plays, seeing *Hamlet* five times, *The Tempest* eight times, and *Macbeth* nine times. It is probable indeed that some of these performances were of the scandalous adaptations of Shakespeare which blot the theatrical record of the Restoration. Davenant, in particular, allowed himself the greatest freedom in adapting Shakespeare's plays to the changed taste of his time. As early as 1661 he re-wrote *Measure for Measure* as *The Law Against Lovers,* introducing Benedick and Beatrice from *Much Ado* and creating a singing and dancing part for a little girl whose performance delighted Mr. Pepys. Later on he laid violent hands on *Macbeth,* writing several new scenes and introducing a "divertissement" of dancing and flying witches which Pepys pronounced "a strange

perfection in a tragedy." Worst of all he and Dryden
converted Shakespeare's lovely *Tempest* into a sort of
comic opera which has been called "the worst perversion of Shakespeare in the two-century history of such
atrocities." *Romeo and Juliet* was equipped with a
happy ending by Howard and for a time it was performed alternately as a tragedy and as a tragi-comedy
—an excellent example of "pay your money and take
your choice." *Lear,* too, was degraded from the realm of
tragedy by Nahum Tate, who in 1681 presented a version which cut out the part of the Fool as violating
neo-classic ideas of decorum, made Edgar and Cordelia
lovers from the start, and united them in marriage at
the close when Lear is happily restored to the throne.
It is an unhappy fact that this perversion in more or
less modified form held the stage for over a century. It
is interesting, however, to note that amid this flood of
adaptations such plays as *Hamlet* and *Othello* held the
stage in unchanged form, except for certain cuts. The
part of Hamlet in fact was one of the great rôles of
Betterton, the foremost actor of the time; "Betterton"
says Pepys "did the prince's part beyond imagination."
The romantic comedies of Shakespeare, alien as they
were to Restoration taste, were for the most part left
untouched and seldom performed.

It is easy to blame Restoration managers and playwrights for their mutilations of Shakespeare; it is only
fair however to recognize the difficulties under which
they labored. They appreciated the great dramatic
power of Shakespeare and attempted to keep his plays
alive upon the stage; yet they knew that in their original
form they would not be accepted by a contemporary
audience. Some remarks by Pepys are illuminating: *A
Midsummer Night's Dream* he called "the most insipid ridiculous play that ever I saw in my life"; *Twelfth Night*

is "a silly play," "one of the weakest that ever I saw";
even *Othello* when compared with the new *Adventures
of Five Hours* was but "a mean thing." If Shakespeare's plays were to draw, they must be purged of
their Elizabethan extravagance of speech; their lack of
decorum and disregard of the unities must be remedied,
and they must be equipped with spectacle and "divertissement." They were acted at least; our age which
reverences the text of Shakespeare sees him all too seldom on the stage.

A change for the better begins to appear about the
middle of the eighteenth century. One by one such
romantic comedies as *Much Ado, As You Like It,* and
Twelfth Night came back to the stage. Macklin in 1741
won fame as "the Jew that Shakespeare drew" by
acting the *Merchant of Venice* in its original form
instead of Lansdowne's travesty, 1701, of that play.

David Garrick, perhaps the greatest of all English
actors, was an enthusiastic admirer of Shakespeare. His
London début, 1741, was in the part of Richard III, and
in the thirty-five years of his stage career he played in
or produced no less than twenty-four of Shakespeare's
plays in which he himself acted seventeen characters.
He was especially successful as Hamlet, as Romeo and
as Lear, but he was also a brilliant comedian; Benedick
in *Much Ado* was one of his favorite parts. Contemporary witnesses praise Garrick for the versatility and the
vigor of his acting. He discarded the traditional stately
declamation of blank verse, and substituted for it a
realistic delivery which rose to passionate heights and
fell to colloquial discourse in accordance with the significance of the text. He began the work of restoring true
Shakespearean versions to the stage; he cleared *Macbeth*
of most of Davenant's additions, and removed much of
Tate's rubbish from *King Lear*. He was not so far in

advance of his age as to discard these traditional versions altogether and he took an actor-manager's liberties
with *Romeo and Juliet* and with *Hamlet*. In the former
he altered the last scene by having Juliet awake before
her lover dies and working up a passionate parting
scene. It was immensely successful on the stage and
persisted well into the next century; in fact it is still
retained in the operatic version of this play. His alteration of *Hamlet* was severely criticized by contemporaries
and by later writers who had never read it. As a matter
of fact it consisted mainly in omitting the Gravediggers'
scene and the rôle of Osric, both of which had become
in the passage of time almost farcical bits of acting. A
unique printed copy of Garrick's version preserved at
the Folger Library shows that he restored many lines
that earlier versions had dropped and added only enough
of his own to fill up the gaps his cut had made. In fact
Garrick deserves real praise for refraining on the whole
to blend new and alien matter with the text of Shakespeare; nothing that he did compares with the enormity
of Tate's adulteration of *King Lear*. Some of Garrick's
arrangements of Shakespeare held the stage for many
years; his *Catherine and Petruchio,* a genially farcical
adaptation of the *Taming of the Shrew,* lingered on till
near the end of the last century. Garrick's brilliant
career as actor, producer and adapter of Shakespeare is
a milestone in the long journey back to the stage presentation of the plays as Shakespeare wrote them, a
journey not yet wholly accomplished; Cibber's travesty
of *Richard III* may still be seen upon the boards.

The age of Kemble follows close on that of Garrick
and while Kemble as an actor was hardly comparable in
range and power with his predecessor, yet as actor-manager and producer he probably did more for Shakespeare
on the stage than any one either before or after him.

Born in 1757 of a theatrical family he was acting at
nineteen, made his début at Drury Lane as Hamlet in
1783 and five years later became manager of that great
theatre. In 1803 he transferred his allegiance to the
rival house, Covent Garden, which he controlled until
his retirement in 1817. Kemble was a devoted lover of
Shakespeare. Unlike Garrick he rejected the neo-classic
drama of the day and bent every effort to restoring
Shakespeare to the stage. He produced at one time or
another some twenty-five of his plays, many of which
had not been acted for years. He was not content simply
to revive old versions of the plays, but himself worked
over and produced an acting version of each text. He
would hardly be regarded as a purist to-day; he retained
much of Tate in his *Lear* and actually introduced passages from Dryden's *All for Love* into his production of
Antony and Cleopatra. Yet on the whole his influence
in purifying the acting versions was for good, and no
manager before him paid such careful attention to the
setting and costuming of the plays, Garrick had acted
Macbeth in the uniform of a British officer and Hamlet
in a costume closely resembling that of an eighteenth-
century clergyman. Kemble was among the first to make
some attempt at historical accuracy both in scenery and
costume.

He was aided throughout his life by his great sister
Sarah, better known as Mrs. Siddons, perhaps the most
famous actress, at least of tragic parts, that ever trod
the English stage. She and her brother were supreme in
such rôles as Macbeth and his wife, Coriolanus and
Volumnia. Mrs. Siddons was the first actress to discard
the fashionable hoops and nodding feathers worn by
stage heroines of the eighteenth century and to model
her costume, especially in classic plays, upon the dra-
pery of antique sculpture.

The genius, combined with the dignity and unblemished character of the Kembles, brother and sister, especially remarkable in the licentious days of the Regency, gave to actors and the stage a position and a recognition unknown since Shakespeare's own day. Their stage career coincides with the period of the romantic critics and both together gave new life to Shakespeare's works. After Coleridge and Hazlitt, after Kemble and Mrs. Siddons, there was no longer a danger that Shakespeare should be considered an "irregular" genius or that his dramas should lie at the mercy of any audacious playwright who aspired to better them.

Edmund Kean, 1787-1833, embodied in his acting the new romantic spirit of the age. He was supreme in passionate and tragic parts; on the stage what Byron was in poetry. To see him act was, Coleridge said: "to read Shakespeare by flashes of lightning." He made his début in 1814 as Shylock and for a brief period the rivalry between him and Kemble ran high until Kean's fervor and intensity eclipsed the somewhat formal and measured inpersonations of his predecessor. Contemporary testimony is unanimous as to the overpowering effect of his acting in such rôles as Shylock, Richard, and Massenger's Sir Giles. Unlike Kemble, he was never a manager or producer. Apart from his acting which, undoubtedly, awoke a new and lively interest in stage performances of Shakespeare, his one great service was in restoring to the acting version the tragic close of *Lear*.

With the passing of the Kembles and of Kean a new era opens. The two great theatres, Drury Lane and Covent Garden, still held their monopoly of so-called legitimate drama. Both houses had been rebuilt and enlarged until the old effects obtained by the intimate relation between actor and audience had become impossible. They began, therefore, to resort to spectacle, to

stress the splendor of their presentations of Shakespeare, and to advertise the accuracy of their costuming
—Planche's costumes for the protagonists in *King John*
and *King Henry IV* were designed after the monumental
effigies of these monarchs. Producers halted the action
to introduce magnificent processions, crowding the stage
with hundreds of people against a scenic background
built up with scrupulous regard to historical accuracy.
All was in vain and by 1843 the failure of both theatres
to maintain their hold on the public led to the abrogation of their long monopoly of presenting the plays of
Shakespeare.

A word must be said in passing, however, on the work
of the actor-manager, Macready, at Covent Garden,
1837-39, and at Drury Lane, 1841-43. A hard-working
and scrupulous producer rather than an actor of genius,
Macready did much to purify the text of the stage versions. Among other changes he finally purged *Lear* of
the Edgar-Cordelia rubbish which even Kean had left
untouched and brought back the character of the Fool,
unseen on the stage since the first performance of Tate's
version. Strangely enough he cast a girl of his company
for this rôle. Macready was, perhaps, the first manager
to institute the system of special productions of Shakespeare's plays, redecorating and recasting a pair of them
each season and relegating others to so-called "stock"
performances. His refusal to allow long-continued runs
to these productions was probably responsible for his
financial failure. He came to realize, as a later bankrupt
manager declared, that "Shakespeare spelled ruin."

With the abrogation of the old patent theatre monopoly a host of new and smaller theatres opened their
doors to Shakespeare. A system of visiting "stars"
sprang up, distinguished actors, like Macready himself,
playing leading parts in various theatres supported as

best they could be, by the regular company of the theatre where they played. Two tendencies, however, were strongly marked.

The most interesting of these was that initiated by Samuel Phelps, once an understudy of Macready, who in 1844 took over what was then the little suburban theatre of Sadler's Wells and for nearly twenty years, until 1862, presented there a succession of Shakespearean performances such as had not been seen since the closing of the Globe and the Blackfriars. During his régime he produced all but six of Shakespeare's plays, and four of these, *Titus* and the three parts of *King Henry VI* were of doubtful authenticity. To these performances he invited a public at what seems to-day incredibly low prices, one shilling for the pit and sixpence for a gallery seat. The long and on the whole successful career of Phelps was rendered possible by his stern discouragement of extravagance in costuming and scenery, by his rigorous training of a small low-salaried stock company, and by his confident reliance on the power of the plays themselves to pack his house. Contemporary criticism of his productions stresses the purity of his texts—he assigned the rôle of Lear's Fool to a man, not a girl as Macready had done, and replaced the Garrick version of *Romeo and Juliet* by Shakespeare's own— and the harmonious effect of the whole performance. Phelps founded a tradition which continues to this day in London where, across the Thames, at the "Old Vic" one may still see the plays of Shakespeare presented by a well-trained stock company, adequate and interesting presentations, too, although undistinguished by the acting of famous "stars" or a background of magnificent scenery. And the "Old Vic" still maintains the Phelps' tradition of popular prices.

The other tendency may be briefly characterized as

one that preferred pageant to poetry. It found its full expression at the Princess's under the direction of Charles Kean, son of the great actor, for about ten years from 1850. Kean continued and exaggerated the methods of Kemble and Macready; he stressed spectacle and ruthlessly cut and re-arranged the scenes of Shakespeare's plays to fit them into the rigid framework of scenery. Lavish expenditure on productions was combined with loudly proclaimed archæological accuracy of costuming and scenery; picturesque tableaux and processions were introduced wherever possible; in short, Kean attempted not without success to turn the auditors of Shakespeare's poetic drama into spectators of his picturization of Shakespeare's plays. He started the system of long runs; his *Midsummer Night's Dream* ran for one hundred and fifty performances; his spectacular *Richard II* for eighty-five. Kean's principles of production were the direct forerunner of those of Irving and Beerbohm Tree.

Irving's brilliant career as actor-manager at the Lyceum, 1878-98, marks a further development of the system of spectacular production combined with the long run. His *Merchant of Venice* ran for two hundred and fifty consecutive performances; his magnificent pageant of *Henry VIII* for over two hundred. He secured the assistance of such famous painters as Ford Madox Brown and Alma Tadema in his productions of *Lear* and *Cymbeline*. He always asserted his devotion to Shakespeare, and as a matter of fact kept his stage versions fairly free from traditional adulteration, but on the other hand he cut the text at will and shifted scenes about to correspond with the elaborate scenic effects. Irving was not an actor of genius, but he was an incomparable manager and had the happy faculty of assembling and training a body of actors equipped as none

has been since his day in acting Shakespearean parts
and giving to Shakespearean verse its full significance
and musical value. Foremost of these was the lovely
and talented Ellen Terry, long Irving's running-mate,
playing Portia to his Shylock—probably his best Shakespearean rôle—and Beatrice to his Benedick.

Irving was at his best in so-called "character" parts;
he was a comparative failure as Hamlet, Macbeth, and
Othello. Perhaps for this reason he often turned aside
from Shakespeare to produce such spectacular plays as
Wills's adaptation of *Faust.* It is interesting to note that
during the first ten years of his management of the
Lyceum he produced only six of Shakespeare's plays.

Whatever fault may be found with Irving's program
it is not to be denied that he produced Shakespeare, at
least in certain plays, with an altogether unprecedented
splendor. His productions became a fashionable rage
in England and in America as well, on his repeated visits
to this country. He was honored as no actor before him
had ever been with the dignity of knighthood and from
1895 on appeared on the stage as Sir Henry. Yet the
tremendous expense of his productions tended to outrun
receipts and in 1898 he was forced to relinquish control
of the Lyceum.

Beerbohm Tree, 1853-1917, continued the work of
Irving. He became the manager of Her Majesty's Theatre in 1897 just as Irving was leaving the Lyceum and
until the outbreak of the World War produced there a
long succession of Shakespeare's plays. Less gifted as
an actor than Irving, he was equally successful as manager and producer. There was, however, nothing new
about his methods. He too engaged great artists to paint
his scenic backgrounds; built up elaborate stage-sets,
and re-arranged the action of the play to fit his scenery.
He was specially fond of spectacular processions and

tableaux, introducing into *King John,* for instance, a dumb-show of the granting of Magna Carta, an incident which Shakespeare for very good reasons (p. 135) had omitted from his chronicle play. Like Irving, Tree enjoyed a great popular reputation and like Irving he received the honor of knighthood; between them they had made it something more than merely respectable to perform the plays of Shakespeare.

With the turn of the century a reaction against this whole system of spectacular production set in. In 1900 F. R. Benson brought a repertoire troupe to the Lyceum and gave a long succession of Shakespeare's plays with weekly changes of the program, a decided innovation in the time of long runs. He actually produced an uncut *Hamlet* which took six hours or so to play, kindly allowing the audience an hour and a half's intermission for dinner, an experiment repeated in this country at the performances of two of O'Neill's long plays. Benson relied neither on spectacle nor on the drawing power of individual actors but on the plays themselves delivered so far as possible in their pristine purity. This principle governed the production of the Elizabethan Society directed by William Poel, which began to present the plays of Shakespeare and his contemporaries with the minimum of scenery on stages more or less resembling that of Shakespeare's theatre. Ben Greet carried a company of young and well-trained actors all over England and across the Atlantic, presenting in the main comedies, sometimes on quite bare stages, with no inconsiderable success. In the main, this principle, the play rather than the spectacle, the words of Shakespeare rather than the performance of a star, governs the annual presentations of the plays at the Stratford Shakespeare Festival.

This survey of Shakespeare on the stage has been necessarily confined to English productions. There have

been great American actors of Shakespeare, notably
Edwin Booth, whose Hamlet was a supreme rendition of
the rôle; but there have been few or no American actor-
managers to initiate and direct a program of Shakespearean performances. Augustin Daly's career as manager of Daly's Theatre in New York, 1879-99, almost
coterminous with that of Irving at the Lyceum, was
marked by a succession of brilliant performances of
Shakespearean comedies, *Taming of the Shrew, As You
like It,* and *Midsummer Night's Dream.* Daly was not
himself an actor, but he gathered and trained probably
the finest company ever assembled in America, including such favorites as Ada Rehan, Maude Adams, and
John Drew. There was nothing novel, however, about
Daly's productions; they were of the school of Irving
with perhaps less stress laid on scenery and more on
ensemble acting.

   Little can be said of Shakespearean production in the
period following the World War. The old spectacular
Irving-Tree tradition has gone by the board; occasional
revivals waver between a faint imitation of its glories
and a half-hearted attempt to introduce a simpler and
more realistic style. Neither in England nor America is
there to-day, with the possible exception of the Old Vic,
a theatre devoted primarily to the production of Shakespeare, nor an actor capable of rendering the greatest
comic and tragic Shakespearean characters. " 'Tis true,
'tis pity."

METRICAL STATISTICS

Iᴛ is improbable that the young student will be much interested in the statistics compiled by investigators of Shakespeare's verse. In accordance with precedent, however, a table of such statistics based upon the work of Fleay, Furnivall, and König is here presented. The student may be warned that the following figures are approximate rather than exact. Counts made by independent investigators differ according to the text used—the *Globe,* for instance, because of its format, gives many more lines of prose than the *Cambridge*—and according to the investigator's subjective interpretation of such phenomena as the "run-on" line and the double, or feminine ending.

In the main, however, the counts come fairly near agreement, and there is substantial concurrence of opinion as to their significance.

A few words in explanation of the following table may not be out of place. The first column shows the total number of lines in a play. It will be noticed that these vary greatly; the early farce, *Comedy of Errors,* shows the lowest figure; *Hamlet,* the largest. It is not likely that these figures represent the exact length of each play as produced on Shakespeare's stage. *Macbeth,* for example, the shortest play after the *Errors,* has been heavily cut in the one text that we have, and it is practically certain that a version of *Hamlet* containing nearly 4,000 lines was never played by Shakespeare's company.

TABLE OF METRICAL TESTS APPLIED TO SHAKESPEARE'S PLAYS

Name of Play	No. of Lines	Prose	Blank Verse	5-Foot Rhymes	% Run-on Lines	% Double Endings	% Speech Ending	No. Light & Weak Endings
L. L. L........	2789	1086	579	1028	18.4	7.7	10.0	3
Com. Er.......	1778	240	1150	380	12.9	16.6	0.6	0
Two Gent.	2294	409	1510	116	12.4	18.4	5.8	0
Tit. And	2523	43	2338	144	9.5	8.6	2.5	5
1 Hen. VI.....	2677	0	2379	314	10.4	8.2	0.5	4
2 Hen. VI.....	3162	448	2562	122	11.4	13.7	1.1	3
3 Hen. VI.....	2904	0	2749	155	9.5	13.7	0.9	3
Rich. III	3619	55	3374	170	13.1	19.5	2.9	4
R. & J.	3052	405	2111	486	14.2	8.2	14.9	7
Mids. Dream ..	2174	441	878	731	13.2	7.3	17.3	1
K. John	2570	0	2403	150	17.7	6.3	12.7	7
Rich. II	2756	0	2107	537	19.9	11.0	7.3	4
Mer. Ven.	2660	673	1896	93	21.5	17.6	22.2	7
Tam. Shrew ...	2649	516	1971	169	8.1	17.7	3.6	14
1 Hen. IV.....	3176	1464	1622	84	22.8	5.1	14.2	7
2 Hen. IV.....	3446	1860	1417	74	21.4	16.3	16.8	1
Much Ado	2826	2106	643	40	19.3	22.9	20.7	2
Hen. V	3380	1531	1678	101	21.8	20.5	18.3	2
Merry Wives ..	3018	2703	227	69	20.1	27.2	20.5	1
J. C.	2478	165	2241	34	19.3	19.7	20.3	10
A. Y. L. I.....	2857	1681	925	71	17.1	25.5	21.6	2
12th Night	2690	1741	763	120	14.7	25.6	36.3	4
T. & C........	3496	1186	2025	196	27.4	23.8	31.3	6
All's Well	2966	1453	1234	280	28.4	29.4	74.4	13
Hamlet	3931	1208	2490	81	23.1	22.6	51.6	8
Meas. Meas. ...	2821	1134	1574	73	23.0	26.1	51.4	7
Othello	3316	541	2672	86	19.5	28.1	41.4	2
K. Lear	3334	903	2238	74	29.3	28.5	60.9	6
Macbeth	2108	158	1588	118	26.6	26.3	77.2	23
A. & C........	3063	255	2761	42	43.3	26.5	77.5	99
Tim. of Ath....	2373	596	1560	184	32.5	24.7	62.8	30
Coriolanus	3410	829	2521	42	45.9	26.4	79.0	104
Pericles	2398	418	1436	225	18.2	20.2	71.0	82
Cymbeline	3339	638	2585	107	46.0	30.7	85.0	130
Wint. Tale	3075	844	1825	0	37.5	32.9	87.6	100
Tempest	2064	458	1458	2	41.5	35.4	84.5	67
Henry VIII ...	2822	67	2613	16	46.3	47.3	72.4	84

The second column shows the number of prose lines in a play. It will be seen at a glance that the number is low for the early comedies, except for the revised *Love's Labors Lost,* and early histories; that it increases with the comedies of the second period—*Merry Wives* is almost entirely in prose—and the contemporary histories—the high figures for *II King Henry IV* and *Much Ado* are due to the prominence of the rôles of Falstaff and Benedict and Beatrice in those plays, all of them prose speakers. It falls off considerably in the tragedies and tragi-comedies.

The third column shows the number of blank verse lines in a play, that is, the number of regular five-foot lines in the so-called iambic pentámetre. This number naturally varies with the amount of prose and of rhyme present in a play; compare, for example, the low figures for *Love's Labour's Lost* and *Merry Wives* with the high figure of *Anthony and Cleopatra,* where there is little prose and much less rhyme.

The fourth column shows the number of five-foot rhymed lines in a play; songs and four-foot lines, such as those of the speeches of the Witches in *Macbeth,* are excluded from this count. The figures vary greatly. On the whole, however, the early plays show a preponderance of rhyme, except for the early histories written under the influence of Marlowe, such as *King John* and *Richard III.* It is most marked in such lyrically poetic plays as *Romeo and Juliet, A Midsummer Night's Dream* and *Richard II.* The extraordinary number in *All's Well* indicates an early date of composition for that revised play. The excessive figures for *Timon* and *Pericles* are due to the inclusion in those plays of a large amount of non-Shakespearean verse containing much more prose and rhyme than was Shakespeare's custom at that date. In *Winter's Tale* there is no rhyme at all except in the

speech of Time as Chorus, and the *Tempest* has only
one pair of rhymed lines in the regular dialogue. It is
safe to say that there is a progressive abandonment of
rhyme, except as a lyrical decoration, as Shakespeare
becomes more and more a master of blank verse.

The fifth column shows the percentage of "run-on"
lines in the total number of blank verse lines in a play.
A "run-on" line is one where both sense and voice are
carried forward without pause into the line that follows.
It is the opposite of the so-called "end-stopped" line.

Thus in such a passage as:

> I am yet
> Unknown to woman, never was foresworn,

The first line is "run-on," the second "end-stopped." A
"stop" is not always indicated by punctuation as here.
Whenever the sense calls for a pause on the last word
of the line, that line is "end-stopped." Naturally the
subjective element comes into play here; a pause seems
necessary to one reader and not to another. This phenomenon, the running on of one line into another, is a
device of Shakespeare's for breaking up the deadly
monotony of the old-fashioned blank verse composed
line by line as a bricklayer imposes one brick upon
another. Even Marlowe, greatest of all the early poet-
playwrights, composed in the main in this fashion, and
those plays of Shakespeare's written under Marlowe's
influence show a small percentage of "run-on" lines as
compared with end-stopped: A good example of their
style is seen in the opening soliloquy of *Richard III,*
where in forty lines there is not a single clear example
of a "run-on." With this compare a speech by Prospero
(*Tempest* V: 33-50), where in seventeen lines there are
about a dozen which might well be counted as "run-on."
A glance at the table will show how this practice in-

creased with Shakespeare until, in his latest plays from *Macbeth* on, over a third of the lines are "run-on."

The sixth column shows the percentage of the double, or feminine ending. A double ending is one where the line instead of closing with the stressed tenth syllable adds an unstressed one. Thus in such a trio of lines as:

> Is this a dagger that I see before me,
> The handle toward my hand? Come, let me
> clutch thee.
> I have thee not, and yet I see thee still.

The first two have the double ending, the last the final stressed syllable. The use of the double ending is another device to vary the monotony of the regular blank verse line; a judicious blend of double endings gives great variety and charm to the verse. There is a definite, though by no means regular, increase in the percentage of double endings from the early to the late plays. Such a low figure, 7.3, in *A Midsummer Night's Dream* is due to the prevalence of rhyme in that play, since double rhymes are comparatively rare in English. In the tragi-comedies the proportion is about one in three. The excessive figure, 47.3, for *Henry VIII* is due to the amount of verse in that play by Fletcher, for the use of the double-ending became a positive mannerism with that author.

The seventh column shows the percentage of the so-called "speech-ending." Earlier writers of blank verse plays, and Shakespeare in his earlier work, used to make each speech end at the close of a line and begin the next speech by another speaker with a new line. As Shakespeare drew further away from the conventional manner of composition, the line-by-line method, he adopted the device of ending a speech midway in a line and completing the line by the first words of the next speaker. This device tended to give a greater air of realism to the spoken dialogue. A good example appears in *Macbeth* V, iv, a short scene of twenty-one lines where every speech ends in the middle of a line. The table shows Shakespeare's progressive employment of this device. The early *Errors* has only six per cent; in the late tragi-comedies the vast majority of speeches are broken in this fashion.

The last column shows the number of light and weak endings in each play. A light-ending is one where an unstressed word, usually a monosyllable, takes the place of the stressed syllable which closes the normal line. Pronouns, auxiliaries, forms of "to be," and a few others constitute the light-endings. Thus in

> If I say sooth, I must report they were
> As cannons overcharged with double cracks.

The first line has a light-ending; the second is normal. The weak ending is a heightening, so to speak, of the light. The last word in the line in this case is so insignificant as to force the running on of the voice into the next line. In this group we find prepositions and conjunctions; *at, in, to, and, if, or,* etc. Thus in

> He hath been in unusual pleasure and
> Sent forth great largesse to your offices.

The first line has a weak ending, the second a normal ending, the stress falling on the tenth syllable.

The trick of light and weak endings, if we may call it so, is a device employed to force *enjambment,* or the running on of line to line. As one might expect, the device is progressively employed. The *Errors* shows no instance of either light or weak endings; light-endings appear for the first time in large numbers in *Macbeth,* many weak endings first in *Anthony and Cleopatra.*

So marked is the increase in his work from about 1606 that this feature has been used to date his latest plays; no play containing over twenty of such endings can well have been written before that time. The comparatively small number in *Timon* is due to the large amount of un-Shakespearean matter in that play.

I have spoken several times in the above paragraphs of a metrical phenomenon as a device employed by Shakespeare. This does not imply that he made a conscious use of any or all of these devices; there is no reason to suppose that he determined at any time to employ a greater proportion of double endings or of "run-on" lines. What happened was that, possibly without his being fully aware of it, he moved steadily in his composition of blank verse in his plays from the rigid regular form of his predecessors to a free and far more varied form. The first was well suited to declamation; we can imagine it being spouted by Alleyn in *Tamburlaine* or Burbage in *Richard III*. The latter was better suited to inter-action of characters upon the stage. We may perhaps suppose that Shakespeare's progress toward freedom corresponded with a movement of his company away from declamation to the audience and toward team-play among themselves. Instead of ranting they came to speak the lines "trippingly on the tongue."

From the point of view of metrical characteristics, Shakespeare's work falls into four periods, which do not, however, correspond exactly with the four periods of his development as a dramatist. The first of these, extending to about 1594,[1] is called by D. L. Chambers, upon whose excellent study *The Metre of Macbeth* I have drawn largely in this brief survey, the *Vanity of Rhyme*.

---

[1] The dates in this paragraph are only approximate; the periods are not sharply divided, but melt into each other. *Macbeth,* for example, is a link between the third and fourth periods.

It includes such plays as *Love's Labour's Lost, A Midsummer Night's Dream, Romeo and Juliet,* and *Richard II.* Early unrhymed plays, such as *Richard III* and *Titus,* also belong here. The second period, *The Balance of Power,* 1594-1600, shows less rhyme, more prose, some increase of double endings and of "run-on" lines. Such plays as *Merchant of Venice, King Henry IV, King Henry V,* and *Julius Cæsar,* and the joyous comedies, belong here. In this period we find "the most even and easy balance of thought and metre." The third period, the *Discordant Weight of Thought,* 1600-1606, shows a still further departure from the normal line; the content of his thought begins to outweigh the poet's facility of expression and we find him breaking up the line, cutting speeches short in mid line, using short and broken lines. At his best in this period, Shakespeare rises to his highest pitch of poetic dramatic expression, but sometimes at the cost of ease and grace. The last period, 1607-1613, the *License of Weak Endings,* shows Shakespeare permitting himself a careless freedom unknown before. The sudden appearance of a host of light and weak endings, about the beginning of the period, seems to mark an almost deliberate attempt to shatter the old norm of the line. At times, especially in passages where there is nothing to fire the poet's imagination, the verse is hardly distinguishable from prose. On the other hand, when Shakespeare catches fire in this period there is nothing in his earlier work quite comparable to the "happy valiancy" of *Antony and Cleopatra* or the grave beauty of the *Tempest.*

CHRONOLOGICAL TABLE

The dates assigned to the plays in the following table are approximate dates of first production. In the main the dates assigned by Chambers (*Elizabethan Stage,* Vol. 3) have been accepted.

The dates of the other literary works, books not plays, are those of publication.

In the dating of Shakespeare's plays the earlier of two possible years is given. Thus a play dating 1594-95 is entered in 1594. If attempts to date a play range over three years the middle date is given here. Thus a play dating 1595-97 is entered under 1596.

Historical Events	Life and Work of Shakespeare	Works of Other Authors
1553. Lyly born (between Oct., 1553 and Jan. 1554.)		
1558. Accession of Elizabeth. Kyd born. Greene born.		
1562.		Norton and Sackville, *Gorboduc.* Brooke, *Romeus and Juliet.*
1564. Marlowe born.	Shakespeare born.	
1566.		Gascoigne, *Supposes.* Painter, *Palace of Pleasure.*
1567.		*Gismond of Salerne.*
1568. First recorded appearance of professional actors at Stratford.		
1572. Massacre of St. Bartholomew.		
1575. Festivities at Kenilworth.		
1576. Erection of first permanent playhouse, Burbage's The Theatre.		
1577. Drake begins circumnavigation of the globe; completed 1580.		
1578.		Holinshed, *Chronicles of England, Scotland, and Ireland.* Lyly, *Euphues, the Anatomy of Wit,* 1578-79. Whetstone, *Promos and Cassandra.*
1579.		North's translation of Plutarch, *The Shepheardes Calendar.*
1580.		Montaigne, *Essais.*
1581.		*Tenne Tragedies* of Seneca.

Historical Events	Life and Work of Shakespeare	Works of Other Authors
1582.	Shakespeare's marriage.	
1583. Queen's Company formed.	Susanna Shakespeare born.	
1584.		Peele, *Araygnement of Paris.* Kyd, *The Spanish Tragedie.*
1585.	Shakespeare's twins, Hamnet and Judith, born.	
1586. Death of Phillip Sidney. Star Chamber decree for licensing of the press.		
1587. Execution of Mary Queen of Scots.		Marlowe, *Tamburlaine.*
1588. Defeat of the Spanish Armada. Robert, Earl of Leicester, died. Principal actors of Lord Leicester's Company join Lord Strange's men.	Shakespeare probably in London.	*The Famous Victories of Henry the Fifth. The Troublesome Raigne of John, King of England.* Marlowe, *Dr. Faustus.* Greene, *Pandosto.* Lyly, *Endimion.*
1589.		Greene, *Friar Bacon and Friar Bungay.* Hakluyt, *Voyages.* Marlowe, *The Jew of Malta.*
1590.	*Comedy of Errors.*	Lodge, *Rosalynde.* Sidney, *Arcadia.* Spenser, *Faerie Queene* (Books I–III).
1591.	*Two Gentlemen of Verona.*	Sidney, *Astrophel and Stella.* Greene, *James IV.*
1592. Plague in London. Theatres closed for three months. Death of Greene.	*1, 2, 3 Henry VI.*	Greene, *Groatsworth of Wit.* Marlowe, *Edward II.*
1593. Plague closes theatres. Lord Strange's men become Earl of Derby's Men. Death of Marlowe.	*Venus and Adonis. Titus Andronicus. Love's Labour's Lost.*	*The True Chronicle History of King Leir.*

Historical Events	Life and Work of Shakespeare	Works of Other Authors
1594. Plague until summer. The Earl of Derby's Men become the Lord Chamberlain's Men. The Lord Chamberlain's Men at The Theatre; the Lord Admiral's Men at the Rose. Death of Kyd.	*Lucrece.* *Richard III.* Shakespeare member of Chamberlain's Company.	*Edward III.*
1595.	*A Midsummer Night's Dream.* *Richard II.*	Spenser, *Amoretti.* Sidney, *Defense of Poesy.*
1596. The Cadiz Expedition.	Shakespeare's father applies for grant of coat of arms. Hamnet Shakespeare dies. *Romeo and Juliet.* *Merchant of Venice.* *King John.*	Spenser, *Faerie Queene* (Books IV–VI).
1597. The Islands Voyage.	Shakespeare purchases New Place, Stratford. *1, 2 Henry IV.* *The Taming of the Shrew.*	Bacon, *Essays* (first version).
1598.	*Much Ado About Nothing.*	Chapman's Translation of the *Iliad* (seven books). Meres, *Palladis Tamia.* Jonson, *Every Man In His Humour.*
1599. Essex in Ireland. Death of Spenser. Lord Chamberlain's Men occupy The Globe.	*Henry V.* *Merry Wives of Windsor.* *Julius Caesar.*	*The Passionate Pilgrim.* Jonson, *Every Man Out of His Humour.*
1600. Alleyn builds Fortune Theatre. Children of Chapel begin playing at Blackfriars.	*As You Like It.* *Twelfth Night.* *Hamlet.*	
1601. Execution of Essex. The War of the Theatres.		Jonson, *The Poetaster.* *The Return from Parnassus*, part II.
1602.	*All's Well That Ends Well.* *Troilus and Cressida.*	

Historical Events	Life and Work of Shakespeare	Works of Other Authors
1603. Death of Queen Elizabeth. Accession of James I. The Lord Chamberlain's Men become the King's Majesty's Servants. Plague stops playing.		Florio's Translation of Montaigne's *Essays.* Jonson, *Sejanus.* Heywood, *Woman Killed with Kindness.*
1604. Theatres reopen in April. Treaty of Peace with Spain.	*Measure for Measure.* *Othello.*	
1605. Gunpowder Plot.	Shakespeare purchases certain fixed rents at Stratford. *King Lear.*	*Eastward Ho.* Bacon, *Advancement of Learning.*
1606. Statute forbidding the use of the name of the Deity on the stage.	*Timon of Athens.* *Macbeth.*	Jonson, *Volpone.*
1607. The bitter winter of 1607-8.	Susanna Shakespeare marries Dr. John Hall. *Antony and Cleopatra.* *Pericles, Prince of Tyre.*	Beaumont, *The Knight of the Burning Pestle.*
1608. Children of Blackfriars disbanded. Burbage leases the Blackfriars.	*Coriolanus.*	Fletcher, *The Faithful Shepherdess.*
1609. Wreck of The Sea Venture off the Bermudas.	*Cymbeline.* Shakespeare's *Sonnets* published.	Beaumont and Fletcher, *Philaster.* Dekker, *The Gull's Hornbook.*
1611.	*The Winter's Tale.* *The Tempest.*	Authorized version of the Bible. Chapmen completes translation of *Iliad.* Beaumont and Fletcher, *King and No King.*
1612. Death of Prince Henry.		Heywood, *Apology for Actors.* Webster, *The White Devil.*
1613. Marriage of Princess Elizabeth. Globe Theatre burnt.	Shakespeare purchases property in Blackfriars. *Henry VIII.* *The Two Noble Kinsmen.*	Webster, *The Duchess of Malfi.*

Historical Events	Life and Work of Shakespeare	Works of Other Authors
1614. Globe Theatre rebuilt.		
1616.	Judith Shakespeare marries. Death of Shakespeare.	
1619.		Pavier attempts a collection of Shakespeare's plays.
1623.	First Folio published.	

BIBLIOGRAPHY

THE following bibliography does not pretend to be exhaustive. It merely suggests a few books, carefully selected, that may prove useful and interesting to the student in connection with the topics discussed in this introduction.

BIOGRAPHY

Adams, J. Q., *A Life of William Shakespeare,* 1923. The standard one volume biography, containing all that is known about the poet.

Brown, Ivor, *Shakespeare,* 1949. One of the most readable of the recent books on Shakespeare. It stresses his personality and power of poetic expression.

Chute, Marchette, *Shakespeare of London,* 1949. A useful and reliable book on Shakespeare's life and career in London.

Chambers, E. K., *William Shakespeare, A Study of Facts and Problems,* 2 vols., 1930. The fullest biography, a book for reference rather than for reading. The second volume reprints important documents.

Dowden, Edward, *Shakespeare, His Mind and Art,* 1875. Old fashioned but still more readable and useful than many modern studies.

Holzknecht, Karl J., *The Backgrounds of Shakespeare's Plays,* 1950. A combination biography and critical handbook to Shakespeare's dramatic writings. Many illustrations.

Raleigh, Walter, *Shakespeare (English Men of Letters),* 1907. Critical rather than biographical, and very good reading.

Wilson, J. Dover, *The Essential Shakespeare,* 1932.

254

A stimulating imaginative reconstruction of Shakespeare's life, particularly interesting in connection with
his youth and his London associations.

CRITICISM

Bradley, A. C., *Oxford Lectures on Poetry,* 1909;
Shakespearean Tragedy, 1904. After half a century
Bradley's criticism of the tragedies is still the best of
its kind. The *Oxford Lectures* contains the criticism of
Antony and Cleopatra, and other Shakespearean studies.

Clemen, W. H., *The Development of Shakespeare's
Imagery,* 1951. A study of the development, forms, and
functions of Shakespeare's images. The most reward-
ing book of its kind.

Granville-Barker, H., *Prefaces to Shakespeare,* 2 vols.,
1946–7. A distinguished work, written from the point of
view of a man thoroughly conversant with the theatre.

Lawrence, W. W., *Shakespeare's Problem Comedies,*
1931. The best study of the so-called "bitter comedies."

Palmer, John, *The Political Characters of Shake-
peare,* 1945. Demonstrates the astuteness of Shakespeare's political observations.

Parrott, T. M., *Shakespearean Comedy,* 1949. A survey of all the plays with a view to determine the degree
and quality of Shakespeare's instinctive genius for
comedy.

Parrott, T. M., and Ball, R. H., *A Short View of
Elizathan Drama,* 1943. Perhaps the most useful of the
shorter histories.

Ralli, A., *A History of Shakespearian Criticism,* 2
vols., 1932. A useful summary with quotations and
paraphrases of Shakespearean criticism from the beginning to the present.

Schuecking, L. L., *Character Problems in Shakespeare's Plays,* 1922. Criticism on historical principles

which attempts to avoid the vagaries of the more personal approach to Shakespeare.

Smart, J. S., *Shakespeare, Truth and Tradition,* 1928. A valuable and suggestive work.

Spencer, Theodore, *Shakespeare and the Nature of Man,* 1942. A poet and scholar's examination of Shakespeare's idea of man's place in the universe.

Spurgeon, Caroline F. E., *Shakespeare's Imagery,* 1936. A statistical study of Shakespeare's images which throws light on Shakespeare's personality and thought, and on the characters and themes of his plays.

Stauffer, D. A., *Shakespeare's World of Images,* 1949. A readable and useful book which traces the evolution of Shakespeare as an ethical playwright and poet.

Stoll, E. E., *Othello: An Historical and Comparative Study,* 1915; *Poets and Playwrights,* 1930; *Shakespeare Studies,* 1927. Stoll's many books are the most distinguished American expression of the school of criticism represented in Europe by Schuecking.

Webster, Margaret, *Shakespeare Without Tears,* 1942. A stimulating work from the point of view of an actress and producer.

THE ELIZABETHAN BACKGROUND

Fripp, E. I., *Shakespeare's Stratford,* 1928. Valuable and interesting notes by a Stratford antiquarian.

Harrison, G. B., *An Elizabethan Journal, 1591–1594,* 1928; *A Second Elizabethan Journal, 1595–1598,* 1931; *A Last Elizabethan Journal, 1599–1605,* 1933. Anthologies of selections from Elizabethan prose and verse describing contemporary manners.

Lee, S., *Stratford-on-Avon,* 1885, 1906. The most interesting historical account of Shakespeare's birthplace.

Madden, D. H., *The Diary of Master William Silence,* 1897. The best account of Elizabethan field sports. Interesting in connection with Shakespeare's youth at Stratford.

Shakespeare's England, by various hands, 2 vols., 1916. A series of essays giving the fullest account of town and country life in Shakespeare's day.

Wright, L. B., *Middle-Class Culture in Elizabethan England,* 1935. An informative study of a part of Elizabethan life too often ignored by students of Shakespeare.

GENERAL

Brooke, C. F. T., *The Shakespeare Apocrypha,* 1908. A collection of the plays once attributed to Shakespeare.

Ebisch, Walter, and Schuecking, L. L., *A Shakespeare Bibliography,* 1931; *Supplement for the years 1930–1935,* 1937. The most satisfactory of the many books of this sort.

McKerrow, R. B., *The Treatment of Shakespeare's Text by His Earlier Editors,* 1933. An interesting essay and an accurate study of the subject.

Onions, C. T., *The Oxford Shakespeare Glossary,* revised edition, 1919. Invaluable for the student of Shakespeare's language.

Pollard, A. W., *Shakespeare's Folios and Quartos,* 1909; *Shakespeare's Fight with the Pirates,* 1917; *A Census of Shakespeare's Plays in Quarto, 1594–1709* (with H. C. Bartlett) 1916. These books laid the foundation of the modern bibliographical and textual study of Shakespeare.

POEMS AND SONNETS

Brooke, C. F. T., *Shakespeare's Sonnets,* 1936. The best re-arrangement of the sonnets. The notes are full and the introductory essay is always aware of the poetry of the sonnets.

Hubler, Edward, *The Sense of Shakespeare's Sonnets,* 1952. An attempt to find out what the sonnets mean, and through the meaning to discover the mind and attitudes of their author.

Rollins, H. E., *The Poems,* New Variorum Edition, 1938; *The Sonnets,* New Variorum Edition, 2 vols., 1944. Excellent texts and thorough compilations of commentary. Useful works of impeccable scholarship.

THE THEATRE

Adams, J. C., *The Globe Playhouse,* 1943. The best description of the theatre where most of Shakespeare's plays were acted.

Baldwin, T. W., *The Organization and Personnel of the Shakespearean Company,* 1927. The standard book on the subject, difficult reading but invaluable for reference.

Bentley, G. E., *The Jacobean and Caroline Stage,* 2 vols., 1941. A continuation of the work begun by Chambers in his study of the Elizabethan Stage. An invaluable reference book.

Chambers, E. K., *The Elizabethan Stage,* 4 vols., 1923. A full account of Elizabethan theatres and of staging in Shakespeare's day. Useful bibliographies.

Harbage, Alfred, *Shakespeare's Audience,* 1941. An excellent book on the character and behavior of Shakespeare's audience.

Nungezer, Edwin, *A Dictionary of Actors . . . before 1642,* 1929.

Odell, G. C. D., *Shakespeare from Betterton to Irving,* 2 vols., 1920. Two and a half centuries of Shakespeare on the London stage. The best book of its kind. Delightful reading.

Sprague, A. C., *Shakespeare and the Actors, The Stage Business in His Plays, 1660–1905,* 1944.

Thorndike, A. H., *Shakespeare's Theatre,* 1916. Excellent one volume study of the Elizabethan theatre.

INDEX

A

Actor, not separated from audience, 87;
  relation to audience, 87
Actors, Elizabethan, 65 f.
Adams, Maud, 239
Addison, *Cato*, 218
Admiral's Company, 72
Adventures of Five Hours, 230
Æsop's Fables, 12
Alchemist, by Ben Jonson, 227
Alcove, the, in early theatre, 78
Aldgate district of London, 24
All's True (Henry VIII), 75, 102
All's Well that Ends Well, 46, 54, 124,
  150, 204, 24?; source of, 151
Alleyn, Edward, 42, 72, 93, 118
Alleyn, Giles, 48
Amphytrion, a Plautine play, 130
Anderson, Mary, 176
Angel, name for room in tavern, 28
Antony and Cleopatra, 85, 170, 171, 172,
  203, 204, 223, 232, 24?, 245, 247; poet-
  ry of, 169; source of, 168
Apollonius of Tyre, 130, 173
Arden, forest of, 5
Arden of Faversham, 104, 118
Arden, Edward, 8
Arden, Mary, 6; married to Shakespeare,
  8
Arden, Robert, 6, 8
Aristotle, 105
Armin, the actor, 70, 148, 160
Arnold, Matthew, 221
Art and Artifice in Shakespeare, *1933*,
  223
As You Like It, 49, 88, 120, 146, 149, 150,
  204, 230, 239; its charm, 148
Aside, the, 88
Aspley, publisher, 204
Aubrey, the antiquary, quoted, 20
Audience, delight in poetry, 98; escape
  from reality, 95; influence on Shake-
  speare, 99; love of conceits, 96; love of
  jests, 96; patriotic, 94
Autograph signatures, 61

B

Bacon, Francis, member of Grays Inn, 31
Balance of Power, 1594–1600, 246
Barry, famous actress, 228
Beaumont, 28, 31, 59, 180, 227, 228
Beauty, romantic passion for, 110
Beeston, Christopher, in Shakespeare's
  company, 20

Beeston, William, tradition from, 20
Benson, F. R., Company at Lyceum, 238
Bestraffte Brudermord, Der (Fratricide
  Punished), 158
Betterton, Eighteenth Century actor,
  229
Betterton, Mrs., famous actress, 228
Bible, the only book studied, 13
Bibliography, 254–258
Bishopsgate, 24
Blackfriars Theatre, 34, 44, 51, 59, 61, 69,
  71, 81, 175, 180, 227, 235
Blount, publisher, 203, 205
Boar's Head Tavern, 30
Booth, Edwin, American actor, 213, 239
Boswell, James, editor of *Third Vario-
  rum*, 212
Bracegirdle, actress, 228
Bradley, *Shakespearean Tragedy*, 223
British Museum, 25
Brooke, Arthur, his long poem source for
  Shakespeare, 138
Brown, Ford Madox, painter, 236
Buc, Sir George, Master of Revels, 175
Burbage, James, 42, 43, 47, 51, 67, 68, 76
Burbage, Richard, 47, 51, 55, 56, 59, 61,
  63, 93, 136, 165
Butter, publisher, 203
Byron, Lord, 233

C

Cambridge, 3, 23, 29, 31
Cambridge Text, edited by W. A. Neil-
  son, 213
Cambridge Shakespeare, edited by Clark,
  Glover, and Wright, 212, 240
Cambyses, 93, 103, 104
Capell, edition of Shakespeare, 212
Carey, George, patron, 72
Carey, Henry, Queen Elizabeth's cousin,
  patron, 72
Catharine and Petruchio, by Garrick, 231
Chamberlain, Lord, Company of, 42, 47,
  53, 226
Chambers, D. L., *Study of Metre of Mac-
  beth*, 245
Chapman, dramatist, 196; his *Conspir-
  acy of Byron*, 59; *the Gentleman Usher*,
  ca. 1062, 60
Characters of Shakespeare's Plays, 221
Charing Cross, 24
Charlecote, country house, 16
Charles II, 228
Change of place indicated in plays, 83

Chaucer, 139; *Knight's Tale*, source of *The Two Noble Kinsmen*, 181; *Legend of Good Women*, 187
Chettle, Henry, friend of Greene's, 39
Children of the Chapel, 34, 58, 71; rise in favor, 51
Chronicle play, English, 104
Chronological Table, 248–253
Cibber, Colley revision of, 136
Cicero, 12
Classical models, influence of, 104, 105; used by university playwrights, 113
Clement's Staples, 31
Clopton, Hugh, citizen of Stratford, 3, 44
Cobber, Travesty of *Richard III*, 231
Cœur de Leon, Richard, 5
Coleridge, Samuel Taylor, 180, 219, 221, 233; his criticism, 219
Colet, Latin Grammar of, 12
Collier, J. P., edition by, 212
Collins, Francis, Shakespeare's lawyer, 63
Comedy, its language, 103; construction of, 105
Comedy of Errors, The, 14, 32, 35, 45, 123, 129, 131, 132, 166, 204, 240, 245; founded on Plautus, 129; ingenious construction of, 131
Company of actors, development of, 66; classes in, 67; expense of, 68
Condell, of Shakespeare's company, 59, 63, 65, 164, 203, 205
Constable, sonnet-sequence of, 191
Contention, 202, 204
Coombe, John, friend of Shakespeare's, 3
Coombe, Tomas, friend of Shakespeare, 56
Coriolanus, 123, 124, 125, 126, 172, 204; characteristics of, 170; source of, 170; British Academy, 1912, 223
Coryat, famous traveler, 74
Covent Garden, 232, 233, 234
Coventry, 5, 16, 101
Crosskeys Tavern, 30
Cruelty of a Step-Mother, The, 104
Curtain, the front, 83
Cymbeline, 14, 76, 78, 84, 123, 126, 174, 175, 204, 227, 236; characteristics of, 174; source of, 174

D

Daly, Augustin, manager, 239
Daly's Theatre, 239
Daniel, Samuel, *Complaint of Rosamond*, 188; sonnet-sequence of, 191
Dark Lady, of the sonnets, 192, 193
Davenant, right to form company, 41, 228, 230; his *Macbeth*, 216
Decameron, a source for Shakespeare, 174
Dekker, Thomas, 29; *The Wonderful Year*, 55; *Shoemaker's Holiday*, 95
Derby's Men, Earl of, 72
Devil, tavern at Temple Bar, 28, 105

DeWitt, his sketch of the Swan Theatre, 74
Digges, L., elegy by, 205, 227
Discordant Weight of Thought, 1600–1606, 247
Dolphin, a room name in taverns, 28
Donne, John, 31
Dorastus and Fawnia, 175
Dowden, *Shakespeare—His Mind and Art*, 1875, 222
Drama, in tavern courtyards, 29–30; the new, 101
Drayton, Samuel, 62, 191
Drew, John, American actor, 239
Droeshout, famous Shakespeare portrait 205
"Drolls," 227
Drury Lane, 232, 233
Dryden, John, 208, 216, 217, 229; *All for Love*, 232
Dudley, Robert, Earl of Leicester, 66
Dunciad, The, 1728, 211

E

Eastward-Ho, 58
Edward I, 5
Edward II, 118, 137
Edward III, 2, 5, 183
Edward VI, 4, 11
Elizabeth, Queen, 8, 27, 63, 145, 182; fount of honor, 33; love of entertainments, 34; interest in theatre, 34; end of glorious period, 50; death of, 52, 226; death of, alluded to perhaps in sonnet, 192
Elizabethan Company, 69
Elizabethan drama, outgrowth of religious drama, 101
Elizabethan Society, 238
Elizabethan time, 214
Endimion, by Lyly, 114
Englishmen for My Money, 94
Enjambment, 247
Essay of Dramatick Poesie, by Dryden, 216
Essex, Earl of, 35, 92, 124; expedition to Ireland, 49; march to London, 50; beheaded, 50
Evans, manager, 51
Every Man, by Jonson, 51
Evidence for dates, metrical, 125
Euphues, by Lyly, 114

F

Faerie Queene, The, 118
Faust, adaptation of, by Wills, 237
Faustus, Dr., 9, 78, 118
Field, Richard, publisher, 21, 41, 184
First Part of the Contention, 127
Fitton, Mary, notion that she was Dark Lady, 193
Fleay, Shakespearean editor, 240

Fletcher, John, (*see* Beaumont and Fletcher), 28, 179, 180, 183, 227, 228; *The Two Noble Kinsmen*, 60

Folger Memorial Library, in Washington, D. C., 128, 203, 231

Fletcher, Lawrence, comedian, 53

Folio, The, first collected edition, 1623, 65, 122, 127, 128, 145, 153, 157, 162, 164, 166, 168, 170, 173, 174, 175, 177, 178, 180, 181, 193, 200, 201, 205, 206, 208, 212, 215; circumstances of printing, 202, 204; defects of, 206; second, 1632, 207; third, 1663, 207; fourth, 1685, 207, 208

Fortune Theatre, 74, 76

Friar Bacon and Friar Bungay, 115

From Henry V to Hamlet, criticism by Granville-Barker, 224

Furness, Howard, editor, 195, 213

Furnivall's Inn, 31

Furnivall, Dr., famous Shakespearean editor, 213, 240

G

"Gags," the, 88

Gallery, uses of, 79

Garrick, David, 147, 230, 231, 232

Gascoigne, produced *Jocasta*, 32; *The Supposes*, 144

Geoffrey of Monmouth, 162

Gesta Romanorum, 141

Gismond of Salerne, 32

Glaucus and Scylla, 186

Globe Theatre, 48, 49, 51, 53, 56, 58, 69, 81, 82, 91, 97, 99, 152, 175, 183, 203, 235; burning of, 61; rebuilt, 61

Globe, text of Shakespeare, 240

Golding, translation of Ovid, 185

Gorboduc, 32, 98, 108

Granville-Barker, 70, 224

Gray's Inn, 31, 129

Great Plague, 153

Greene, Robert, 37, 38, 43, 60, 109, 127; quoted, 38; influence of, 115; contribution to new comedy, 116; *James IV*, 139; *Pandosto*, 175

Greenwich, Queen's Court at, 22

Gresham, Sir Thomas, builder of The Royal Exchange, 23

Groatsworth of Wit bought with a Million of Repentance, by Greene, 38

"Groundlings," 76, 97

Guild, at Stratford, 4 f.

Guild of the Holy Cross, 2

Guild School, 11, 20

Guildhall, 7

H

Halliwell-Phillips, editor, 213

Hamlet, 14, 64, 78, 83, 86, 95, 118, 120, 156, 157, 158, 159, 160, 161, 167, 172, 198, 200, 206, 228, 229, 231, 238, 240

Hampton Court, residence of the King, 55

Harrison, Master, entry in Stationer's Register, 187

Harvey, Gabriel, quoted, 157

Hathaway, Anne, daughter of Richard, bride of Shakespeare, 17

Hazlitt, William, 219, 233; a practical critic of Shakespeare, 221

Heminge, of Shakespeare's Company, 48, 59, 63, 65, 164, 203, 205, 206, 227

Henley Street, in Stratford, 5, 10

Henry IV, 21, 28, 35, 45, 95, 124, 143, 145, 202, 206, 227, 228, 234, 242, 247; creation of Falstaff, 142

Henry V, 35, 49, 71, 86, 89, 95, 124, 125, 126, 127, 142, 144, 145, 146, 155, 198, 200, 202, 206, 247; creation of Falstaff, 142; development of this character by Shakespeare, 143

Henry VI, 38, 46, 123, 126, 127, 136, 202, 204, 235

Henry VIII, 102, 123, 125, 180, 183, 204, 236, 244; presentation of, 60; accepted as partly by Shakespeare, 178; theories as to, 179

Henslowe, owner of theatre, 68, 69, 71, 75, 128; *Titus and Ondronicus*, 128

Herald's Office, 8, 43

Herbert, Lord William, Lord Chamberlain, 193, 202

Hero and Leander, 118, 120

Heywood, Thomas, 196, 197; quoted; *Apology for Actors*, 47

"His Majesty's Players," 53

Holinshed, chronicle of, 166, 168, 174

Holland, Hugh, sonnet by, 205

Holy Trinity, Church of, 2

Horace, dicta of, 105

Horestes, 104

Howard, Lord Charles, 66, 229

I

Ibsen, plays for "picture-frame" stage, 73

Inns of Court, 30, 92, 105, 106, 152; influence of, 32

Irving, Henry, actor, 180, 236, 237, 238, 239

J

Jaggard, printer and publisher, 46, 203, 205, 206

James IV, 115

James, King, 67, 166; accession of, 53; assistance to Shakespeare, 35; love of theatre, 53

Jew of Malta, The, 118

Jocasta, by Gascoigne, 32

John, King, 45, 119, 122, 136, 204, 234, 238, 242

John, King, the Troublesome Reign of,
134; appeal to patriotism, 134; re-
writing of an old play, 134
Johnson, Dr. Samuel, 96, 180, 217, 218;
edition of Shakespeare, 211
Jonson, Ben, 5, 13, 28, 32, 51, 62, 77, 99,
196, 197, 200, 202, 205, 214; *Every
Man out of his Humour,* 49; *Sejanus,*
54; his *Bartholomew Fair,* 95; *Every
Man in* and *Every Man Out of His
Humour,* 146; *Every Man In,* 205;
Poetaster, 152; *Masque of Oberon,* 175
Judith, Shakespeare's daughter, mar-
riage of, 62, 63
Julius Cæsar, 125, 126, 155, 168, 172,
204, 227, 228, 247

K

Kean, Charles, 236
Kean, Edmund, actor, 222, 233
Kemble, John, actor, 231, 232, 233, 236
Kemp, actor, 42, 48, 70, 93,
Kenilworth, Queen Elizabeth at, 17
Killigrew, manager, 228
King's Men, 59, 157, 201, 203, 226, 227
Kinwelmersh, with Gascoigne, produces
Jocasta, 32
Kipling, Rudyard, suggestion of, 177
Knack to Know a Knave, A, 128
Knight, edition of Shakespeare, 212
Knight of the Burning Pestle, The, 75, 88
Koenig, a Shakespearean critic, 240
Kyd, Thomas, dramatist, 43, 104, 107,
109, 111, 120, 127, 158, 215; *Spanish
Tragedy,* 21; success of, 117; contribu-
tion of, 118

L

Lamb, Charles, 180, 219, 220, 221, 222
Langley, Francis, builder of the Swan
Theatre, 43
Lansdowne's travesty, 230
Law Against Lovers, The, 228
Lear, King, 54, 60, 70, 86, 97, 124, 160,
161, 162, 163, 164, 165, 172, 199, 200,
201, 202, 203, 206, 226, 229, 230, 231,
232, 233, 236
Lee, Sidney, biographer of Shakespeare,
213
Leir, King, the old play of, 162
License of Weak Endings, 1607–1613, 246
Lincoln's Inn, 31
Livy, his prose, as a source for Shake-
speare, 187
Locrine, spurious play, 207
Lodge, Thomas, *Rosalynde,* 148
London, 4, 19, 71, 104, 122, 127, 128,
129, 177, 185, 235; in Shakespeare's
day, 22; a city of churches, 25; addicted to pleasure, 27; taverns in, 27–
28; courtyard in taverns, 29; theatres
of, 29

London Bridge, 23
London Prodigal, The, 207
London Tower, the, 24, 55
Lord Leicester's Company, 71
Lord Strange's Men, 126
Love's Labours Lost, 12, 35, 45, 56, 71,
115, 129, 133, 147, 191, 196, 206, 226,
242, 247; a new type of comedy, 132
Love's labours wonne, 45, 156
Lover's Complaint, The, 189
Lucan, translated into English, 118
Lucian, *Timon, the Misanthrope,* 165
Lucrece, 21, 128, 134, 157, 184, 187, 189
Lucy, Sir Thomas, tradition concerning,
19
Ludgate district in London, 24
Lyceum Theatre, 236, 237, 239
Lyly, John, dramatist, 12, 21, 43, 106,
112, 113, 133, 186, 215; his notion of
high comedy, 114; popularity of, 114

M

Macbeth, 54, 60, 82, 85, 86, 95, 163, 164,
166, 167, 172, 204, 228, 230, 240, 242,
244, 245, 246; source of, 166
Macklin, actor, 230
Macready, actor, 234, 235, 236
Madden, *Diary of Master William Silence,* 16
Malone, edition of Shakespeare by,
(1790), 212
Marlborough, Duke of, knowledge of
history from Shakespeare, 95
Marlowe, Christopher, 9, 38, 43, 104,
109, 110, 111, 112, 117, 120, 122, 127,
135, 142, 150, 215; greatest of predecessors of Shakespeare, 118; contribution to Elizabethan tragedy, 119; *Jew
of Malta,* 141; *Hero and Leander,* 186
Marston, John, dramatist and satirist,
92, 196
Massacre at Paris, The, 118
Massinger, Philip, 196
Master of the Revels, 66, 69, 175, 196,
206
Measure for Measure, 54, 56, 125, 153,
159, 204, 228
Menaechmi of Plautus, 130
Merchant of Venice, The, 35, 45, 142, 150,
202, 206, 230, 236, 246; characteristics
of, 140; the creation of Shylock, 141
Meres, Francis, 124, 128, 144, 146, 150,
191, 196; *Palladis Tamia, Wits Treas-
ury,* 44
Mermaid tavern, 28, 99
Merry Wives of Windsor, The, 14, 35, 146,
198, 200, 202, 206, 226, 242; tradi-
tion of its origin, 145
Metrical statistics, 240 f.
Midas, play by Lyly, 114
Middle Temple, 30
Middleton, Thomas, dramatist, 29, 164,
166

Midsummer Night's Dream, 14, 45, 71, 83, 124, 140, 150, 202, 206, 227, 229, 236, 239, 242, 244, 247; complete success of, 139; contrasted with *Jew of Malta*, 141
Milton, John, 190, 193
Miracle plays, 101
Misfortunes of Arthur, The, 32, 107
Molière, plays for the "tennis-court" theatre, 73
Moorfields, suburb of London, 24
More, Sir Thomas, controversy over, 181, 183
Morgann, his famous essay, 1777, 219
Mother Bombie, by Lyly, 114
Much Ado About Nothing, 25, 35, 49, 83, 95, 146, 149, 150, 206, 227, 230, 242; characteristics of, 147
Munday, Anthony, author, 181
Murderous Michael, 104

N

Narrative in Elizabethan drama, 86
Nashe, Thomas, playwright, 38, 116
New Place, bought by Shakespeare, 8, 19, 44, 58
New Variorum, (*see* Variorum), Dr. Howard Furness, 195, 213
Newgate, district in London, 24
North, Sir Thomas, Plutarch's *Lives*, 1579, 124, 155, 168, 170
Norton, author of *Gorboduc*, 32
Novelle, Italian, 111

O

"Old Vic," 235, 239
O'Neill, Eugene, 195, 238
Othello, 54, 56, 60, 70, 78, 86, 160, 161, 162, 163, 167, 172, 174, 176, 200, 206, 218, 227, 228, 229, 230; contrasted with *Hamlet*, 159; characters in, 160; masterpiece of construction, 160
Ovid, 12, 118; *Amores*, 185; *Metamorphoses*, 185; *Fasti*, 187
Oxford, 3, 13, 23, 29, 31, 166
Oxford, edited by W. J. Craig, 213
Oxford Lectures on Poetry, 223

P

Painter, *Palace of Pleasure*, 151
Palladis Tamia, by Meres, 123
Passionate Pilgrim, The, 47
Paul's, St., Cathedral, 25, 71
Pavier, Thomas, issues plays in quarto form, 202, 203
Peele, George, dramatist, 34, 43, 109, 127, 128, 134
Pembroke, Philip, Shakespeare's patron, 35, 66, 127
Pembroke, William, Shakespeare's patron, 35
Pembroke, his company, 40, 198

Pepys, Samuel, 228, 229, 235
Pericles Prince of Tyre, 60, 89, 124, 172, 173, 200, 201, 202, 203, 204, 205, 207, 209, 212
Philaster, by Beaumont and Fletcher, 174
Phillips, of Shakespeare's Company, 43, 48
Phœnissœ, of Euripides, 32
Plautus, plays of, 12, 105, 114, 131
Play publishing in Shakespeare's day, 195 f.
Plays, in tables showing dates of quarto editions, 201
Plutarch, (*see* North), 13, 139; *Lives*, Sir Thomas North's translation, 155; *Life of Antony*, 165, 168
Poel, William, director of Elizabeth Society, 238
Poems Written by Wil. Shakespeare Gent., 190
Poetaster, by Jonson, 51
Pope, Alexander, 43, 48, 211, 217, 218; edition of Shakespeare, 209
Promos and Cassandra, 153
Puritan, The, 207

Q

Quiney, Thomas, married to Judith Shakespeare, 62

R

Raleigh, Sir Walter, 118, 153
Ralph Roister Doister, 106
Rape of Lucrece, success of, 42
Ravishment of Lucrece, The, 187
Realism, demand for, 101; homely, of Elizabethan drama, 102
Red Bull, London tavern, 30, 227
Register, The Stationer's, 187, 199
Rehan, Ada, American actress, 239
Renaissance, 142, 189, 192, 194; spirit of the, 111
Restoration, the, 229
Rice, John, actor, 65
Richard II, 5, 45, 49, 50, 119, 137, 142, 143, 196, 206, 236, 242, 247
Richard III, 5, 45, 119, 137, 138, 150, 196, 206, 227, 231, 242, 243, 246, 247; characteristics of, 135
Roberts, J., printer, 199, 203
Roman de la Violette, 174
Romantic impulse, the, 109
Romeo and Juliet, 45, 46, 78, 93, 129, 139, 140, 150, 169, 191, 198, 200, 206, 209, 229, 231, 235, 242, 247; characteristics of, 138; its theme romantic love, 138; contrasted with Brooke's play, 138
Rosalynde, 186
Rose Theatre, 28, 41, 72, 68
Rowe, Nicholas, biographer and editor of Shakespeare, 15; edition 1709, 207; characteristics of his edition, 208

Royal Exchange, the, 23
Rümeslin, German, 223
Run-on lines, 242 f.
Ruskin, famous chapter of, 215
Rutland, Lord, friend of Shakespeare, 92
Rymer, Thomas, *Tragedies of the Last Age*, 215, 216

S

Sackville, author of *Gorboduc*, 31, 32
Sadler's Wells, theatre of, 235
Sappho, 114
Saxo Grammaticus, 158
Scottish History of James IV Slain at Flodden, 116
Schücking, Shakespearean critic, 224
Schücking's *Character Problems in Shakespeare's Plays*, 223
Secunda Pastorum, 102
Seneca, 12, 107, 119, 138, 158; model for English tragedy, 107 f.; a psychological dramatist, 108; influence on blank verse, 108; technique of, 108
Shakespeare, Ann, sister of William, 11
Shakespeare, Edmund, brother of William, 11
Shakespeare, Gilbert, brother of William, 10
Shakespeare, Judith and Hamnet, children of William, 37; baptism of, 18
Shakespeare, Hamnet, death of, 19
Shakespeare, Joan, sister of William, 11
Shakespeare, John, father of William, 6, 11, 15, 17, 18, 44; shoemaker in Stratford, 6; failure of, 7
Shakespeare, Richard, brother of William, 10
Shakespeare, Susanna, daughter of William, 62, 63; birth of, 18; marriage of, 58
Shakespeare, William, 2, 3, 5, 9, 13, 15, 16, 17, 19, 20, 22, 28, 34, 43, 48, 57, 58, 59, 62, 71, 84, 86, 90, 92, 94, 96, 99, 101, 104, 109, 110, 113, 119, 121, 128, 129, 131, 135, 136, 142, 144, 148, 154, 155, 157, 160, 162, 163, 164, 167, 168, 170, 174, 175, 176, 177, 178, 179, 180, 182, 183, 184, 186, 187, 188, 189, 192, 193, 195, 197, 198, 202, 206, 208, 214, 218, 220, 226, 231, 234, 238; his first stage play, 7; his mother, 8; gentleman, 8; early life of, 10 f.; his brothers and sisters, 10; baptism of, 10; education of, 11; knowledge of Greek and Latin, 13; the boy, 14; probably apprentice, 15; familiarity with sports, 15; his bride, 17; leaves Stratford, 19; in touch with aristocracy, 35; "Lost Years" of, 37; selects patron, 40; *Venus and Adonis*, published, 41; sonnets of, 42; coat-of-arms of, 43; return of, to Stratford, 44; plays named by Meres, 45; change in fortunes, 47; in company formed by Cuthbert, 48;

silent on death of Queen, 50; new period of, 53; signs of royal favor, 54; receives grant of red cloth, 55; his Company, at the Globe Theatre, 56; possibly receives silver-gilt bowl, 56; increase of personal fortune, 57; living in London, 1602–1607, 57; drawn into lawsuit, 57; removal of, in London, 57; profits of, 59; possible breakdown of, 59; his romances, 60; in London, 1613, 61; income of, 62; changes in his will, 63; death of, 63; signatures of, 63; burial in Stratford church, 63; monument, 64; descendants of, 64; as playwright, 65; his company, 69; theatre of, 73; plays, length of, 85; his audience, 91 f.; language of, 96; use of songs, 97; references to musical instruments, 97; poetry of plays, 97; representative of his age, 99; debt to university playwrights, 112; compared to Marlowe, 122; development of, 122 f.; evidence for dates of plays, 123; periods of his work, 126; his company, 127; technique of comedy, 129; plot from classical comedies, 130; contribution of realism, 130; compared with Marlowe, 137; summary of his tragic period, 171; his England, 186; and the sonnets, 192; text of, 195 f.; table of plays, 201; Rowe's edition of, 208; text, editors and editions of, 208 f.; first biography of, 209; Pope's edition of, 209; edition by Capell, 211; Theobald's edition of, 211; edition by Malone, 212; edition by Samuel Johnson, 212; criticism of, 214 f.; criticism by Johnson, 218; his plays, popularity of, 227
Shakespeare Quarto Facsimiles, 213
Shakespeare Restored, 210
Shakespeare, On the Tragedies of, 1810, 221
Shakespeare, the Man, 223
Shakespeare's Dramatic Art in *Companion to Shakespeare Studies*, 224
Shakespeare's Theatre and Audience, 223
Shakespearean Studies, 1874, 223
Shakespearean Tragedy, by Bradley, 223
Shaw, G. Bernard, 195
Shepheard's Calendar, 186
Short View of Tragedy, 215
Siddons, Mrs., actress, 222, 232, 233
Sidney, Philip, 31, 86, 92, 108, 192; *Arcadia*, 148, 162; *Astrophel and Stella*, 191
Sir John Oldcastle, old chronicle play, 202, 207
Slye, of Shakespeare's company, 59
Smithwick, publisher, 204
Soliloquy, the, 88
Sonnets, 131, 183, 187, 189, 191; theories as to, 192; poetic values of, 193

Southampton, Earl of, 35, 49, 92, 184, 187, 192; patron of Shakespeare, 40; dedication to, 41; condemned to death, 50

Southwark, suburb of London, 24

Spanish Armada, 94, 104

Spanish Tragedy, by Kyd, 21, 75, 94, 117, 158

Specimen of English Dramatic Poets, 220

Spencer, Gabriel, fellow-actor of Jonson, 93

Spenser, *Shepheard's Calendar*, 110; verse forms of, 186, 192; *Amoretti*, 191

Stage, influence of structure on dramatic technique, 84

Stanley, Ferdinando, Lord Strange, noble of Shakespeare's day, 35, 37, 71

Strange, Lord, his company, (*see* Stanley), 37, 40

Stationer's Register (*see* Register), 39, 123, 124, 168, 172, 184, 187, 189, 199, 204

Strand, London, 23

Stratford, 1, 3, 4, 10, 13, 15, 16, 19, 20, 36, 37, 43, 57, 60, 61, 63, 145, 176, 179, 183, 184; Collegiate Church of, 2; John of, 2; Ralph of, Bishop of London, 2; Robert of, 3

Stratford, Shakespeare Festival, 238

Stoll, Professor, Shakespearean critic, 223

Substance of Tragedy, by Bradley, 223

Supernatural, preference for, 109

Survey, metre introduced by, 108, 193

Swan Theatre, 43, 74, 81; sketch of, 74, 77, 78

Swinburne, *A Study of Shakespeare*, 175, 222

T

Tadema, Alma, painter, 236

Tales from Shakespeare, by Charles and Mary Lamb, 220

Tamburlaine, by Marlowe, 75, 110, 118, 246

Taming of the Shrew, 46, 124, 204, 227, 231, 239; characteristics of, 145

Tancred and Gismonda, 32

Tarleton, Dick, famous clown, 67, 93

Tate, Nahum, 229, 230, 231, 232, 234; adaptation of, 163

Tempest, The, 60, 76, 78, 99, 122, 123, 178, 185, 204, 226, 227, 228, 229, 243; source of, 177; a unique play, 178

Temple Bar, 28

Tennyson, Lord, 173, 175, 194

Terence, read in school, 12, 105

Terry, Ellen, actress, 237

Theobald, Lewis, Shakespeare editor, 210, 211; his work recognized, 211

Theatre, the (*see* names of different theatres), 68, 76, 91, 99; closing of, 40; reopening of, 42; closed by the plague, 55; stage of, 74; plans of, 76 f.; properties of, 82; reopened, 134; Her Majesty's, 237

Third Variorum, 1821, 212

Thomas Lord Cromwell, 207

Thorpe, Thomas, publisher, 189, 190

Thyestes, by Seneca, 109

Tilney, Edward, Master of Revels, 182

Timon of Athens, 124, 172, 204, 242, 246; theories to account for, 164; source of, 165

Titus Andronicus, 45, 46, 94, 123, 124, 125, 127, 128, 188, 206, 235, 247; presented, 41

Tonson, publishers, 208, 209

Tragedy, little of popular, 103; realism of, 104; influence of classics, 106; subjects of, 106; beginnings of romantic, 111

Tree, Beerbohm, actor, 180, 236, 237, 238

Trinity Church in Stratford, 18

Troilus and Cressida, 54, 123, 151, 187, 200, 201, 204, 206

True Tragedy, owned by Thomas Pavier, 202

True Tragedy of Richard Duke of York, 127

Twelfth Night, 32, 49, 144, 146, 150, 204, 227, 229, 230; characteristics of, 149

Two Gentlemen of Verona, 45, 129, 132, 204; characteristics of, 131

Two Noble Kinsmen, The, 183, 205, 227; source of, 180

U

"University playwrights," 112

Upper-stage, 79

V

Vanity of Rhyme, 245

Variorum Shakespeare (*see* New Variorum), 212

Venus and Adonis, 12, 21, 40, 41, 128, 134, 184, 185, 187, 188, 189

Vice, the, 103, 104, 105

Virgil, read in school, 12

Volpone, by Jonson, 227

W

"War of the Theatres," 51

Ward, John, Stratford vicar, 62

Warwick, Earl of, company of, 66

Warwick castle, near to Stratford, 5

Wayte, William, petition of, 43

Westminster, Whitehall in, 22

Whetstone, George, author of *Promos and Cassandra*, 153, 154

Whitehall in Westminster, 22, 32, 55

Whole Contention, The, 202

Whore of Babylon, The, by Dekker, 9

Wilkins, George, playwright, 172
William the Conqueror, 5
Wilmcote, village near Stratford, 6
Winter's Tale, The, 60, 175, 176, 178, 204, 206, 226, 227, 242; masterpiece of tragi-comedy, 176
Witch, The, by Middleton, 166
Woman Killed With Kindness, A, 104
Worcester, Earl of, company of, 66

Works of Benjamin Jonson, The, published, 1616, 197
Wotton, Henry, quoted, 75
Wriothesley, Henry, theory as to identification of W. H., 193

Y

"Yard," 81
Yorkshire Tragedy, A, 202, 207